Financial Reporting
1994–95:
A Survey of
UK Reporting Practice

Financial Reporting 1994–95: A Survey of UK Reporting Practice

Edited by

D. J. Tonkin

Managing Director,

Company Reporting Limited

and

L. C. L. Skerratt

Professor of Accounting and Finance,

Department of Accounting and Finance,

University of Manchester

The Institute of Chartered Accountants

in England and Wales

Gloucester House

399 Silbury Boulevard

Central Milton Keynes MK9 2HL

Tel: 01908 248000

1995

Copying and reproduction

In the interests of research and education, permission is granted for the reproduction of sections of this survey provided such reproduction is restricted to the purposes of research, private study or discussion.

Written permission from one of the Editors should be obtained for reproduction for any other purpose.

In all cases, reproduction of sections of this survey must indicate adequately the source stating, in particular, the name of the contributor of the section and crediting The Institute of Chartered Accountants in England and Wales.

No responsibility for loss occasioned to any person acting or refraining from action as a result of any material in this publication can be accepted by the editors, contributors or publisher.

© 1995 The Institute of Chartered Accountants in England and Wales

ISBN 1 85355 549 5

Typeset by LBJ Enterprises Ltd, Chilcompton, Somerset
Printed in Great Britain by Bell and Bain Ltd, Glasgow

ACKNOWLEDGEMENTS

This publication is sponsored by The Institute of Chartered Accountants in England and Wales, and does not necessarily represent the views of the Institute.

The Institute and the Editors gratefully acknowledge the assistance of all concerned in the preparation of the work.

Contributors

The selected topics were prepared and written by:

Peter Chidgey	Partner, Stoy Hayward
James W Dean	Price Waterhouse
Clive Goodhead	Senior Manager, Touche Ross
Rowan Jones, MA, PhD, IPFA	The University of Birmingham
Guy F Loveday, BSc FCA	Partner, Professional Training Partnership
Nic Nicandrou	Price Waterhouse
Andrew Piper, BCom, FCA, FCMA	The University of Birmingham

The survey tables and examples were prepared and written by:
David J Tonkin, MA, PhD, FCA   Managing Director, Company Reporting Ltd

INTRODUCTION

This is the twenty-sixth edition of this series of reviews of the financial reporting practices of large UK companies. The work is divided into two parts. In Part I selected contributors analyse current practice on topics in which each is known to have specialist expertise. Part II contains a systematic survey of current accounting practice. For each of the areas covered by this part of the survey there are two components: (i) tables which analyse the financial reports of a sample of industrial and commercial companies, and (ii) a series of examples of current reporting practice.

Part I Selected topics

This part of the survey addresses some of the "issues of the day". In an ever-changing financial environment it is important that there be a number of response mechanisms. Consequently, the editors have aimed to give each contributor maximum freedom to review the selected topic. The review is conducted on the basis of the contributor's own day-to-day experience and is supported liberally by examples which "have crossed his desk", so to speak. The examples are an important part of this review and are taken from the leading edge of current practice. In many cases, the contributor's discussion of examples is forthright and outspoken; the aim is not to offend, but to stimulate a healthy and dynamic review. A cumulative contents list of these and previous selected topics is given in the Appendix.

Part II Survey tables and examples

Survey tables

As a companion to the selected topics the editors have aimed to conduct a background monitoring of financial reporting practice in order to ensure that current debate is supported by, and benefits from, the facts. In many areas of practice there is variability which may or may not be fully understood and which may or may not change over the years. It is important that any trends are identified and debate is informed. Each of the tables in the survey focuses on an important area of accounting practice; in conjunction with previous editions of this publication the editors hope to provide a unique perspective on accounting disclosure and measurement. The analysis is based on the financial reports of 300 industrial and commercial companies published during the year to 30 June 1994. Details of the sample selection procedure are contained in the Appendix at the end of the book.

Survey examples

The presentation of each survey table is followed by a selection of examples from current reporting practice. The examples are taken from the same company sample as for the survey tables and each is chosen as representative of the particular practice identified in the table. The editors have aimed to illustrate each of the significant practices identified in the survey tables.

PREFACE

In recent years, financial reporting in Britain has been characterised by change. This has resulted partly from the actions of the Financial Reporting Council and partly from changes in the underlying business environment. Prominent among the new developments is the increased disclosure in many areas of company annual reports. The following chapters feature discussion of areas where increased disclosure is apparent, areas where change has begun to take place, and of areas where substantial change is still required.

In Chapter 1, Peter Chidgey identifies the increasing trend among companies to include auditors' and directors' statements of responsibility. Recent auditing standards encourage companies to make a distinction between the responsibilities of auditors and those of directors. It is hoped that such disclosures will narrow the so-called "expectations gap". Chidgey argues that variations in disclosure practice among companies has led to confusion over the purpose of responsibility statements. He argues that in attempting to comply with other disclosure requirements, companies have diluted the directors' responsibility statements. There are also signs that separate auditors' statements of responsibility are beginning to disappear; Chidgey suggests that these statements are victim to the competition for space in company reports.

"The writing is on the wall for the operating lease", prophesies Guy Loveday in his discussion of lease accounting in Chapter 2. At present companies appear to be adopting the SSAP 21 90 per cent rule to distinguish between operating and finance leases. Under SSAP 21, if a lease is deemed an operating lease then both the leased asset and the lease obligations remain off balance sheet. If a lease is deemed a finance lease then both the asset and the liability are brought onto the balance sheet as if the asset had been purchased. Obviously, the choice of classification can have a major effect on the appearance of the balance sheet. Of concern to Loveday is the fact that companies are reluctant to disclose details of lease classification and the use of discounting techniques (for the purpose of the 90 per cent rule). With the emphasis in accounting steadily moving from form to substance, Loveday suggests that it may be a matter of time before the rights and obligations arising from all lease arrangements will be capitalised.

Statements prompted by the Cadbury Committee's voluntary Code of Best Practice could pose problems for auditors and readers of accounts, according to Andrew Piper and Rowan Jones. In Chapter 3 they explain how the London Stock Exchange has added requirements concerning the Code to its listing rules. Specifically, companies should state whether they have complied with the Code, identify and explain areas of non-compliance, and have the statement of compliance reviewed by the auditors. Companies are not required to disclose the results of the auditors' review, and readers may therefore be unaware of the scope of the review and its conclusions. Furthermore, Piper and Jones point out that auditors perform a difficult role in reviewing the directors' statement of compliance. Auditors are required to review the directors' statement of compliance but not the actual actions of directors which are taken to achieve compliance. Piper and Jones suggest that auditors may be concerned that, if they do report on their review, their sanction of the statement of compliance could be interpreted as confirmation of compliance with the Code itself. The end result is merely the publication of the directors' opinions, possibly ambiguously stated, on whether or not the Code is being complied with.

Extraordinary items are now virtually extinct – a result which should please the Accounting Standards Board. Through FRS 3, the ASB attempted to virtually abolish extraordinary items, which were accounted for "below the line". FRS 3 requires almost all transactions to be accounted for above the line. The ASB's assault on extraordinary items was intended to counter the abuse of extraordinary items (companies were temped to take unfavourable results below the line) and to counter user fixation with the single earnings per share number as a performance measure. Clive Goodhead, in Chapter 4, reviews current practice and concludes that the ASB appears to have achieved its objective. He notes that a variety of presentations are still possible within FRS 3's framework, allowing companies to present measures they believe are the most useful.

Financial reporting for life assurance business profits has been in a state of transition in recent years. Moves in reporting practice have been prompted by recognition of the inadequacies of the traditional statutory solvency basis of accounting (based on cash flows). In Chapter 5, James Dean and Nic Nicandrou report that companies are moving away from the solvency basis to profitability bases of accounting. Most banks and building societies have adopted the new approaches, which usually take the form of the "embedded value" or "accruals" methods. Dean and Nicandrou note that there is some diversity in company reports regarding the accounting treatment and disclosure of methodology and assumptions. They argue that such divergence restricts the usefulness of the reports. While consultation is taking place regarding acceptable methods for life assurance accounting, industry continues to work towards acceptable bases for recognising profits along the lines of embedded value and the accruals basis. Dean and Nicandrou suggest that a hybrid of these two methods, the "convergence" basis, may be a likely successor.

It is clear that some of the radical changes taking place in financial reporting have resulted in a variety of disclosure and measurement practices. The authors have argued that this diversity often contributes to confusion for readers. It is to be exptected that such substantial developments in financial reporting practice will take time to bed down as companies find their feet in the new reporting environment. Furthermore, the variety of practices may suggest that companies are really thinking about what they are disclosing in company reports, rather than simply "trotting off" standard statements – a practice that would devalue company reports. It is hoed that in time the process of change will result in a distillation of the best quality information for annual report users.

Bill Robertson and David Tonkin
November 1994
Edinburgh

CONTENTS

Auditors' review of Cadbury compliance statements *Andrew Piper and Rowan Jones*

Life profit reporting *James W. Dean and Nic Nicandrou*

PART II SURVEY TABLES AND EXAMPLES

Part I

SELECTED TOPICS

by

selected contributors

SAS 600 AUDITORS' AND DIRECTORS' RESPONSIBILITY STATEMENTS

Peter Chidgey

INTRODUCTION

The inclusion of auditors' and directors' responsibility statements in companies' annual financial statements is one of the most noticeable new trends in financial reporting. Whereas in 1990 it would have been difficult to find more than odd examples of such statements, they are now invariably to be found in the financial statements of all listed companies.

This has been driven by the development and issue of:

- SAS 600 – the Statement of Auditing Standards introducing a new form of audit report; and
- the Cadbury Report accompanied by the Stock Exchange requirement that listed companies report compliance with its Code of Best Practice.

The motivation for these changes comes from an attempt to narrow the so called "expectation gap" between what users expect from an audit report and what it actually delivers.

AUDITING STANDARDS

The APB in developing the revised audit report saw three sides to the "expectation gap", being misunderstandings:

- of the nature of audited financial statements;
- as to the type and extent of work undertaken by auditors; and
- about the level of assurance provided by auditors.

The proposed revisions to the audit report were aimed at the second and third of these. One of the APB's stated aims, in its development of an expanded form of audit report, was to clarify the respective responsibilities of auditors and directors regarding the financial statements.

Detailed proposals were contained in an ED SAS which was published in May 1992. This included an example of a directors' responsibility statement. It also included a lengthy example of an auditors' responsibility statement for inclusion in the audit report. This Exposure Draft had an immediate effect in practice as companies began to include statements based upon it in their financial statements.

SAS 600: "Statement of Auditing Standards: Auditors' Reports on Financial Statements" was issued in May 1993 and became mandatory for audits of financial statements for periods ending on or after 30 September 1993. This was based on the ED SAS and, amongst other changes, required a new form of audit report containing a statement distinguishing between the respective responsibilities of directors and auditors.

As can be seen by the examples below, it is clearly the APB's intention that the directors' responsibilities would be set out in a separate statement cross referred to in the audit report. Only if the directors did not explain their responsibilities adequately in the financial statements would auditors be expected to include a description in their own report.

The standard includes, as a non-mandatory Appendix, an example of a statement of directors' responsibilities which is reproduced in Figure 1.

Figure 1:
Directors' Responsibilities

> Company law requires the directors to prepare financial statements for each financial year which give a true and fair view of the state of affairs of the company and of the profit or loss for that period. In preparing those financial statements, the directors are required to:
>
> - select suitable accounting policies and then apply them consistently;
> - make judgements and estimates that are reasonable and prudent;
> - state whether applicable accounting standards have been followed, subject to any material departures disclosed and explained in the financial statements;
> - prepare the financial statements on the going concern basis unless it is inappropriate to presume that the company will continue in business.
>
> The directors are responsible for keeping proper accounting records which disclose with reasonable accuracy at any time the financial position of the company and to enable them to ensure that the financial statements comply with the Companies Act 1985. They are also responsible for safeguarding the assets of the company and hence for taking reasonable steps for the prevention and detection of fraud and other irregularities.

The SAS also contains an example of an audit report which is based on the standards, with a "model" paragraph referring to the directors' statement and providing an example of what auditors may say about their own responsibilities.

> As described on page ... the company's directors are responsible for the preparation of financial statements. It is our responsibility to form an independent opinion, based on our audit, on those statements and to report our opinion to you.

There was one important difference in this from the Exposure Draft. The Exposure Draft had contained a much extended version of the auditors' responsibility statement. The main differences from the final version being that the Exposure Draft covered the full legal responsibility of the auditors to report if:

- the company has not kept proper accounting records;
- the financial statements are not in agreement with the accounting records;
- the auditors have not obtained all the information and explanations (which to the best of their knowledge and belief are necessary for the purpose or their audit);
- the contents of the directors' report are not consistent with the financial statements.

This was left out of the final standard in the interests of brevity – to allow most unqualified and qualified reports to fit on to a single page.

CADBURY

The other main influence on practice in this area is the report of the Committee on Corporate Governance under the chairmanship of Sir Adrian Cadbury and more particularly the Code of Best Practice issued with the report, with which listed companies must report compliance or non compliance from 30 June 1993. The report, which had been exposed in draft form in May 1992 and was issued in December 1992, also recommends that financial statements contain separate statements of responsibilities by auditors and directors. The Code, in addition, recommends that the directors' statement of responsibility for preparing the financial statements is placed next to a statement by the auditors about their reporting responsibilities. This has led in practice to most companies either showing directors' responsibility statements above the auditors' report or on a facing page.

The Cadbury Report sets out in an Appendix the areas which such a statement should cover. These are:

(a) the legal requirement for directors to prepare financial statements for each financial year which give a true and fair view of the state of affairs of the company (or group) as at the end of the financial year and of the profit and loss for that period;

(b) the responsibility of the directors for maintaining adequate accounting records, for safeguarding the assets of the company (or group), and for preventing and detecting fraud and other irregularities;

(c) confirmation that suitable accounting policies, consistently applied and supported by reasonable and prudent judgements and estimates, have been used in the preparation of the financial statements;

(d) confirmation that applicable accounting standards have been followed, subject to any material departures disclosed and explained in the notes to the accounts.

This differs from SAS 600 in respect of the last two points. Whereas the examples in SAS 600 were merely statements of responsibility, the Cadbury example calls for confirmations that suitable accounting policies have been consistently applied and accounting standards followed. This goes one step further than a statement of responsibilities and such a statement serves a different purpose to SAS 600 as it does not formally acknowledge all the directors' responsibilities.

Further, the Cadbury report suggests that such confirmations should be extended in that this statement would be a suitable vehicle for reporting on internal controls and the applicability of the going concern concept, once suitable guidance has been developed.

OTHER INFLUENCES – LAW SOCIETY

The Company Law Committee of the Law Society has also had an influence in this area. Motivated by a concern that directors were publishing these statements without taking appropriate legal advice, they produced, in November 1993, a draft form of statement which is reproduced in Figure 2.

Figure 2:
Statement of Directors' Responsibilities in Relation to Financial Statements

> The following statement, which should be read in conjunction with the auditors' statement of auditors' responsibilities set out below, is made with a view to distinguishing for shareholders the respective responsibilities of the directors and of the auditors in relation to the financial statements.
>
> The directors are required by the Companies Act 1985 to prepare financial statements for each financial year which give a true and fair view of the state of affairs of the Company and the Group as at the end of the financial year and of the profit and loss for the financial year.
>
> Following discussions with the auditors, the directors consider that in preparing the financial statements, the Company has used appropriate accounting policies, consistently applied and supported by reasonable and prudent judgements and estimates, and that all accounting standards which they consider to be applicable have been followed (subject to any explanations and any material departures disclosed in the notes to the financial statements).
>
> The directors have responsibility for ensuring that the Company keeps accounting records which disclose with reasonable accuracy the financial position of the Company and which enable them to ensure that the financial statements comply with the Companies Act 1985.
>
> The directors have general responsibility for taking such steps as are reasonably open to them to safeguard the assets of the Group and to prevent and detect fraud and other irregularities.
>
> The directors, having prepared the financial statements, have requested the auditor to take whatever steps and undertake whatever inspections they consider to be appropriate for the purpose of enabling them to give their audit report.

This contains some elements of the SAS 600 version reworded to bring the duties closer to the precise wording of company law and also contains elements of the Cadbury recommendations particularly in respect of directors' confirmations.

This version of the statement may be seen as having two main flaws:

- it draws auditors into the directors' choice of accounting policies and as such appears to have moved away from distinguishing auditors and directors' responsibilities;
- the final paragraph appears to indicate that the scope of the audit is at the directors' request rather than being determined by company law.

After protest about these points the committee published a modification to its view on these two paragraphs, which amounted to a minor climb down, saying that such wording should only be used where "it can accurately reflect what has occurred in practice". It went on to say:

> It is particularly important that any wording describing the process should not be capable of being interpreted as a comment on the legal responsibilities of those concerned.

and to warn directors and their advisers that auditors may wish to clarify this matter in their reports if they consider the words capable of misinterpretation.

6

PRACTICE

Practice in the UK has passed through two distinct phases:

- in 1992 and early 1993 financial statements, in response to the various proposals, there was an increasing trend of directors' and auditors' responsibility statements outside the auditors' report;
- in late 1993 and 1994 financial statements there have been separate statements of directors' responsibilities (either free standing or in the directors' report) and a decreasing number of separate auditors' responsibility statements – these being replaced by the statement included in the audit report.

A typical example of those following the standard wording recommended in the audit standard, is BOC see Example 1.

Example 1
The BOC Group plc   *30 September 1993*
Responsibility of the directors'

Company law requires the directors to prepare financial statements for each financial year which give a true and fair view of the state of affairs of the Company and of the Group and of the profit or loss of the Group for that period. In preparing those financial statements, the directors are required to:

- select suitable accounting policies and then apply them consistently.
- make judgements and estimates that are reasonable and prudent.
- state whether applicable accounting standards have been followed subject to any material departures disclosed and explained in the financial statements.
- prepare the financial statements on the going concern basis unless it is inappropriate to presume that the Group will continue in business.

The directors are responsible for keeping proper accounting records which disclose with reasonable accuracy at any time the financial position of the Company and to enable them to ensure that the financial statements comply with the Companies Act 1985. They are also responsible for safeguarding the assets of the Group and hence for taking reasonable steps for the prevention and detection of fraud and other irregularities.

To the members of   We have audited the financial statements on pages 52 to 77.
The BOC Group plc
Respective   As described opposite the Company's directors are
responsibilities of   responsible for preparation of financial statements. It is our
directors and auditors   responsibility to form an independent opinion, based on our
audit, on those statements and to report our opinion to you.

Practice, however, varies from this orthodox model in two main ways:

- the inclusion of separate auditors' responsibility statements;
- changes in the form of the directors' responsibility statements.

AUDITORS' RESPONSIBILITY STATEMENTS

A decreasing number of companies include a separate auditors' responsibility statement in addition to the "standard" reference in the audit report. Those companies that still do, tend to restrict themselves to the reporting responsibilities of the "auditors" set out in the ED SAS 600. **Example 2 Albert Fisher plc**, includes a statement in an auditors' page which also contains auditors' reports on the Corporate Governance Statement and on the financial statements. The statement of responsibilities is reproduced below:

Example 2
Albert Fisher Group plc *31 August 1993*
Statement of auditors' responsibility

> The auditors are required to form an independent opinion on the financial statements presented by the directors based on their audit of whether the financial statements give a true and fair view and comply with the Companies Act 1985 and also to report their opinion to shareholders. The Companies Act 1985 also requires the auditors to report to shareholders if the following requirements are not met:
>
> a) that the company has maintained proper accounting records;
> b) that the financial statements are in agreement with the accounting records;
> c) that the auditors have obtained all the information and explanations which, to the best of their knowledge and belief, are necessary for the purpose of their audit;
> d) that the contents of the Directors' Report are consistent with the financial statements.

This statement is of somewhat doubtful parentage; it refers throughout to "the auditors" but is inserted between two statements made by the auditors only the last of which (the audit report) is signed separately. It therefore appears as a directors' statement from the text but an auditors' statement from its position.

By contrast, **Example 3 Dixons plc** includes a statement of auditors' responsibilities which is clearly made by the directors and is positioned between the directors' statement and the audit report. The Dixons statement is on similar lines to Albert Fisher although it additionally refers to responsibilities under Schedule 6 Companies Act 1985.

Example 3
Dixons plc *1 May 1993*
Extract from auditors' responsibilities statement

> The auditors are required to give, as far as they are reasonably able to do so, a statement giving the required particulars if the requirements of Schedule 6 of the Companies Act 1985 (which relate to disclosure of emoluments and other benefits of directors and others) are not complied with in the financial statements.

M J Gleeson Group plc, Wickes plc, Wolseley plc and TSB plc (not reproduced) contain similar statements to Dixons whilst The Greenals Group plc contains no reference to this additional responsibility. Close Brothers Group plc in its 31 July 1993 statements contains a statement of responsibilities combining the directors and auditors statements. The directors part being based on SAS 600 similar to **Example 1 BOC Group plc** whilst the auditors' responsibilities are similar to **Example 2 Albert Fisher plc**. An interesting feature in respect of all these statements is that they do not refer to the statement in the auditors' report nor are they referred to in it.

As indicated above, one noticeable trend in this area is a reduction in the number of these statements. Following the introduction in SAS 600, of the reduced size of auditors' responsibilities statements, a number of companies have dropped the fuller additional statements included in their 1992/93 financial statements. Examples of such companies are Gleeson Group plc, Tesco plc, Williams Holdings plc, STV plc and Coats Vyella plc.

This has been seen by some as an unfavourable effect of the SAS as the shortened form of responsibility statement, included in the audit report, conveys significantly less information about auditors' responsibilities than the original proposal upon which most of the separate auditors' statements were and, where still found, are based.

VARIATIONS TO DIRECTORS' RESPONSIBILITIES

The greatest variation in practice is in the statements of directors' responsibilities. Although there are many examples of companies using the example from SAS 600 (see **Example 1 BOC plc** above) a large number of companies follow the Cadbury recommendation. These include in their statement a confirmation with regard to the selection of suitable accounting policies and the use of applicable accounting standards rather than acknowledging their responsibility for doing so. Some go further and confirm other matters. **Example 4 Allders plc**, make such a statement which extends to confirming that proper accounting records have been kept.

Example 4
Allders plc *30 September 1993*
Extract from directors' report

> In preparing these financial statements, the directors confirm that they have:
>
> – selected suitable accounting policies and applied them consistently;
> – made judgements and estimates that are reasonable and prudent;
> – stated that applicable accounting standards have been followed;
> – prepared the financial statements on a going concern basis.
>
> The directors also confirm that proper accounting records, which disclose with reasonable accuracy at any time the financial position of the Group and enable them to ensure that the financial statements comply with the Companies Act 1985, have been kept.

Example 5 Y J Lovell plc is another company which goes beyond Cadbury, also including "the preparation of accounts" requirements in its confirmation.

Example 5
Y J Lovell Holdings plc *30 September 1993*
Extract from statement of directors' responsibilities in respect of the accounts

> Company Law requires directors to prepare accounts for each financial year which give a true and fair view of the state of affairs of the Company and the Group and of the profit or loss of the Group for that period. In preparing those accounts, the directors are required to:
>
> • select suitable accounting policies and then apply them consistently;

- make judgements and estimates that are reasonable and prudent;
- state whether applicable accounting standards have been followed, subject to any material departures disclosed and explained in the accounts;
- prepare the accounts on the going concern basis unless it is inappropriate to presume that the Group will continue in business.

The directors confirm that the accounts will comply with the above requirements.

Other companies, whilst confirming that they have selected suitable accounting policies, exclude confirmations concerning accounting standards and use of the going concern basis. This is presumably because such statements are included in the accounting policies or notes to financial statements in each case.

LAW SOCIETY RECOMMENDATIONS

There are a number of examples of directors' statements based on the Law Society recommendation. The most interesting ones being where directors have used the paragraphs referred to above dealing with accounting policies and the scope of the audit. **Example 6 Bass plc** includes the recommended paragraph on "accounting policies" in its entirety which prompted a variation of the audit report from Ernst and Young to emphasise the responsibility of the directors for these choices, the insertion of the word "solely" clarifying the directors' statement.

Example 6
Bass plc *30 September 1993*
Extracts from statement of responsibilities and report of the auditors

Statement of Responsibilities
Following discussions with the auditors, the directors consider that, in preparing the financial statements on pages 30 to 58 inclusive, the Company has used appropriate accounting policies, consistently applied and supported by reasonable and prudent judgements and estimates, and that all applicable accounting standards have been followed. The financial statements have been prepared on a going concern basis.

Report of the Auditors: Respective Responsibilities of Directors and Auditors
As described above, the Company's directors are solely responsible for the preparation of the financial statements including the selection of suitable accounting policies.

This may be compared with **Example 7 Lookers plc**, which uses almost identical wording but with no response in the audit report. Lookers also refers to the extent of the audit examination, picking up the final paragraphs from the Law Society recommendations but has modified this to take out the phrase "have requested" and replace it with the more descriptive "understand that". This wording as a result does not imply the directors are able to restrict the scope of auditors.

Example 7
Lookers plc *30 September 1993*
Extract from statement of directors' responsibilities

The directors, having prepared the financial statements, understand that the auditors take whatever steps and undertake whatever inspections they consider to be appropriate having regard to Auditing Standards and Guidelines, for the purpose of enabling them to give their audit report.

This contrasts with Albert Fisher which reproduces the Law Society wording on this issue as do both Compass Group plc and Ocean Group plc.

On the other hand **Example 8 Burmah Castrol plc** provides a good example of a statement based on the Law Society model with both references to auditors excised.

Example 8
Burmah Castrol plc   *31 December 1993*
Statement of directors' responsibilities in relation to financial statements

The following statement, which should be read in conjunction with the auditors' responsibilities set out below, is made with a view to distinguishing for shareholders the respective responsibilities of the directors and of the auditors in relation to the financial statements.

The directors are required by the Companies Act 1985 to prepare financial statements for each financial year which give a true and fair view of the state of affairs of the company and the group as at the end of the financial year and of the profit or loss for the financial year.

The directors consider that in preparing the accounts on pages 29 to 49, the company has used appropriate accounting policies, consistently applied and supported by reasonable and prudent judgements and estimates, and that all accounting standards which they consider to be applicable have been followed.

The directors have responsibility for ensuring that the company keeps accounting records which disclose with reasonable accuracy the financial position of the company and which enable them to ensure that the financial statements comply with the Companies Act 1985.

The directors have general responsibility for taking such steps as are reasonably open to them to safeguard the assets of the group and to prevent and detect fraud and other irregularities.

Glynwed plc amongst others follows this approach.

Other companies have included modified versions based on the Law Society Model. **Example 9 Glaxo Holdings plc** provides a succinct version of the statement.

Example 9
Glaxo Holdings plc   *30 June 1993*
Directors' statement of responsibility in relation to accounts

The directors are required by law to prepare accounts for each financial year which give a true and fair view of the state of affairs of the Company and the Group as at the end of the financial year and of the profit or loss for that year. They are responsible for maintaining adequate accounting records, for safeguarding the assets of the Group and for preventing and detecting fraud and other irregularities.

The directors confirm that suitable accounting policies have been consistently applied, that reasonable and prudent judgements and estimates have been used in the preparation of the accounts and that applicable accounting standards have been followed.

Example 10 M J Gleeson Group similarly take a minimalist line to the statement.

Example 10
M J Gleeson Group plc *30 June 1993*
Directors' responsibilities

<table>
<tr><td>In respect of the preparation of financial statements</td><td>The directors are required by law to prepare accounts each year which give a true and fair view of the state of affairs of the Group at the end of the financial year and of its profit or loss for the year.</td></tr>
<tr><td></td><td>The directors are responsible for maintaining adequate accounting records, safeguarding the assets of the Group and preventing and detecting fraud and other irregularities.</td></tr>
<tr><td></td><td>The directors confirm that the accounts have been prepared in accordance with applicable accounting standards and using suitable accounting policies, consistently applied and supported by reasonable and prudent judgements and estimates.</td></tr>
</table>

Neither of these companies use the wording recommended in the SAS (or by the Law Society) in relation to the obligation to keep proper accounting records which disclose with reasonable accuracy at any time the financial position of the company and which ensure financial statements comply with the Companies Act 1985. Instead they restrict themselves to the term "adequate accounting records".

Other companies for example, **Example 11 Booker plc** follow SAS 600 but use the first paragraph of the Law Society recommendation to put the statement in its true context. The Law Society noted when recommending this paragraph that its inclusion may limit the use to which the responsibilities statement may be put.

Example 11
Booker plc *1 January 1994*
Statement of directors' responsibilities

The following statement, which should be read in conjunction with the Report of the Auditors, is made with a view to distinguishing for shareholders the respective responsibilities of the directors and of the auditors in relation to the financial statements.

Example 12 M&G Group plc, in contrast, acknowledges a wider degree of responsibility by including before their standard statement the following:

Example 12
M&G Group plc *30 September 1993*
Extract from directors' responsibility statement

The prime responsibility of the directors is to direct the management of the Group in such a way as to maximise the long term return to shareholders. They are also required, however, to ensure that proper regard is given to the interests of the Group's customers, its staff and community.

CONCLUSIONS

As may be seen from the above, there are a number of variations in practice in what should be a simple area in which to achieve uniformity. SAS 600 has a single purpose in this area which is for companies to show separate statements of responsibilities for directors and auditors.

This relatively simple purpose has been subverted for good and bad reasons. The Cadbury proposals aim to make directors confirm that they have lived up to certain of their responsibilities. However, they call for a mixed statement of confirmation and responsibilities rather than simple statements of responsibilities. This dilutes the educational message.

The Law Society, in an apparent attempt to clarify, initially served to confuse by attempting to join auditors into the choice of accounting policies. Although their advice was not widely followed, this again has served to deflect preparers from the true purpose of the statements.

This area has potential for more confusion when the relevant Cadbury guidance is introduced. To add reporting on internal control and going concern will mean that the responsibility statements will be in danger of becoming all things to all men.

Given the purpose of these statements, this area does appear to be one where a repetition of "boiler plate" language is useful to reinforce the message. By the same token, variations to the "boiler plate" can lead to confusion. By far, the most desirable development in this area would be for there to be a clear agreement on the purpose of directors' responsibility statements between APB and those responsible for implementing Cadbury.

It is possible to sympathise with those who are responsible for preparing company reports. The number of additional statements that now need to be included, for example, the operating and financial review, the Cadbury compliance statements and the responsibility statement, leads to a natural desire to provide multi-purpose statements combining wherever possible. However, to do this with the directors' responsibility statement dilutes its purposes and loses a valuable educational opportunity.

There is some scope for improvement and embellishment of these statements. It is odd that one of the areas where the expectation gap is highest in relation to fraud and error is not covered explicitly in the auditors' statement although it is covered in the directors' responsibilities. This is understandable given the difficulties experienced in developing guidance as it is obviously a difficult area in which to frame a suitable statement for auditors. It is one, however, in which a useful message could be conveyed to the readers of audit reports.

It is also interesting to note that directors' responsibilities have been embellished on occasions (see **Example 12 M&G Group plc**) although this development is one about which directors ought to be somewhat wary. Directors have many responsibilities, some legal some not. To try to incorporate them all in a single statement is probably too complex an undertaking to consider. The statement serves its purpose best by dealing with accounting responsibilities. Corporate goals and the directors' role in achieving them are best dealt with in a specific statement elsewhere.

It is also unfortunate to note that the onset of SAS 600 has meant that auditors' statements of responsibilities, included separately within financial statements, have begun to disappear. Those examples where one is used are a useful expansion of the message in the audit report and help delineate the auditors' territory from that of the directors. It is perhaps inevitable, however, that such non-mandatory disclosures are the first victims of the competition for space in company reports.

LEASING

Guy F. Loveday

INTRODUCTION

1. SSAP 21, Accounting for leases and hire purchase contracts

In his introduction to SSAP 21 (issued August 1984), the then chairman of the Accounting Standards Committee Ian Hay Davison said that:

> "It is sometimes argued that leased assets should not be recognised on a company's balance sheet as the company does not have legal title to the asset. Whilst it is true that a lessee does not have legal ownership of the leased asset, however, he has the right to use the asset for substantially the whole of its useful economic life. These rights are for most practical purposes equivalent to legal ownership."

In one sense then, the standard is emphasising the substance of the arrangement. Leasing an asset for substantially all of its useful life is in substance similar to purchasing the asset and holding it for substantially all of its useful life and hence should be accounted for in the same way. But, pioneering as it was in the United Kingdom, the standard only goes so far. According to SSAP 21, leasing an asset for rather less than substantially all of its useful life is not in substance similar to purchasing the asset and holding it for a shorter period of time and accordingly the standard does not require it to be accounted for in the same way.

Thus the distinction between the finance lease (which is in substance similar to a purchase) and the operating lease (which is not) was introduced into United Kingdom standard practice. Whilst the finance lease will result in the recognition of an asset and a related liability in the balance sheet, the operating lease will not. With hindsight it is easy to see that companies were bound to probe the grey area at the boundary between these lease types. Companies inevitably prefer classification as operating leases if possible, with assets and liabilities remaining off balance sheet; rather than as finance leases with the resultant increases in balance sheet gearing.

Lease classification hinges on whether or not a lease is deemed to transfer to the lessee substantially all the risk and rewards associated with the ownership of the asset which is the subject of the lease. Typical rewards of ownership are the right to the unrestricted use of the asset during the period of ownership, the right to keep the profits generated by this use and the right to the proceeds of sale of the asset at the end of the period of ownership. Typical risks of ownership are the losses resulting from the asset being unreliable or unsuitable, the danger of the asset becoming obsolete such that any outlay is no longer recoverable in full and the possibility that the asset will not be worth as much as anticipated at the end of the period of ownership.

In practice, many leases are classified fairly easily. If an asset is leased for only a small fraction of its total useful life and then returned to the lessor, it is clear that significant rewards (right to material sales proceeds) and risks (residual value materially lower than anticipated) are not transferred to the lessee and that the arrangement is an operating lease. If however an asset is leased for virtually all of its total useful life then the non-transference of those same risks and rewards becomes irrelevant since they would be immaterial towards the end of the asset's useful life. It would be fair to say that whilst not all, at least substantially all of the risks and rewards have been transferred. The risks and rewards not transferred would have little commercial effect. The arrangement is clearly a finance lease.

2. SSAP 21's "90% test"

When a lease cannot be classified easily from its terms and conditions, SSAP 21 provides a present value test to aid classification. The test is that a lease is presumed to be a finance lease if, at the outset, the present value of the minimum lease payments – discounted at the interest rate implicit in the lease – amounts to substantially all of the fair value of the leased assets. The standard indicates that "substantially all" is normally 90% or more. Not surprisingly, the test has become known as the 90% test.

Although not emphasised by the standard, the test can perhaps be best understood by seeing it as an equation:

Fair value of = Present value of + Present value of
leased asset   minimum lease   unguaranteed estimated
                payments   residual amount

It can then be seen that the present value (or 90%) test is a test of the materiality of the unguaranteed estimated residual amount. If the present value of the unguaranteed residual amount is greater than 10% of the fair value of the asset it is deemed to be a significant reward of ownership, the non-transference of which has caused a presumption that the arrangement is an operating lease.

3. Technical Release 664, Implementation of SSAP 21

In 1987, the ICAEW published Technical Release (TR) 664 concerning the perceived practice of auditors accepting the result of the 90% test as a strict rule. The text of TR 664 is particularly interesting bearing in mind the approach taken more recently by FRS 5 "Reporting the substance of transactions". TR 664 states:

"Lease agreements give rise to a set of rights, rewards, risks and obligations and can be complex. The package must be analysed with greater weight given to the aspects of the agreement which are likely to have a commercial effect in practice".

With respect to the presumptive 90% test, TR 664 stated "This presumption does not . . . provide a strict mathematical definition of a finance lease".

4. FRS 5, Reporting the Substance of Transactions

FRS 5 issued in April 1994 states that in determining the substance of a transaction, "all its aspects and implications should be identified and greater weight given to those more likely to have a commercial effect in practice".

The point is of course that the 90% test is only a test as to the significance of one reward of ownership, i.e., one aspect of the transaction and what TR 664 encourages and FRS 5 requires is consideration of all the aspects of the leasing arrangement. This could result in leases failing the 90% test but still being classified as finance leases and hence causing the recognition of assets and liabilities at the outset of the agreements. Indeed, FRS 5 lays down an approach to determining the substance of a transaction which entails identifying whether the transaction has given rise to new assets or liabilities. On the basis that FRS 5 defines liabilities as "an entity's obligations to transfer economic benefits as a result of past transactions or events" it seems hard to escape from the position that all leasing agreements give rise to obligations and hence should, at least in principle, result in the recognition of liabilities (and assets) in the balance sheet of the lessee. The essential difference between SSAP 21 and FRS 5 is that whilst both standards emphasise the importance of considering the substance of transactions, SSAP 21 only allows recognition of assets and liabilities if substantially all the risks and rewards of ownership have been transferred to the lessee; whilst FRS 5 (in the absence of SSAP 21) would require recognition of assets and liabilities to the extent that risks and rewards have been transferred.

5. Reconciling SSAP 21 and FRS 5

There is then a conflict between SSAP 21 and FRS 5. However, FRS 5 states that where the substance of a transaction or the treatment of any resulting asset or liability falls not only within the scope of FRS 5 but also directly within the scope of another FRS or SSAP, then the standard that contains the more specific provisions should be applied. But which standard contains the more detailed provisions? The explanation section of FRS 5 contains guidance stating that in general SSAP 21 contains the more specific provisions governing accounting for stand-alone leases, although the general principles of FRS 5 will also be relevant in ensuring that leases are classified as finance or operating leases in accordance with their substance. The guidance goes on to say that for some lease arrangements (particularly for those that are merely one element of a large arrangement) FRS 5 will contain the more detailed provisions.

Unfortunately, the approach taken by companies and their auditors will rarely be apparent from the stated accounting policy. It is only when leases are reclassified from operating to finance that we will be able to see the impact that FRS 5 is having in this area. Such reclassifications have, in the past been rare although in 1991 The Burton Group plc changed their treatment of certain sale and lease back arrangements from operating to finance leases in view of what they foresaw as likely developments in accounting practice. Clearly if a company has limited reliance on operating leases then there is no danger that significant assets and liabilities are languishing off balance sheet. Conversely, if a company has substantial operating lease commitments, then under current standard practice no assets and liabilities will be recognised with respect to those commitments. For such companies if reclassification as finance leases were ultimately required, this would inevitably cause increases in balance sheet gearing.

ANALYSIS

1. Operating lease rentals - accounting policy

As regards operating leases, SSAP 21 requires rentals to be charged on a straight line basis, even if payments are not made on this basis, unless another systematic and rational basis is more appropriate.

If a lessor grants a period of reduced rentals or even a rental holiday at the outset of a lease, then payments will not be made on a straight line basis and simply charging rentals as they are incurred would not seem to be an alternative systematic and rational basis.

The capitalisation of lease premiums as tangible fixed assets and their depreciation on a straight line basis over the lease term will result in a straight line recognition of the premium which is clearly appropriate.

In more recent years, some new operating leases have included reverse lease premiums as incentives to the lessee to enter the agreement. A proposed Urgent Issues Task Force Abstract suggests that such reverse premiums should also be spread on a straight line basis over the lease term. One company that already does this is **Example 1 James Beattie plc**.

Example 1
James Beattie plc   *31 January 1994*
Extract from accounting policies

> **Leases**
> The Company's principal leased assets are properties held under operating leases and the annual rentals are charged directly to the profit and loss account. Reverse premiums are treated as deferred income and released to the profit and loss account evenly over the period up to the first rent review of the lease concerned.

Whilst many companies state unambiguously that operating lease rentals are charged to the profit and loss account on a straight line basis, some companies do not, and consequently the precise policy adopted is unclear.

Example 2 Inchcape plc merely state that rental payments arising from operating leases are charged to the profit and loss account but do not mention the basis used.

Example 2
Inchcape plc   *31 December 1993*
Extract from accounting policies

> **(i) Leases –**
> (i) As Lessee – Assets held under finance leases are treated as if they had been purchased at the present value of the minimum lease payments. This cost is included under tangible fixed assets and depreciation is provided accordingly. The corresponding obligations under these leases are included within borrowings. The finance charge element of rentals payable is charged to the profit and loss account. Rental payments arising from operating leases are charged to the profit and loss account.

Example 3 Capital Industries plc state that operating lease rentals are charged as incurred.

Example 3
Capital Industries plc   *31 December 1993*
Extract from accounting policies

(d) Leased assets
Assets acquired under finance leases and hire purchase agreements are capitalised and depreciated in accordance with the group's depreciation policy. The capital element of future lease payments is included in the balance sheet as obligations under finance leases. The finance element of lease payments is charged to the profit and loss account.

Rentals under operating leases are charged to the profit and loss account as incurred over the lease term.

Example 4 Bromsgrove Industries plc state that operating lease rentals are written off in the year to which they relate.

Example 4
Bromsgrove Industries plc   *31 March 1993*
Extract from accounting policies

Leasing and hire purchase
Assets acquired under finance leases and hire purchase arrangements are capitalised and the related liability included in creditors. Finance charges in respect of such assets are charged in the profit and loss account over the shorter of the estimated useful life of the asset or the aggregate of the primary and secondary lease periods. Operating lease rentals are written off in the year to which they relate.

Example 5 Burmah Castrol plc have changed the wording of their accounting policy to clarify that rentals are (and presumably always have been, since no change of policy is indicated) charged on a straight line basis having previously stated that rentals were charged as incurred.

Example 5
Burmah Castrol plc   *31 December 1993*
Extract from accounting policies

Leases
The cost of assets held under finance leases is included within tangible fixed assets and depreciation is provided in accordance with the group's normal depreciation policy. The capital element of future lease rentals is included in creditors. Rental payments in respect of operating leases are charged to profit and loss account on a straight-line basis over the lease term.

Example 6 Hanson plc, despite having significant operating lease commitments discloses no accounting policy for operating lease rentals.

Example 6
Hanson plc *30 September 1993*
Accounting policies and extract from the notes to the accounts

22 Commitments   The annual commitment under non-cancellable operating leases was:

	Land and buildings		Plant and equipment	
	1993	1992	**1993**	1992
Leases expiring:	£ million		£ million	
Within one year	**11**	5	**4**	3
Within two to five years	**33**	21	**18**	16
After five years	**28**	40	**9**	7
	72	66	**31**	26

If a company pays rent on a vacant property, prudence might require that provision be made for future rentals payable in excess of any likely amounts receivable on disposal of the leasehold interest. This would appear to be a more appropriate basis than straight line recognition. A proposed Urgent Issues Task Force Abstract on this subject was dropped as a result of difficulties in establishing a general rule that would ensure appropriate treatment in all diverse circumstances.

2. Operating lease rentals – profit and loss account disclosure

SSAP 21 requires the disclosure of operating lease rentals charged in the profit and loss account, analysed between amounts payable in respect of hire of plant and machinery and in respect of other operating leases.

Example 7 Bowater plc disclosed amounts payable in respect of leases of land and buildings rather than "other" operating leases – which is helpful and informative if it is presumed that these are their only other leases.

Example 7
Bowater plc *31 December 1993*
Extract from the notes to the accounts

2 Operating Expenses
The analysis of operating expenses between continuing and discontinued businesses is as follows:

	1993 Continuing £m	1993 Discontinued £m	1993 Total £m	1992 Continuing £m	1992 Discontinued £m	1992 Total £m
Materials	954.6	6.7	961.3	679.0	12.6	691.6
Employee costs	545.7	6.2	551.9	378.7	10.9	389.6
Depreciation	85.3	0.9	86.2	60.2	1.6	61.8
Other operating costs	338.0	7.4	345.4	238.0	12.8	250.8
Other operating income	(26.2)	(0.2)	(26.4)	(24.3)	(0.1)	(24.4)
	1,897.4	21.0	1,918.4	1,331.6	37.8	1,369.4

Continuing operations in 1993 include the following relating to acquisitions; materials £138.2 million, employee costs £79.3 million, depreciation £11.1 million, other operating costs £52.8 million and other operating income £1.7 million.

	1993 £m	1992 £m
Materials	961.3	691.6
Change in stock of finished goods and work in progress	1.5	(3.6)
Employee costs (Note 3)	551.9	389.6
Other expenses	311.2	229.8
Depreciation: owned assets	81.4	54.9
leased assets	4.8	6.9
Operating lease rentals: plant and machinery	9.2	6.6
land and buildings	13.3	10.1
Research and development	6.8	5.0
Auditors' remuneration: audit services — UK	1.0	1.1
— Overseas	1.6	1.2
non-audit services — UK	0.3	0.4
— Overseas	0.5	0.2
Share of associated undertakings' operating profits	(3.0)	(5.5)
Income from listed investments	(0.2)	(0.8)
Net rental income	(6.6)	(6.0)
Other income	(16.6)	(12.1)
	1,918.4	1,369.4

Audit fees of £1.4 million (1992: £1.4 million) and other United Kingdom fees of £0.3 million (1992: £0.4 million) were payable to the group auditors, Ernst & Young.
Auditor's remuneration, includes £0.2 million (1992 £0.2 million) for audit services provided to the parent company.

Example 8 Hanson plc discloses the amounts payable in respect of computers, plant and machinery but not amounts in respect of other operating leases (such as properties) despite the existence of such leases.

Example 8
Hanson plc *30 September 1993*
Extract from the notes to the accounts

		1993		1992	
		Continuing	Discontinued	Continuing	Discontinued
		£million	£million	£million	£million
3 Costs and	Changes in stock of finished	**92**	**6**	38	5
overheads	goods and work in progress				
less other	Raw materials and	**4,616**	**13**	4,214	97
income	consumables				
	Employment costs (note 4)	**1,478**	**22**	1,295	80
	Depreciation	**288**	**16**	228	20
	Depreciation of finance leases	**6**	**–**	6	–
	Other operating charges	**2,249**	**15**	1,708	57
	Share of profit of associated undertakings	**(19)**	**–**	(18)	–
		8,710	**72**	7,471	259
	Discontinued per above	**72**		259	
		8,782		7,730	

The total figures for continuing operations in 1993 include the following charge (credits) relating to acquisitions; changes in stock £(2)mn, raw materials and consumables £69mn, employment costs £16mn, depreciation £8mn and other operating charges £15mn.
Other operating charges include hire of computers, plant and machinery £108mn (£90mn), remuneration of auditors £6mn (£5mn) and expenditure on reserach and development of £20mn (26mn). Income from listed investments amounted to £5mn (21mn)
Non audit fees paid to Ernst & Young in the UK amounted to £1mn (£1mn)

3. Operating lease commitments

In respect of operating leases, SSAP 21 requires disclosure of payments which the lessee is committed to make during the next year, analysed between those in which the commitment expires within that year, in the second to fifth years inclusive and over five years from the balance sheet date. Commitments in respect of leases of land and buildings are to be shown separately from those in respect of other operating leases.

Example 9 Inchcape plc discloses the required information but without comparatives. The Companies Act 1985 Sch 4 para 58(2) does require corresponding amounts in respect of items stated in the notes.

Example 9
Inchcape plc *31 December 1993*
Extract from the notes to the accounts

31 REVENUE COMMITMENTS	Land and Buildings £m	Other Tangible Fixed Assets £m
Operating lease rentals payable in 1994 are in respect of commitments expiring:		
Within one year	14.3	4.1
Between one and five years	32.0	9.2
In five years or more	21.0	–
	67.3	13.3

The Group has, in the ordinary course of business, commitments under forward foreign exchange and interest rate contracts relating to the hedging of transaction and interest exposures and overseas earnings.

Example 10 Gestetner plc disclosed commitments in respect of plant and equipment rather than "other" operating leases presumably on the basis that these are their only other operating leases.

Example 10
Gestetner plc *31 October 1993*
Extract from the notes to the accounts

	GROUP		COMPANY	
	1993	1992	1993	1992
NOTE 24 OPERATING LEASE COMMITMENTS	£m	£m	£m	£m
At the balance sheet date, there were annual commitments under the operating leases expiring as follows:				
LAND AND BUILDINGS				
WITHIN ONE YEAR	2.1	2.6	....	....
BETWEEN ONE AND FIVE YEARS	13.0	14.2	....	....
AFTER FIVE YEARS	4.8	7.1	....	1.6
	19.9	23.9	....	1.6
PLANT AND EQUIPMENT				
WITHIN ONE YEAR	2.4	2.5	....	....
BETWEEN ONE AND FIVE YEARS	9.6	10.6	....	....
AFTER FIVE YEARS	0.1	0.2	....	....
	12.1	13.3	....	....

4. Finance leases – initial recording

As regards finance leases, SSAP 21 requires the initial recording of an asset and liability at the present value of the minimum lease payments. To do this whenever an asset is leased for less than its useful life and any residual value accrues to the lessor, the company would need to know the interest rate implicit in the lease. The standard allows the fair value of the asset to be used instead of the present value of the minimum lease payments if it is a close approximation (i.e., if the residual value accruing to the lessor is immaterial as will usually be the case).

Example 11 Inchcape plc records finance leases at the present value of minimum lease payments.

Example 11
Inchcape plc   *31 December 1993*
Extract from accounting policies

(i) Leases
(i) As Lessee – Assets held under finance leases are treated as if they had been purchased at the present value of the minimum lease payments. This cost is included under tangible fixed assets and depreciation is provided accordingly. The corresponding obligations under these leases are included within borrowings. The finance charge element of rentals payable is charged to the profit and loss account. Rental payments arising from operating leases are charged to the profit and loss account.

Example 12 Bromsgrove Industries plc states that assets acquired under finance leases are capitalised but do not stipulate how.

Example 12
Bromsgrove Industries plc   *31 March 1993*
Extract from accounting policies

Leasing and hire purchase
Assets acquired under finance leases and hire purchase arrangements are capitalised and the related liability included in creditors. Finance charges in respect of such assets are charged in the profit and loss account over the shorter of the estimated useful life of the asset or the aggregate of the primary and secondary lease periods. Operating lease rentals are written off in the year to which they relate.

5. Finance leases – apportionment of rentals between capital and interest

The standard requires rentals payable under finance leases to be apportioned between the finance charge and a reduction of the capital obligation so as to produce a constant rate of charge on the remaining capital obligation or a reasonable approximation thereto. Using the interest rate implicit in the lease will produce a constant rate if the lease is initially recorded at the present value of the minimum lease payments. A sum-of-the-digits (rule of 78) basis will produce a reasonable approximation as long as the lease term is no longer than about seven years.

Example 13 Capital Industries plc is one of many companies that does not stipulate a method for allocating rentals between capital and interest.

Example 13
Capital Industries plc *31 December 1993*
Extract from accounting policies

(d) Leased assets
Assets required under finance leases and hire purchase agreements are capitalised and depreciated in accordance with the group's depreciation policy. The capital element of future lease payments is included in the balance sheet as obligations under finance leases. The finance element of lease payments is charged to the profit and loss account.

Rentals under operating leases are charged to the profit and loss account as incurred over the lease term.

Example 14 Bromsgrove Industries plc do not stipulate a method for allocating rentals between capital and interest but do state that finance charges are allocated over the shorter of the estimated useful life of the asset and the aggregate of the primary and secondary lease periods. This would appear to be a more suitable policy for the allocation of depreciation rather than finance charges.

Example 14
Bromsgrove Industries plc *31 March 1993*
Extract from accounting policies

Leasing and hire purchase
Assets acquired under finance leases and hire purchase arrangements are capitalised and the related liability included in creditors. Finance charges in respect of such assets are charged in the profit and loss account over the shorter of the estimated useful life of the asset or the aggregate of the primary and secondary lease periods. Operating lease rentals are written off in the year to which they relate.

Example 15 Gestetner plc states that rentals are apportioned using the rule of 78 method.

Example 15
Gestetner plc *31 October 1993*
Extract from accounting policies

TANGIBLE FIXED ASSETS AND DEPRECIATION
Tangible fixed assets, including assets acquired under finance leases, are stated at cost or subsequent revaluation. Tangible assets acquired under finance leases are capitalised with outstanding obligations due under such leases, net of finance charges, included within other creditors. Rentals payable thereon are apportioned, using the Rule of 78 method, between a reduction of the outstanding obligation and finance charges.

Example 16 Prism Leisure Corporation plc state that finance charges are written off over the period of the agreement with reference to the written down value of the capital amount – but do not stipulate how this is done.

25

Example 16
Prism Leisure Corporation plc *28 March 1993*
Extract from accounting policies

Finance leases
Where assets are financed by leasing agreements that give rights approximating to ownership and are retained for use by the Group, the assets are treated as if they had been purchased outright. The amount capitalised is the present value of the minimum lease payments payable during the lease term. The corresponding leasing commitments are shown as finance lease obligations. Finance charges are written off over the period of the agreement with reference to the written down value of the capital amount.

6. Finance leases – depreciation

The standard requires that assets leased under finance leases be depreciated over the shorter of the lease term and the useful life.

Example 17 Inchcape plc simply state that assets leased under finance leases are depreciated.

Example 17
Inchcape plc *31 December 1993*
Extract from accounting policies
(i) Leases –
(i) As Lessee – Assets held under finance leases are treated as if they had been purchased at the present value of the minimum lease payments. This cost is included under tangible fixed assets and depreciation is provided accordingly. The corresponding obligations under these leases are included within borrowings. The finance charge element of rentals payable is charged to the profit and loss account. Rental payments arising from operating leases are charged to the profit and loss account.

Example 18 Westland Group plc state that assets leased under finance leases are depreciated in accordance with the group's depreciation policy – which is based on useful life.

Example 18
Westland Group plc *1 October 1993*
Extract from accounting policies

7 Tangible assets, depreciation and leases

Certain land and buildings are included in the accounts at revalued amounts.

Depreciation is calculated to write off the cost or valuation of fixed assets, by equal instalments, over their expected useful lives on the following bases:

Freehold buildings	up to 40 years
Leasehold land and buildings	40 years or period of lease if shorter
Plant, machinery, fixtures, fitting, helicopters and equipment	4 to 15 years

Expenditure on production tooling not specifically recovered under contracts is written off as follows:

Development standard tooling	as incurred
Production standard tooling	4 to 10 years

Freehold land is not depreciated.

Tangible assets held under finance leases, which give rights equivalent to ownership, are capitalised and depreciated in accordance with the Company's depreciation policy. Leasing payments compromise interest and capital elements. Interest is charged to revenue and the capital element of future lease payments is included in creditors.

Rental payments under operating leases are charged against revenue as incurred.

CONCLUSION

It is apparent then, that 10 years on from the introduction of SSAP 21 companies are complying with the standard but are perhaps a little reticent to give away too much detail about the process of lease classification and the extent of usage of actuarial principles (discounting techniques) rather than simpler approximations. Where then do we go from here?

The ICAEW's Financial Reporting and Accounting Group, when asked by the ASB to review SSAP 21 for practical problems concluded (in 1992) that if treatment as finance leases is to continue to be triggered by the transference of substantially all the risk and rewards of ownership – then the 90% test should be replaced with a series of qualitative tests. I believe that the ASB will go further than this – the conflict between SSAP 21 and FRS 5 must surely be resolved by reference to the Statement of Principles for Financial Reporting (upon which FRS 5 is based). This will entail moving away from the idea of recognition of assets and liabilities once a point has been reached to the idea of progressive recognition as more risks and rewards are transferred (i.e., the asset is leased for more and more of its useful life). SSAP 21 could be amended to encompass this change but it could just as easily be done away with altogether with the scope of FRS 4 on Capital Instruments being widened to bring in leases.

Perhaps ASB Chairman Sir David Tweedie gave the game away back in March 1994 at the ICAS Festival of Accounting when he said:

"One of the oldest off balance sheet techniques is leasing. It has been partially curbed by the requirement to capitalise finance leases. Yet is there any point in capitalising only finance leases? If a company has a binding obligation to pay lease rentals these result in a liability even if the lease does not fall within the existing definition of a finance lease."

LEASING

The writing is very much on the wall for the operating lease. It is now apparent that whilst SSAP 21 did require us to consider more than just the legal form of a transaction it stopped short of requiring us to always reflect the economic substance of that transaction. It can only be a matter of time before we have to do so.

AUDITORS' REVIEW OF CADBURY COMPLIANCE STATEMENTS

Andrew Piper and Rowan Jones

INTRODUCTION

The auditors' review of Cadbury compliance statements is currently the subject of the pronouncements of the following bodies:

- Cadbury Committee on the Financial Aspects of Corporate Governance
  - Report
  - Code of Best Practice
  - Notes to the Code
- London Stock Exchange
  - Listing Rules
- Auditing Practices Board (APB)
  - Bulletin 1993/2

The Cadbury Committee was set up in May 1991 by the Financial Reporting Council, the London Stock Exchange and the accountancy profession. After considering submissions made following the issue of an interim report, its final report was published on 1 December 1992. This includes a Code of Best Practice and the Committee recommends that the boards of all listed companies registered in the United Kingdom should comply with the Code. The Code is as follows:

1   The Board of Directors

1.1   The board should meet regularly, retain full and effective control over the company and monitor the executive management.

1.2   There should be a clearly accepted division of responsibilities at the head of a company, which will ensure a balance of power and authority, such that no one individual has unfettered powers of decision. Where the chairman is also the chief executive, it is essential that there should be a strong and independent element on the board, with a recognised senior member.

1.3   The board should include non-executive directors of sufficient calibre and number for their views to carry significant weight in the board's decisions.

1.4   The board should have a formal schedule of matters specifically reserved to it for decision to ensure that the direction and control of the company is firmly in its hands.

1.5   There should be an agreed procedure for directors in the furtherance of their duties to take independent professional advice if necessary, at the company's expense.

1.6 All directors should have access to the advice and services of the company secretary, who is responsible to the board for ensuring that board procedures are followed and that applicable rules and regulations are complied with. Any question of the removal of the company secretary should be a matter for the board as a whole.

2 Non-Executive Directors

2.1 Non-executive directors should bring an independent judgement to bear on issues of strategy, performance, resources, including key appointments, and standards of conduct.

2.2 The majority should be independent of management and free from any business or other relationship which could materially interfere with the exercise of their independent judgement, apart from their fees and shareholding. Their fees should reflect the time which they commit to the company.

2.3 Non-executive directors should be appointed for specified terms and reappointment should not be automatic.

2.4 Non-executive directors should be selected through a formal process and both this process and their appointment should be a matter for the board as a whole.

3 Executive Directors

3.1 Directors' service contracts should not exceed three years without shareholders' approval.

3.2 There should be full and clear disclosure of directors' total emoluments and those of the chairman and highest-paid UK director, including pension contributions and stock options. Separate figures should be given for salary and performance-related elements and the basis on which performance is measured should be explained.

3.3 Executive directors' pay should be subject to the recommendations of a remuneration committee made up wholly or mainly of non-executive directors.

4 Reporting and Controls

4.1 It is the board's duty to present a balanced and understandable assessment of the company's position.

4.2 The board should ensure that an objective and professional relationship is maintained with the auditors.

4.3 The board should establish an audit committee of at least 3 non-executive directors with written terms of reference which deal clearly with its authority and duties.

4.4   The directors should explain their responsibility for preparing the accounts next to a statement by the auditors about their reporting responsibilities.

4.5   The directors should report on the effectiveness of the company's system of internal control.

4.6   The directors should report that the business is a going concern, with supporting assumptions or qualifications as necessary.

Note: References to the notes to the Code have been excluded.

The Committee recommends in the introduction to the Code that listed companies reporting in respect of years ending after 30 June 1993 should make a statement in their report and accounts about their compliance with the Code and identify and give reasons for any areas of non-compliance.

The Code also sets out as Notes a number of further recommendations on good practice, which do not form part of the Code. Note 14 recommends that the company's statement of compliance should be reviewed by the auditors before publication insofar as it relates to paragraphs 1.4, 1.5, 2.3, 2.4, 3.1 to 3.3, and 4.3 to 4.6 of the Code. Notwithstanding this, Note 13 states that the "companies will not be able to comply with paragraphs 4.5 (internal control) or 4.6 (going concern) until the necessary guidance has been developed"; at the time of writing the necessary guidance has not been issued.

In itself, the report of the Cadbury Committee is voluntary; indeed, the report makes clear that "the Code is to be followed by individuals and boards in the light of their own particular circumstances. They are responsible for ensuring that their actions meet the spirit of the Code and in interpreting it they should give precedence to substance over form" (para 7). The Committee remains responsible for reviewing the implementation of its proposals (para 6).

However, the London Stock Exchange has taken elements of the Cadbury Report and introduced them into its Listing Rules (February 1994). Listed companies must, of course, issue an annual report and accounts (12.41) and the report and accounts of a company incorporated in the UK must, unless the Exchange otherwise agrees, include the following (12.43(j)):

• A statement as to whether or not it has complied throughout the accounting period with the Code of Best Practice;
• A company that has not complied with the Code, or has complied with only part of the Code, or (in the case of requirements of a continuing nature) had complied for only part of the accounting period, must specify the paragraphs with which it has not complied and (where relevant) for what part of the period such non-compliance continued, and give reasons for any non-compliance.

In addition, 12.43(j) requires that the company's statement of compliance must be reviewed by the auditors before publication insofar as it relates to paragraphs 1.4, 1.5, 2.3, 2.4, 3.1–3.3 and 4.3–4.6 of the Code. It is important to note that this last listing requirement does not refer to the manner in which the auditors' review is reported on.

In December 1993, the Auditing Practices Board issued a Bulletin (1993/2) on "Disclosures Relating to Corporate Governance". The purpose of all of the APB's bulletins is to provide auditors with timely guidance on new or emerging issues; they are persuasive rather than prescriptive; they are indicative of good practice; and they are likely to be developed into Statements of Auditing Standards (with which auditors are required to comply) or Practice Notes ("The Scope and Authority of APB Pronouncements", May 1993).

PRESENTATION OF THE COMPLIANCE STATEMENT

No specific form has been recommended or required by the Committee, the Stock Exchange or the accountancy profession. This has led to a flexible approach which companies have interpreted in very different ways. These can be classified into three types:

(a)   a new separate statement, sometimes on a separate page;
(b)   a statement included under a separate heading as part of the Directors' report; and
(c)   a statement included in the Chairman's statement.

Non-compliance with the Code, as might be expected given its newness, occurs frequently. The stated reasons also recur. A common reason was the lack of formal recording of existing procedures; many companies have reported that existing procedures, which complied with those recommended but were not previously recorded, have now been formally recorded. Others have stated that their size is too small to justify the appointment of three non-executive directors so they do not comply with 4.3, which requires an audit committee of at least three non-executive directors. This "size" justification is recognised by the Cadbury Committee itself: paragraph 8 states that "smaller listed companies may initially have difficulty in complying with some aspects of the Code"; the implication is, however, that they will comply at some future date.

The disclosure of the paragraphs of the Code that have not been complied with and the disclosure of non-compliance for part-periods have varied significantly.

PRESENTATION OF THE REPORT OF THE AUDITORS' REVIEW

The Cadbury Committee recommends that the company's statement of compliance should be reviewed by the auditors before publication but that the review should only cover those stated paragraphs of the Code that can be objectively verified (para 4); as we have seen, these recommendations have been put into the Stock Exchange's "Listing Rules".

On the matter of reporting on the result of the review, Cadbury proposed that the auditors need only report on that non-compliance which has not been properly disclosed. As we will see below, the APB has taken a different position.

The APB, in Bulletin 1993/2, has provided guidance for auditors in relation to this review. In relation to reporting on the auditors' review, the APB's main concern is with situations in which "auditors are known to have reviewed the information but readers of that information are unaware of the scope of the review and its conclusion" (para 22).

Consequently, the APB considers it desirable, but not obligatory, for the annual reports to include a report from the auditors, preferably separate from their report on the financial statements, regarding their review of the statement of compliance (para 22). However, the Board also states that an acceptable alternative to a published report on the review is for the directors to include in the statement of compliance a reference to the fact that the auditors have reviewed that statement (para 24).

While the Board prefers the auditors themselves to report and to issue a review report separate from the audit report on the financial statements, it allows the possibility of combining these two provided that "it is made clear that the review is additional to and separate from the audit" (para 23).

The Bulletin further states that if auditors are either:

- Not satisfied as to the form and context of the directors' reference, or
- Not satisfied that the directors' statement appropriately reflects the company's compliance with the paragraphs of the Code specified for the auditors' review

they should report on their views (para 25).

Finally, in respect of paragraphs 4.5 (internal control) and 4.6 (going concern) of the Code, the APB states that, when directors make no statements about these two issues, the auditors' report should make no reference to paras 4.5 and 4.6. The Board also "strongly advises auditors not to report publicly on any statements by the directors concerning these two paragraphs". If directors do make such statements, *any auditors' reports issued* should "make it clear that the auditors' review does not include such statements, and that the auditors do not comment thereon" (para 30); it may be important to note that this guidance means that, in such circumstances, the auditors' views may not be publicly available – because the auditors' report is not published and the directors have taken the option of publicly referring to the fact of the review having taken place.

The APB Bulletin provides illustrative examples of review reports.

In relation to reporting on the auditors' review, there are four main situations encountered:

(a) review report is included as an additional item in the statutory audit report;
(b) there is a separate signed review report referring to the compliance statement;
(c) the company makes reference to the auditors' review; and
(d) there is no reference in the annual report to the auditors' review.

PRACTICE AND COMMENT

Some statements on corporate governance, of which the compliance statement is often only a small part, and reports are reproduced below with brief comments. The examples have been considered under the following headings but many of them relate to more than one area of discussion:

1. Report of review presented as a separate statement.
2. Report of review included in the audit report.
3. Reference in the statement of compliance.
4. Positive report by auditors.
5. No reference to report on review.

6. Reference to a specific date.
7. Non-compliance.
8. Introduction of formal procedures.
9. Insufficient non-executive directors.
10. No audit committee.
11. Separation of roles of chairman & chief executive.
12. No signature.
13. Detailed description of compliance.
14. Other matters included in the corporate governance statement.
15. Internal controls.

1. Report of review as a separate statement

The APB preference is for a separate report of the review by the auditor. **Example 1 BBA Group plc** follows exactly the example provided by the APB. It might be possible to quibble about the review report referring to the directors' statement of compliance when the statement above is called Directors' Statement on Corporate Governance. It was unfortunate that the third non-executive director resigned but the fact remains that at the time of the statement and review report the company was not in compliance with the Code; some readers might expect this to be highlighted and more readily apparent. However, the APB's preferred form of reporting does not require non-compliance to be emphasised.

Example 1
BBA Group plc *31 December 1993*
Separate, after directors' report (p 22)

DIRECTORS' STATEMENT ON CORPORATE GOVERNANCE

When making their preliminary announcement of the Company's performance in 1990, the directors re-affirmed their management style to be one "characterised by honesty and openness", and those qualities, together with a determination to remain constantly answerable to the Company's shareholders, continue to dictate the manner in which the Board conducts its stewardship. Consequently, the Cadbury Committee's Report concerning the financial aspects of corporate governance was welcomed.

With regard to the Code of Best Practice accompanying that Report, the majority of its provisions were already reflected in the practices of the Company; the Board having long recognised the wisdom, in terms of effective governance, of, amongst other things, separating the roles of Chief Executive and Chairman, appointing independent non-executive directors of high calibre, subjecting executive directors' remuneration to the scrutiny of a Remuneration Committee and encouraging a rigorous and objective audit.

However, having had regard to the structure of the Board (then two executive and three non-executive members), the directors took the view that unreserved compliance with the Code's provisions ought not to be undertaken without some diligent examination of the implications of so doing, both in terms of cost and further internal procedures which might be necessitated.

The outcome of that examination was the Board's decision on 21 September 1993 to establish an audit committee (to comprise three non-executive directors of the Company) as contemplated by provision 4.3 of the Code and to regulate in greater detail the terms and manner of appointment of non-executive directors so as to secure compliance with provisions 2.3 and 2.4.

Excepting the consequence of Mr L J Stammers' resignation referred to below, and those provisions where the necessary guidance for compliance has yet to be published, the Board is satisfied that the Company continues to comply with the Code in full.

On 1 December 1993, Mr L J Stammers tendered his resignation as a non-executive director of the Board. This resignation, which was wholly unforeseen, resulted in the membership of the Board's audit committee being reduced to two (Mr R H Cooper and Mr V E Treves) contrary to the requirement of provision 4.3 of the Code. No appointment to that committee, in place of Mr Stammers, has yet been made.

REVIEW REPORT TO BBA GROUP PLC

In addition to our audit of the financial statements we have reviewed the directors' statement above concerning the Company's compliance with the Code of Best Practice, insofar as it relates to the specific paragraphs of the Code which the London Stock Exchange has specified for our review. We carried out our review having regard to the Bulletin "Disclosures relating to corporate governance" issued by the Auditing Practices Board.

The purpose of the directors' statement is to give readers information which assists them in forming their own views regarding the governance of the Company. In respect of the paragraphs of the code specified for our consideration, we are required to draw attention to any aspects of the Company's non-compliance with the Code which the directors have not properly disclosed. We are not required to review, and have not reviewed, the effectiveness of the Company's governance procedures.

Through enquiry of certain directors and officers of the Company, and examination of relevant documents, we have satisfied ourselves that the directors' statement appropriately reflects the Company's compliance with the specified paragraphs of the Code.

KPMG Peat Marwick
Chartered Accountants
Bradford

24 March 1994

Note that this Review report was placed directly underneath the Directors' statement on Corporate Governance. See also **Example 16**.

2. Report of review included in the Audit Report

This is not the APB's preferred form of presentation, ostensibly because of possible confusion by the readers of the difference between an audit and a review. The APB's second example has broadly been followed by **Example 2 Bass plc** and clearly distinguishes the "Corporate Governance matters" from the audit opinion; however, it has omitted the sentence "We carried out our review having regard to the Bulletin, 'Disclosures relating to corporate governance' issued by the Auditing Practices Board". This could be considered an unfortunate omission as its inclusion by the APB was to indicate what a review meant, and readers might consider that an audit had been completed. It should also be noted that the report is addressed to the members of Bass plc and states that "We are not required to review, and have not reviewed, the effectiveness of the Company's governance procedures". The conclusion is "that the Directors' statement appropriately reflects the Company's compliance with the specified paragraphs of the Code". This is surprising given that the governance statement

Example 13 Bass plc mentions internal controls: the APB clearly states that if directors do mention internal controls, the review report should make it clear that the auditors' review does not include such statements (para 30). Experts know that the "specified paragraphs" do not relate to internal controls but it is unreasonable to expect the average shareholder to know.

Example 2
Bass plc *30 September 1993*
Included in the Report of the Auditors to the members of Bass plc

REPORT OF THE AUDITORS
to the members of Bass plc

We have audited the financial statements on pages 30 to 58, which have been prepared under the historical cost convention as modified by the revaluation of certain fixed assets and on the basis of the accounting policies set out on pages 30 to 32.

RESPECTIVE RESPONSIBILITIES OF DIRECTORS AND AUDITORS
As described above, the Company's Directors are solely responsible for the preparation of the financial statements including the selection of suitable accounting policies. It is our responsibility to form an independent opinion, based on our audit, on those financial statements and to report our opinion to you.

BASIS OF OPINION
We conducted our audit in accordance with Auditing Standards issued by the Auditing Practices Board. An audit includes examination, on a test basis, of evidence relevant to the amounts and disclosures in the financial statements. It also includes an assessment of the significant estimates and judgements made by the Directors in the preparation of the financial statements, and of whether the accounting policies are appropriate to the Company's circumstances, consistently applied and adequately disclosed.

We planned and performed our audit so as to obtain all the information and explanations which we considered necessary in order to provide us with sufficient evidence to give reasonable assurance that the financial statements are free from material misstatement, whether caused by fraud or other irregularity or error. In forming our opinion we also evaluated the overall adequacy of the presentation of information in the financial statements.

OPINION
In our opinion the financial statements give a true and fair view of the state of affairs of the Company and the Group as at 30 September 1993 and the Group's profit for the year then ended and have been properly prepared in accordance with the Companies Act 1985.

CORPORATE GOVERNANCE MATTERS
In addition to our audit of the financial statements, we have reviewed the Directors' statement on page 26 concerning the Company's compliance with the Code of Best Practice, insofar as it relates to the paragraphs of the code which the London Stock Exchange has specified for our review.

The purpose of the Directors' statements is to give readers information which assists them in forming their own views regarding the governance of the Company. In respect of the paragraphs of the Code specified for our consideration, we are required to draw attention to any aspects of the Company's non-compliance with the Code which the Directors have not properly disclosed. We are not required to review, and have not reviewed, the effectiveness of the Company's governance procedures.

Through enquiry of certain directors and officers of the Company, and examination of relevant documents, we have satisfied ourselves that the Directors' statement appropriately reflects the Company's compliance with the specified paragraphs of the Code.

Ernst & Young
Chartered Accountants
Registered Auditor
London
30 November 1993

3. Reference in the statement of compliance

Many companies include a reference to the report of the auditors' review within their statement on corporate governance. This is not the preferred choice of the APB but their third choice. **Example 3 The Shell Transport and Trading Company plc** is a relatively brief statement which clearly separates the compliance statement by the Board, and their statement regarding the review by the auditors.

Example 3
The Shell Transport and Trading Company plc   *31 December 1993*
Part of the Report of the Directors

Code of Best Practice – effective from July 1, 1993
The Board considers that Shell Transport has fully complied with the Code of Best Practice published by the Committee on the Financial Aspects of Corporate Governance with the exception of the provisions relating to the commentary on internal controls and the going concern basis of the accounts, in respect of which the guidelines recommended by that Committee have yet to be finalized.

The Company's auditors, Ernst & Young, have reviewed the above statement insofar as it relates to the paragraphs of the Code of Best Practice which The London Stock Exchange has specified for their review. They have reported to the Board that they concur with the above statement.

See also Examples 7, 8, 11, 12, 14, 15, 18, 20.

Although reference should be made to the complete examples, it is of interest to summarise briefly the key phrase used by the report of the auditor as quoted by the directors:

Example
3 . . . they concur . . .
7 . . . appropriately reflects . . .
8 . . . they concur . . .
11 . . . appropriately reflects . . .
12 . . . this statement is properly made.
14 . . . they concur . . .
15 . . . they concur . . .
18 . . . appropriately reflects . . .
20 . . . it is reasonable for the directors to make this statement.

4. Positive report by the auditors

Example 4 Croda International plc states "They have reported to the Board that they are of the opinion that it is appropriate for the directors to make the statement that the Group complies with these aspects of the Code". It is perhaps an example of all that needs to be said when there is no non-compliance, and the auditors have agreed that the "Group complies". The more usual wording is that "it is appropriate for the directors to make the statement" whether or not there is full compliance.

Example 4
Croda International plc   *31 December 1993*
Part of Directors' report (p 21)

> **Corporate governance**
> The Cadbury Committee report on the Financial Aspects of Corporate Governance was published in December 1992 together with its Code of Best Practice which came into effect after 30 June 1993. The Board supports the highest standards in corporate governance and confirms that the Group complies with all provisions of the Code for which external guidance has so far been given.
>
> The Group's auditors, Price Waterhouse, have reviewed our compliance with the specific matters in the Code which the London Stock Exchange requires that the auditors should review. They have reported to the Board that they are of the opinion that it is appropriate for the directors to make the statement that the Group complies with those aspects of the Code.

See also **Example 6**.

5. No reference to report on review

Example 5 The Boots Company plc has a very brief compliance statement as part of the Chairman's Statement. There is no "heading" to this item to bring it to the notice of the reader, and there is no reference to the auditors' review. Since there is no other reference to the auditors' review in the report and accounts, it would seem to contravene the requirements of the APB Bulletin.

The omission of any reference to the review by the auditor would appear to be the second most popular choice and presumably reflects the lack of a reporting requirement in the listing rules.

Example 5
The Boots Company plc   *31 March 1994*
Included in Chairman's Statement (p 5)

> We have further reviewed the composition and terms of reference of our board committees and in particular have adopted the suggestion in the Cadbury Report on the Financial Aspects of Corporate Governance that the Nominations Committee should advise the board on executive as well as non-executive appointments. We continue to comply with the Code of Best Practice in that report, except for reporting on internal controls and the going concern status of the company neither of which can be pursued without further guidance from the accountancy profession.

6. Reference to a specific date

The listing rule basically requires a statement of compliance and this could be, and often is, a very short statement. Early in 1993 the listing rule referred to the annual report and accounts for accounting periods ending after 30 June 1993 and the Code published in December 1992. There was not much time for companies whose accounting period ended on 31 December 1993 to make changes to ensure full compliance for the whole year.

The listing rule (12.43(j)) requires that when a company complied with the Code for only part of an accounting period (in the case of requirements of a continuing nature), it should specify for what part of the period such non-compliance continued, and give reasons for the non-compliance.

The Draft Guidance for directors (October 1993) . . . produced by the Working Group of the ICAEW Internal Control and Financial Reporting discussed the problems of the date or period to which the statement should apply. **Example 6 Reckitt & Colman plc** refers to the changes they have made and quotes a specific date by which they were in full compliance with all the provisions of the Code other than those for which guidance is awaited.

Example 6
Reckitt & Colman plc *1 January 1994*
In the Annual Review part of the Operating Review (p 13)

Corporate governance
During the year the directors of Reckitt & Colman carried out a full review of the company's compliance with the Code of Best Practice issued by the Cadbury Committee on the Financial Aspects of Corporate Governance on 1 December 1992. Following that review, procedures were formalised with regard to the selection and appointment of non-executive directors and the ability of directors to take independent professional advice. A minor amendment was made to directors' service agreements. On 1 January 1994 Reckitt & Colman was in full compliance with all the provisions of the Code, other than those items (namely going concern and internal control) for which guidance is awaited. The company's auditors, Price Waterhouse, have reviewed the company's compliance with the specific matters in the Code which the London Stock Exchange requires that the auditors should review. They have reported to the board that they are of the opinion that it is appropriate for the directors to make the statement that the company complies with those aspects of the Code.

See also **Example 11**.

7. Non-compliance

Individual areas of non-compliance have been considered below. **Example 7 The Gieves Group plc** illustrates a situation where the emphasis of "we comply except for . . ." which is so prevalent in financial reporting should be changed to say "we only comply with . . .". Thus, the company complies with paragraphs 3.1 to 3.3 but does not comply with paragraphs: 1.4 (reserved board matters); 1.5 (professional advice for directors); 2.3 (specified terms for non-executive directors); 2.4 (selection of non-executive directors); 4.3 (an audit committee of at least three non-executive directors).

It should be noted that despite the non-compliance for no doubt adequate reasons there is the same wording in the review report from the auditors: "appropriately reflects the Company's compliance with the paragraphs of the Code . . .". While this is in accordance with the Bulletin, readers might prefer something more positive from the auditors' review report.

In passing we note that this company appears to assume that the Code requires the roles of chairman and chief executive to be split (see also **Examples 12** and **13**).

Example 7
The Gieves Group plc *31 January 1994*
Included in the Report of the Directors (p 14)

Corporate Governance

The Company complies as far as practicable with the Code of Best Practice embodied in the Cadbury Report. The principal responsibilities of the board are to agree overall strategy and investment policy, to approve major capital expenditure, to monitor the performance of the senior management and to ensure that there are proper internal controls in place.

The five non-executive directors bring an independent viewpoint and create overall balance, operating in the interest of both the Company and its shareholders.

A remuneration committee comprising the chairman and three non-executive directors has been in existence for a number of years, responsible for sanctioning the remuneration and benefits of the executive directors.

As envisaged by paragraph 3.15 of the Cadbury Report, the Company has not deemed it practicable to implement certain recommendations of the Code. In particular the Company has not formed either an audit committee nor split the roles of chief executive and chairman, although the two operating subsidiaries have their own managing directors. The directors consider that in view of the size of the Company the disadvantages of implementing these recommendations would outweigh the benefits.

Notwithstanding the above, the Company complies with paragraphs 3.1 to 3.3 but does not comply with paragraphs 1.4, 1.5, 2.3, 2.4 and 4.3. The Company will consider its compliance with items 4.5 (effectiveness of the Company's system of internal control) and 4.6 (directors to report that the business is a going concern) of the Code, when the guidelines for these two items have been developed.

Grant Thornton have reviewed this statement of compliance and have reported to the Board that it appropriately reflects the Company's compliance with the paragraphs of the Code that are specified for consideration by the Company's auditors.

8. Introduction of formal procedures

The separate statement on its own page, reproduced in **Example 8 BTR plc** explains the actions that have been taken in one area (independent professional advice) of non-compliance, to ensure compliance and reasons in another area (composition of the audit committee which is good practice as described in the Notes rather than "best practice" and part of the Code) for not changing. The statement concludes "The auditors have reported to the Board that to the extent of their review they concur with this statement of the company's compliance with the Code". It is also interesting to compare the location of the statement with **Example 9 BTR plc** for the previous year where it appears within the signed Shareholders Report.

Example 8
BTR plc *31 December 1993*
After the signed (by the Chairman and the Managing Director) Shareholders Report (p 8)

CORPORATE GOVERNANCE

In December 1992 the Cadbury Committee published its report on the Financial Aspects of Corporate Governance, including a recommended Code of Best Practice ("the Code").

The Board has had for many years group controls and standing orders which set down the authority the Board reserves to itself either as a Board or as approved Committees of the Board for specific items.

There are three key committees. The Audit Committee consists of all directors and will meet twice a year; the Nominations Committee consists of all directors and meets as requested; the Compensation Committees, where non-executive directors are majority members, meet as required.

During 1993, BTR did not have a formally constituted Audit Committee, however, the auditors presented annually to the entire Board on all and any matters considered relevant by them regarding the Company's affairs. Also in 1993, there was no formal procedure in place for directors, in furtherance of their duties, to take independent professional advice at the Company's expense. In 1994, however, the Board has introduced formal procedures regarding both the above. The Notes to the Code make certain recommendations regarding the composition of Audit Committees, but BTR believes all directors should be aware of and accept the responsibility for matters dealt with in this Committee. The auditors may raise any relevant issue with any of the directors, just as all directors have access to the auditors.

The analysis of directors' emoluments may be read in Note 6 on page 47 of these accounts.

With the exception of those proposals that await guidance from the accounting and auditing profession, and the comments above relating to the Audit Committee and independent professional advice for directors in 1993, BTR has complied with the Code since its introduction.

This statement of compliance with the Code has been reviewed by the Company's auditors to the extent recommended by the London Stock Exchange.

The auditors have reported to the Board that, to the extent of their review, they concur with this statement of the Company's compliance with the Code.

Example 9
BTR plc *31 December 1992*
Within the signed (by the Chairman and the Managing Director) Shareholders Report (p 8)

CORPORATE GOVERNANCE

The discharge of your Board's responsibilities for the good governance of the Company is again well evidenced by this Report & Accounts.

The introduction of a Code bearing on this one facet of the corporate crystal, however well-intentioned, cannot ensure integrity or competence — the twin towers of an enduring business structure.

Caveat investor.

See also **Example 11**.

9. Insufficient non-executive directors

Another statement which explains non-compliance is **Example 10 Dares Estates plc**. This does not contain any reference to the review by the auditors, although they have expressed their willingness to continue in office. It is a very small company with only seven employees and would clearly seem to be a valid example of an alternative Code for smaller companies.

Example 10
Dares Estates plc   *31 December 1993*
Included in Directors' report (p 8 and 9)

> **Compliance with Code of Best Practice on Corporate Governance**
> The Company is supportive of the Code of Best Practice recommended by the Cadbury Committee on the Financial Aspects of Corporate Governance and complies with most of the Code's requirements.
>
> The Company has a separate Chairman and managing Director. The only other Board member is an independent non-executive, who is required under the present Board structure to seek re-election at every second Annual General Meeting. The Company has only four other members of staff and the Directors are intimately involved in all of the day to day decision making. Consequently the Board has not prepared a formal schedule of matters specifically reserved to it for decision, nor have the Board specifically agreed a procedure for the Directors to take independent advice, if necessary, at the Company's expense.
>
> Furthermore, as the Company has only one non-executive Director, the Company is clearly unable to establish either an audit committee or remuneration committee which complies with the requirements of the Code. Accordingly, the Board of Directors carries out the proper functions of such committees, for these purposes, under the chairmanship of the non-executive Director.
>
> The Board considered it inappropriate to seek the appointment of additional non-executive Directors of the required calibre at a time when its financial viability was wholly dependent upon a financial restructuring. The restructuring having now been achieved, it is the intention of the Board to increase the number of non-executive Directors when it is able to put forward proposals for the expansion of the Company.
>
> When the Company has appointed suitable non-executive Directors it is the Company's intention to put in such additional procedures as are required to enable the Company to comply with the Code in full.

10. No audit committee

Although reporting non-compliance, **Example 11 Huntleigh Technology plc** explains what has been changed to ensure compliance since 1 July 1993 in two of the four areas. Formal procedures have been introduced to provide compliance. In the third, the board is considering increasing the numbers of non-executive directors but in the fourth area the directors believe that because of the size of the group it does not require a remuneration or an audit committee. It is also reported that the company's auditors are satisfied that the statement "appropriately reflects the company's compliance". Readers might prefer something more positive from the auditors' review report notwithstanding the fact that this is in accordance with the Bulletin.

Example 11
Huntleigh Technology plc *31 December 1993*
Included in Report of the Directors (p 19)

Corporate governance

Following the issue of the Code of Best Practice ('the Code') of the Cadbury Committee on The Financial Aspects of Corporate Governance, the directors have reviewed the company's compliance with the Code from 1 July, 1993. The board supports the principles contained in the Code. With the exception of the proposals that await guidance from the accounting and auditing profession, the company has complied with the provisions of the Code, save as outlined below:

- The board approves the annual budget, the long term plans and all major investment and finance matters of the group. Board meetings are held on a regular basis and, following the issue of the Code, a formal schedule of matters to be reserved for decision by the Board is currently being prepared.

- No formal procedure previously existed for directors in the furtherance of their duties to take independent professional advice, if necessary, at the company's expense. However, it has been normal practice that professional advice is sought whenever necessary and a procedure has now been implemented.

- The board has currently one non-executive director who has been in office for many years without specific terms. He is subject to re-election by rotation as are all other directors. The board is currently considering increasing the number of non-executive directors and their selection will be considered by the board as a whole.

- The company does not have a remuneration or an audit committee as recommended by the Code. The directors believe that because of the size of the group and the management and control structure it does not require such committees at this time; however, this recommendation will be regularly reviewed.

The company's auditors, BDO Binder Hamlyn, have reviewed this statement. Based on their review they are satisfied that the statement appropriately reflects the company's compliance with the paragraphs of the Code which the London Stock Exchange has specified for their review.

See also **Example 10**.

11. Separation of the roles of Chairman and Chief Executive

Holding of these roles by one person is not prohibited by the Code although 1.2 includes "there should be a ... division of responsibility ... such that no one individual has unfettered powers of decision". Several companies have recently separated the roles citing Cadbury as part of the reason. **Example 12 Marks & Spencer plc** refers to the Cadbury Report for justification of their existing practice, and similarly in **Example 13 Bass plc**.

Example 12
Marks and Spencer plc *31 March 1994*
Included in Report of the Directors (p 27)

Corporate Governance – Cadbury Report

The Company complied throughout the financial year with the Code of Best Practice in the Report of the Committee on the Financial Aspects of Corporate Governance ("the Cadbury Report") with the exceptions of paragraphs 4.5 and 4.6 for which official guidance on compliance has not yet been issued.

In accordance with the recommendation in paragraph 4.9 of the Cadbury Report in cases where the roles of Chairman and Chief Executive are not separated, the Board includes non-executive directors of great experience. They make a valuable contribution to the Board's discussions and represent a source of strong and independent judgement: they constitute the Audit Committee and they serve as a majority on the Compensation Committee.

The Company's auditors, Coopers & Lybrand, have reviewed this Compliance Statement as to those paragraphs of the Code where compliance is subject to auditors' review. They have confirmed that based upon their review they are satisfied that this Statement is properly made.

Example 13
Bass plc *30 September 1993*
Included in Directors' Report (p 27)

CORPORATE GOVERNANCE

The Company complies with the Code of Best Practice incorporated in the Report of the Committee on the Financial Aspects of Corporate Governance in all aspects of which the report has been brought into application, and has done so since 30 June 1993. In those areas where further guidance is awaited, for example on internal controls, the Directors believe that existing systems and standards are such that there will be no difficulty in complying.

As recommended by the Report for companies where the Chairman is also the Chief Executive, Bass has experienced non-executive Directors, who represent a source of strong independent judgement. The four non-executive Directors, who all have significant commercial and other interests outside Bass, gain knowledge of the Company and its operations from regular presentations by the operating divisions outside Board meetings and from visits to the divisions. This provides the background which is necessary for effective and regular involvement in strategy, management succession and analysis of internal controls.

12. No signature

Where the statement of compliance is a separate statement, i.e., not included in the report of the directors or the chairman's statement, there is (as far as we have seen) no signature to indicate any personal responsibility. This is the case shown in **Example 14 The British Petroleum Company plc** where a whole page is devoted to corporate governance. The second paragraph would be adequate as a compliance statement and it should be noted that the report of the auditors' review has been placed next to the statement of compliance paragraph.

Example 14
The British Petroleum Company plc *31 December 1993*
After the Chairman's Letter, before the Group Chief Executive's Review (i.e., no signature) (p 4)

Corporate Governance

The company's auditors, Ernst & Young, have reviewed the directors' statement concerning the company's compliance with those paragraphs of the Cadbury Committee's Code of Best Practice that are specified for their review. The auditors have reported to the directors that, based on their review, they concur with the directors' statement.

At the end of 1992, the Cadbury Committee issued its report on corporate governance – the system by which companies are directed and controlled. Effective corporate governance has long been practised by BP's board. Indeed, the Chairman was able to state in the group's 1992 annual report that we already substantially complied with the Cadbury recommendations.

The core of Cadbury is a 19-point Code of Best Practice. The London Stock Exchange requires each listed company to tell its shareholders how far it has complied with the Code in reports for accounting periods ending after 30 June 1993. We are pleased to confirm that, from 1 July, we did so fully, other than for the two points on which official guidance to all companies is awaited.

The Code has two main tenets. First, there should be a clear division of responsibilities at the head of a company. Second, the board should include independent, non-executive directors of sufficient calibre and number for their views to carry significant weight. Both apply to BP's case.

Biographies of the company's directors appear on pages 8 and 9. Seven are managing directors and eight, including the part-time Chairman, are non-executive directors. BP is unusual among UK-listed companies in having a majority of non-executive directors on its board.

The board, which meets at least monthly, has a formal schedule of matters reserved to it. The most important of these are the determination of strategy and policy for the company, and the allocation of its financial resources. Other matters are delegated formally to committees of the board:

- **The Audit Committee** is concerned with the adequacy and effectiveness of BP's internal controls and the compliance of the group's accounts with statutory and other requirements. Chaired by Sir Patrick Sheehy, it reviews the half-year and annual accounts and, from 1994, will also review the first and third quarter results. It ensures that BP's relationship with its auditor remains at arm's length.

- **The Compensation Committee** sets the compensation and other terms and conditions of managing directors' contracts, and makes recommendations on the remuneration of other senior employees. Chaired by Lord Ashburton, it obtains independent advice on rates of pay and compensation packages in comparable companies, and sets performance targets for the managing directors and monitors progress towards them.

- **The HSE Audit Committee** is chaired by Sir James Glover. It ensures that BP's Health, Safety and Environmental policies are complied with company-wide. BP has been a leader among British companies in recognising the importance to all its stakeholders of having developed policies on these vital issues.

- **The External Affairs Committee** is chaired by Lord Wright. It reviews BP's external affairs strategy and reputation, and considers the implications for BP of external events and political trends.

Membership of the committees is listed on page 9. With one exception, only non-executive directors sit on them, although the managing director responsible for the particular topic attends their meetings.

There is also a **Nominations Committee**. It recommends to the board candidates for appointment as directors and whether current directors should be put forward for re-election at the AGM. Membership is normally the Chairman and Group Chief Executive, plus one managing and one non-executive director.

13. Detailed description of compliance

In addition to the compliance statement some companies report in considerable detail how that compliance has been satisfied. **Example 15 British Telecommunications plc** provides information about the Board of Directors (personal details are included elsewhere) and the Audit and Remuneration Committees.

Example 15
British Telecommunications plc *31 March 1994*
Report of the directors (p 13 and 14)

Corporate governance
In December 1992, the *Committee on the Financial Aspects of Corporate Governance* (the *Cadbury Committee*) produced its report which contained a *Code of Best Practice*, recommending best practice in the way in which listed companies, such as BT, should be governed.

Such companies are now required to include a statement of compliance with the Code in their annual report and accounts, giving details of any areas of non-compliance.

The directors consider that BT has fully complied with the Code since the date of the 1993 Annual Report, except for those items in the Code on which final guidance is awaited. BT's auditors, Coopers & Lybrand, have confirmed to the directors that they have reviewed this statement in accordance with Auditing Practices Board guidance and they concur with this view so far as it relates to those paragraphs of the Code which the London Stock Exchange has specified for their review.

The Board will review BT's compliance with those items of the Code on which final guidance is awaited when that guidance is available. These items will require the directors to report that the business is a going concern, and to report on the effectiveness of the company's system of internal control.

BT's compliance with the main items in the *Code of Best Practice* is as detailed below:

Board of Directors
The Board meets regularly to consider matters specifically reserved for its attention, so that it may control key issues and monitor the group's overall performance.

The majority of the Board's members are non-executive, with experience at senior level variously in international, financial, legal, marketing, government and diplomatic affairs. Most of these non-executive directors are independent of the management of BT, being free from any business or other relationships which could materially interfere with the exercise of their judgement. A formal nomination and selection process has been established for the appointment of non-executive directors; their contracts of appointment are normally for three years, at the end of which period the Board carries out a review.

The non-executive directors provide a strong independent element on the Board, with Mr Bosonnet, Deputy Chairman, as senior member. However, the Board operates as a single team.

The executive directors have service agreements for fixed periods, which do not exceed three years and which are reviewed annually. The emoluments paid to the directors and to the chairman are disclosed in note 24 to the financial statements.

The Board has agreed and established a procedure for directors, in the furtherance of their duties, to take independent professional advice, if necessary, at the company's expense. In addition, all directors have access to the advice and services of the company secretary, the removal of whom would be a matter for the whole Board.

Audit and Remuneration Committees
The Board has an Audit Committee, consisting solely of non-executive directors, which is chaired by Mr Bosonnet. The Audit Committee has written terms of reference; these include reviewing annually the services and fees of the company's auditors, to ensure that an objective and professional relationship is maintained.

There are also two Board remuneration committees. The Board Committee on Executive Remuneration consists solely of non-executive directors and is also chaired by Mr Bosonnet. It reviews annually the remuneration and service agreements of the chairman and the other executive directors.

The other committee reviews the remuneration of the non-executive directors.

Reporting
A statement by the directors of their responsibilities for preparing the accounts is included on page 15.

14. Other matters included in the corporate governance statement

Other matters included by **Example 16 Scottish Power plc** are the directors' responsibility for the financial statements and a description of auditors' responsibilities. Also included under the same heading of corporate governance was the report of the review by the auditors. This is not addressed to anyone in particular and does not follow exactly **Example 1** – a separate report from the auditors, suggested by the APB. The presentation in the annual review rather than in the separate directors' report and accounts may not have been expected. It is interesting to see that in **Example 17 the Annual Review of Scottish Hydro-Electric plc** there is a brief mention of corporate governance as part of the chairman's statement but the main reference is in **Example 18 Scottish Hydro-Electric plc**.

Example 16
Scottish Power plc   *31 March 1994*
In the Annual Review 1993–94 (p 16 and 17)

It does NOT appear in the separate Directors' Report and Accounts 1993–94 to which the readers of the Annual Review are referred.

Corporate Governance

Statement of compliance

Under London Stock Exchange listing rules, a company incorporated in the UK must state in its Annual Report and Accounts whether it has complied throughout the accounting period with the Code of Best Practice published in December 1992 by the Committee on the Financial Aspects of Corporate Governance ("the Cadbury Report").

The directors of ScottishPower confirm that the company has complied with the Code with the following exceptions. The directors are not yet required to report on the effectiveness of the company's system of internal control nor are they required to report that the business is a going concern (as requested by paragraphs 4.5 and 4.6 of the Code) because the necessary guidance for companies has not been developed as recommended in the Cadbury Report.

While criteria for measuring the effectiveness of internal controls are proving difficult for the accountancy profession to establish for universal application, going concern is an issue which requires to be considered by companies in relation to their particular circumstances. The directors of ScottishPower are able to confirm that the company remains a going concern on the basis of adequate cash flow forecasts.

Board control

The Corporate Governance structure within ScottishPower ensures that there is a well balanced division of reponsibilities at Board level and that the ultimate power and authority for decision making remains securely vested in the collective responsibility of the full Board.

The Board of Directors, comprising the Chairman, four other non-executive directors and five executive directors, meets at least 11 times during the year. Through these meetings, the Board retains full and effective control over the company and is responsible for overall strategy, investment policy, major capital expenditure and other significant financial issues. There is an agreed schedule of matters requiring Board approval.

The operational management of the company is delegated by the Board to the Chief Executive and operated via the Chief Executive's Committee which includes the four other executive directors (supported by other non-Board executives). Ten separate accountable businesses, each headed by a Managing Director, provide day to day control over the company's operations. The Chief Executive's Committee monitors and gives guidance to the separate businesses and takes all major company decisions within the framework of policies approved by the Board.

Audit Committee

The significant presence on the Board of widely experienced, independent, non-executive directors provides expertise which complements the skills of the executive directors. The non-executive directors play an active role in forming major policy decisions and in determining the strategic direction of the company. They alone form the Audit Committee and the Emoluments and Nominations Committee (membership details appear on page 32).

The Audit Committee acts in an advisory capacity to the Board. It has written terms of reference which enable it to form an independent opinion of the appropriateness of the company's accounting policies and it also reviews the auditors' findings.

Emoluments and Nominations Committee

The Emoluments and Nominations Committee is responsible for making recommendations to the Board on the appointment of main Board directors and the employment terms and level of remuneration of such directors. The committee gives its view to the Board on the general salary structure, remuneration and employment terms of senior management. It is responsible for recommending to the Board the basis on which the executive directors' performance related incentive scheme will operate and for reviewing the executive directors' performance against previously agreed targets. It also reviews and makes recommendations to the Board on the company's share option schemes.

Directors' responsibility for the financial statements

The directors are required by UK company law to prepare financial statements for each financial year which give a true and fair view of the state of affairs of the company and the group as at the end of the financial year and of the group's profit or loss.

The directors confirm that suitable accounting policies have been used and applied consistently and that reasonable and prudent judgements and estimates have been made in the preparation of the financial statements for the year ended 31 March 1994. The directors also confirm that applicable accounting statements have been prepared on the going concern basis.

The directors are responsible for ensuring that proper accounting records are kept, for safeguarding the assets of the company and the group and hence for taking reasonable steps for the prevention and detection of fraud and other irregularities.

Auditors' responsibilities

The company's registered auditors, Coopers & Lybrand, are responsible for forming an independent opinion on the financial statements of the group presented by the directors and for reporting their opinion to the shareholders. The auditors are required to report to the shareholders if the following requirements are not met:
– that the group has maintained proper accounting records
– that the financial statements are in agreement with the accounting records
– that the contents of the Directors' Report are consistent with the financial statements
– that directors' emoluments and other transactions with directors are properly disclosed in the financial statements
– that they have obtained all information and explanations which, to the best of their knowledge and belief, are necessary for the purpose of their audit.

Report by the Auditors on the statement of compliance with the Code of Best Practice

We have reviewed the directors' statement concerning the company's compliance with the Code of Best Practice published by the Committee on the Financial Aspects of Corporate Governance, insofar as it relates to those paragraphs of the Code which the London Stock Exchange has specified for our review. We carried out our review having regard to the Bulletin "Disclosures relating to corporate governance" issued by the Auditing Practices Board.

Our procedures primarily comprised enquiry of appropriate directors and officers and examination of relevant documents. We are not required to review, and have not reviewed, the effectiveness of the company's governance procedures.

Based on our review we have satisfied ourselves that the directors' statement appropriately reflects the company's compliance with the specified paragraphs of the Code.

Coopers & Lybrand
Chartered Accountants and Registered Auditors
Glasgow
11 May 1994

Example 17
Scottish Hydro-Electric plc *31 March 1994*
Part of the Chairman's Statement in the Annual Review and Summary Financial Statement
(p 9)

Corporate Governance
In Hydro-Electric we have made sure that we comply fully with all applicable sections
of the much discussed Cadbury Code of Best Practice, most of which reflects practice
which already applied within the Company. So far as the Board is concerned, we have
an Audit Committee consisting of all the non-Executive Directors chaired by myself; a
Remuneration Committee constituted so that nobody decides on their own pay, and a
Nomination Committee to consider new appointments to the Board. Other parts of the
Company's methods of operation have been reviewed to ensure that they are in line
with the Cadbury recommendations.

Example 18
Scottish Hydro-Electric plc *31 March 1994*
Part of the Report of the Directors in the Directors' Report and Accounts (p 5)

Corporate governance
Following the publication in December 1992 of the Code of Best Practice by the
Committee on the Financial Aspects of Corporate Governance, the Board has reviewed
the Company's compliance during the year ended 31 March 1994.

To ensure full compliance for the future the Board approved the following at a meeting
held on 8 July 1993:

(a) a procedure to allow Directors to take independent professional advice at the
Company's expense in the furtherance of their duties;

(b) revised terms of reference for its Audit Committee and Remuneration Committee;

(c) the establishment of a Nomination Committee.

At the Board Meeting held on 2 December 1993 the Board adopted a written Schedule
of matters reserved to it for approval.

Other than as referred to above, and for the provisions of the Code regarding reports
by the Directors on the Company's internal controls and that the business is a going
concern (for which the necessary guidance is not yet available), the Company has
complied with the requirements of the Code throughout the financial year.

The auditors, KPMG Peat Marwick, have confirmed to the Directors that this statement
appropriately reflects the Company's compliance with the Code of Best Practice, in so
far as it relates to the paragraphs of the Code which the London Stock Exchange has
specified for their review.

15. Internal controls

Guidance as to the requirements for compliance with the recommendations on internal
control have not yet been published.

Nevertheless some companies do make reference to the area. **Example 19 Burnfield
plc** after an extremely brief statement of compliance includes details about board
committees, directors and internal control.

Again there is no reference to the report of the review by the auditors and the APB "strongly advises auditors not to report publicly on any statements by the directors concerning the effectiveness of the company's systems of internal control".

In **Example 20 Rentokil Group plc** the corporate governance item in the report of the directors consists of three paragraphs. The first paragraph ends with the sentence that the auditors "have confirmed to the directors . . . it is reasonable for the directors to make this statement".

The second and third paragraphs relate to internal control and the going concern areas, but while there may be a presumption that these two areas are not covered by the auditors' review the APB would prefer the report of the review to be specific in its exclusion of these two areas from the review.

Example 19
Burnfield plc   *31 December 1993*
Separate statement (p 10)

STATEMENT OF CORPORATE GOVERNANCE

Burnfield plc complies with the Code of Best Practice within the Cadbury Report.

The Board
The Board normally meets monthly to review not only the current state of the business but also to determine its future strategic direction. The Board has a formal schedule of matters specifically reserved for its decision which can only be amended by the Board itself. Specific arrangements have been made to cover exceptional circumstances when decisions reserved to the Board are required between monthly meetings.

Board Committees
Two committees of the Board, both of which comprise all of the non-executive directors, chaired by B D McGowan are in place.

1. Audit Committee
The Committee, which has been given specific terms of reference, meets at least twice a year and may be attended by any director. The auditors are invited to attend each meeting.

2. Remuneration Committee
The Committee determines the annual remuneration levels of the executive directors. Remuneration levels include basic salary, bonus (if any), share options and service contracts.

Directors
There is a clear division of responsibility between the Chairman and Managing Director such that no one individual has unfettered powers of decision.
No service contracts for executive directors exceed one year. The pay of the directors, as agreed by the Remuneration Committee, is disclosed in note 10 of the financial statements. The appointment and removal of a director is a matter for the Board as a whole and a formal process exists for the appointment of non-executive directors.
The Board has three experienced, independent non-executive directors whose opinions are valued. The non-executive directors do not benefit from share options or pension provision. They have formal access to all information and, if required, external advice, at the expense of the company. Their fees reflect their involvement

in the business and their terms of office are renewable, at the discretion of shareholders, when seeking re-election at annual general meetings.

All directors have access to the Company Secretary, whose removal and appointment is a matter for the Board as a whole and who is responsible to the Board for ensuring that agreed procedures and applicable rules and regulations are observed.

Internal Controls

The Cadbury Report recognised that guidelines would have to be developed to provide a framework for companies to report on their internal control systems. Although these guidelines have not yet been developed, the directors are satisfied that the group has effective systems of internal control, including clearly documented delegation of authority from the Board to subsidiaries and defined procedures for obtaining approval for major transactions. In addition, the group has established procedures for planning and budgeting and for monitoring the performance of the group against the approved plans and budgets.

Example 20
Rentokil Group plc *31 December 1993*
Included in Report of the Directors (p 36)

Corporate Governance The board has reviewed the areas where, during the year ended 31st December 1993, the company was not in compliance with the provisions of the Code of Best Practice published by the Cadbury Committee on the Financial Aspects of Corporate Governance ("the Code"). The areas concerned (apart from that mentioned below) were those relating to the composition of the audit committee, the procedure for enabling directors to take independent advice and the process for appointing non-executive directors. The company now complies in all respects with the Code save that, of the non-executive directors (as shown on page 31), three (one of whom will be retiring at the annual meeting) are also directors of Sophus Berendsen A/S, the company's majority shareholder, and one is a partner in the company's principal legal advisers (paragraph 2.2 of the Code). The auditors, Price Waterhouse, have confirmed to the directors that, in relation to those aspects of the Code which are capable of objective verification, it is reasonable for the directors to make this statement.

The company maintains a system of internal controls, including suitable monitoring procedures, in order to provide reasonable, but not absolute, assurance of the maintenance of proper accounting records and the reliability of the financial information used within the business or for publication. The directors are satisfied that these controls generally operated effectively during the period covered by the accounts.

After making enquiries, the directors have a reasonable expectation that the company has adequate resources to continue operations for the foreseeable future. For this reason, they continue to adopt the going concern basis in preparing the accounts.

CONCLUSIONS

The role of the auditors in reviewing the directors' statement of compliance is clearly a difficult one. It is probably also fair to say that the task for readers of the statement is even more difficult. The essence of the difficulties is that the policy-makers appear to be ambivalent about the part to be played by users of the annual report and accounts.

The Code is voluntary and it emphasises that what matters is that the actions of directors meet the spirit of its recommendations. In a similar spirit, the Stock Exchange has made no rules about the directors' actions in this regard; instead, it has simply given them the responsibility for reporting on their own actions. How they choose to effect this report is in no way circumscribed, except to say that their statement will appear in the annual report and accounts.

The Stock Exchange requires the auditors to review this statement – but there is no requirement to disclose the results of the review. This raises two reporting issues for the companies, auditors or others to resolve. The first is that whereas the listing rules do not distinguish between the auditors *qua* auditors of the financial statements and auditors *qua* reviewers of the statements of compliance, the auditing profession does. The second relates to the manner in which readers of the report and accounts are to be informed of the directors' actions.

Both the Code and the Listing Rules emphasise that the auditors' role relates only to such compliance that can be "objectively verified". What this is saying is that for matters of opinion, it is the directors' opinions that count: the auditors are only required to review matters of fact. But whereas the Cadbury Committee and the Stock Exchange are content to include compliance with paragraphs 4.5 and 4.6 as matters of fact, the auditing profession may well be justified in being reluctant to become involved. There is no doubt that the two paragraphs refer to matters of fact (because they only refer to reporting on the issues, not compliance with the issues themselves), but auditors could argue that any association of their name with such compliance is likely to be interpreted as confirmation that the internal controls are effective and that the company is a going concern.

All three groups of policy-makers involved can be taken to approve of this emphasis on the objectively verifiable and, given the environment being addressed, this is not difficult to understand. But it does appear to lead to very real problems for those who are neither directors nor auditors; the matters of fact, and the auditors' review of those facts, can be entirely obscured from the readers.

The APB has attempted to deal with both of these reporting issues but the relevant guidance does not seem to have had significant influence, as yet. It is entirely possible, of course, that the Cadbury Code is being implemented broadly in the way anticipated by the policy-makers. On the basis of the review offered here, however, it is difficult to offer anything other than the directors' opinions, often ambiguously stated, on whether it is or not.

DISCLOSURE OF EXCEPTIONAL AND EXTRAORDINARY ITEMS UNDER FRS 3

Clive Goodhead

INTRODUCTION

Financial Reporting Standard No 3 "Reporting financial performance" (FRS 3) was the first "home grown" accounting standard to emerge from the Accounting Standards Board (ASB). FRS 1 and FRS 2 were both effectively inherited from the old ASC. FRS 3 makes fundamental changes to the way in which financial performance, in particular the profit and loss account, is presented; there is significantly less emphasis on earnings per share. In the past earnings per share has received undue attention from many analysts, at the cost of a fuller understanding of a company's performance. The obsession with earnings per share and trends in earnings per share put pressure on many companies to account for large unusual items as extraordinary items so that they did not distort such calculations and trends. Even exceptional items that were positioned "above the line" were often disclosed in a manner that encouraged analysts to add them back when calculating headline earnings figures.

At the launch of FRS 3, David Tweedie, Chairman of the ASB, said:

"FRS 3 is a landmark standard. It changes fundamentally the presentation of a company's financial performance. The standard moves the emphasis away from simple headline numbers to a presentation of the components of profit, thereby making possible more mature analysis of a company's performance than the previous reliance on a single number such as the 'bottom line' or profit on ordinary activities after taxation. In the Board's view the performance of a company simply cannot be encapsulated in a single number.

In this standard the Board has virtually abolished the extraordinary item which has been the source of so much confusion and manipulation. Ensuring that almost all transactions will be recorded 'above the line' will relieve preparers of accounts from having to meet competitive pressures by stretching to breaking point the definitions of exceptional (above the line) and extraordinary (below the line) items. We believe that the proposals of FRS 3 will dispose of most of the arguments over the definition of extraordinary and exceptional items and will remove one of the major abuses of UK accounting".

It was hoped that the changes would provide companies with a framework to communicate a wider base of relevant information to investors and other users of their financial statements and encourage analysts to make a more thorough analysis of reported profits. Exceptional and extraordinary items are a very important part of this analysis; this chapter examines how companies are reporting such figures and how they are reflecting such items in the presentation of earnings per share.

EXTRAORDINARY ITEMS

All the formats set out in the Companies Act 1985 (the Act) require separate disclosure on the face of the profit and loss account of information relating to extraordinary items. Extraordinary items are not defined in the Act, but are defined in the EC Fourth Company Law Directive as "income and charges that arise otherwise than in the course of the company's ordinary activities". The definition now used for UK financial reporting is that contained in FRS 3. FRS 3 states that extraordinary items are:

"Material items possessing a high degree of abnormality which arise from events or transactions that fall outside the ordinary activities of the reporting entity and which are not expected to recur. They do not include exceptional items nor do they include prior period items merely because they relate to a prior period."

This definition is more restrictive than that in the Directive since it introduces the additional test concerning the expectation of recurrence.

The critical distinction between an extraordinary item and one that is included within ordinary activities is whether the item derives from transactions or other events that fall outside the ordinary activities of the reporting entity or from transactions or events that fall within those activities. FRS 3 defines ordinary activities as:

"Any activities which are undertaken by a reporting entity as part of its business and such related activities in which the reporting entity engages in furtherance of, incidental to, or arising from, these activities. Ordinary activities include the effects on the reporting entity of any event in the various environments in which it operates, including the political, regulatory, economic and geographical environments, irrespective of the frequency or unusual nature of the events."

This definition of ordinary activities is more wide ranging than the definition contained in FRS 3's predecessor standard, SSAP 6. One of the implicit intentions of FRS 3 is that there should be a severe decrease in the number of items reported as extraordinary.

The ASB was unable to envisage any extraordinary items and accordingly FRS 3 does not give any examples; the ASB believes that the extraordinary item has effectively been abolished.

The reporting of extraordinary items has, as envisaged by the ASB, been extremely rare. Indeed, the publication Company Reporting has reported only one instance of a listed company reporting extraordinary items (and then only in the comparative figures following their restatement to comply with FRS 3). The "Financial Summary" set out in the 1993 Annual Report and Accounts of **Example 1 Fairway Group plc** indicates extraordinary items in 1990, 1991 and 1992.

Example 1
Fairway Group plc *31 December 1993*
Extract from the financial summary

	1993 £'000	1992 £'000	1991 £'000	1990 £'000	1989 £'000
Turnover	42,250	29,269	19,759	8,363	5,846
Profit before tax	2,246	1,513	1,768	1,053	756
Tax	(737)	(516)	(587)	(381)	(283)
Minority interest	16	24	—	—	—
Extraordinary items	—	(162)	83	(130)	—
Attributable profit	1,525	859	1,264	542	473
Dividends	1,058	953	926	439	335
Shareholders' funds	6,354	6,013	9,597	3,444	5,570
Earnings per share	4.79p	2.90p	5.50p	3.36p	2.83p
Dividends per share (net)	3.35p	3.15p	3.15p	3.00p	2.75p

Note:
Earnings per share for all years is stated after adjustment for the bonus element of subsequent rights issues and previous years have been restated to include extraordinary items as required by Financial Reporting Standard number 3.

The extraordinary items reported in the years 1990 to 1992 are as follows:

	1992 £'000	1991 £'000	1990 £'000
Costs of aborted acquisitions	(162)	(2)	(65)
Profit on sale of quoted investment		97	
Write down in value of quoted investment			(65)
Residual expenses on closure of Wokingham office		(12)	
	(162)	83	(130)

The notes to the 1993 accounts stated, in respect of the 1992 amounts, that "The above items fell outside the ordinary activities of the Company and are not expected to recur". Apart from this short statement, there is no real indication why the directors and the auditors, Beavis Walker, believe the items reported as extraordinary do not derive from the company's ordinary activities given the new extremely wide-ranging definition of such activities.

EXCEPTIONAL ITEMS

FRS 3 defines exceptional items as:

"Material items which derive from events or transactions that fall within the ordinary activities of the reporting entity and which individually or, if of a similar type, in aggregate, need to be disclosed by virtue of their size or incidence if the financial statements are to give a true and fair view."

SSAP 6 included a list of items which may have been exceptional and a list of those which may have been extraordinary. Under FRS 3, these are all exceptional items. The lists included:

- Abnormal charges for bad debts, stock obsolescence or losses on long-term contracts.
- Redundancy and reorganisation costs unrelated to the discontinuance of a business segment.
- Previously capitalised intangible assets written off other than as part of a process of amortisation.
- Amounts transferred to employee share schemes.
- The expropriation of assets.
- Surpluses arising on settlement of insurance claims.
- Amounts received in respect of insurance claims for consequential loss of profits.
- Change in basis of taxation, or significant change in government fiscal policy.

Exceptional items fall within the ordinary activities of a reporting entity and, therefore, it follows that they should be charged or credited in arriving at the "profit or loss on ordinary activities". Prior to FRS 3, exceptional items were often aggregated under one heading of exceptional items. FRS 3 requires them to be included under the natural statutory format heading to which they relate unless they fall within one of the three categories of "non-operating exceptional items" listed in paragraph 20 of FRS 3 (profits or losses on the sale or termination of an operation; costs of a fundamental reorganisation or restructuring; and exceptional profits or losses on the disposal of fixed assets). Unlike some of the forms of presentation often adopted under SSAP 6, the FRS 3 approach does not conflict with the requirement of the Act to give the full amount of income and expenditure in respect of each of the statutory format headings.

FRS 3 requires the amount of each exceptional item, either individually or as an aggregate of items of a similar type, to be disclosed separately by way of note, or on the face of the profit and loss account if that degree of prominence is necessary to give a true and fair view. The items should also be attributed to continuing or discontinued operations as appropriate and an adequate description of each item should be given to enable its nature to be understood. In showing the amount of each exceptional item, individual items or groups of items should not be combined if separately they relate to continuing and to discontinued operations. In practice, it appears that most exceptional items are disclosed on the face of the profit and loss account rather than disclosed only in the notes to the accounts.

Exceptional items that fall within operating profit
The most straightforward disclosure of an exceptional item is illustrated by **Example 2 The Burton Group plc**. In the early 1990s the fortunes of The Burton Group declined dramatically. The new chief executive, who was appointed in 1992, decided that the group needed to concentrate on improving efficiency and in January 1993 the "Best Practice" programme was announced. Part of the costs of this programme were to be met from reorganisation provisions set up in financial years prior to 1993. However, the costs exceeded the provisions with the result that the 1993 cost of sales included a net charge of £14.6 million in respect of the programme. The Burton Group disclosed this

charge as an exceptional item on the face of the profit and loss account. The disclosure on the face of the profit and loss account includes the total cost of sales (£1,749.9 million), as required by the Companies Act; the nature of the exceptional item is explained in note 2 to the accounts.

Example 2
The Burton Group plc *28 August 1993*
Extract from the consolidated profit and loss account

	Note	1993 £m	1992 (Restated) £m
For the financial year ended 28th August 1992	Note		
Turnover		**1,893.1**	**1,764.6**
Cost of sales — Ongoing		(1,735.3)	(1,625.2)
Exceptional	2	(14.6)	—
Total		(1,749.9)	(1,625.2)
Gross profit		143.2	139.4

Extract from note 2 to the accounts

2 Cost of sales — exceptional
Exceptional costs included as part of cost of sales comprise one off redundancy and other costs of £21.6 million, associated with the implementation of the 'Best Practice' programme announced in January 1993, offset by the release of £7.0 million of provisions brought forward from previous years.

The recent recession has affected not only retailers such as The Burton Group but also companies in a wide range of other business sectors. Many companies have over the last couple of years reported diminutions in the values of properties held as operating assets. **Example 3 Pearson plc** illustrates this. In the year ended 31 December 1993 Pearson's profit and loss account included a £20 million charge in respect of a permanent diminution in the value of a property used by one of the group's operating subsidiaries, *The Financial Times*. Because the property is used within the group's operations the charge in the profit and loss account was made prior to arriving at operating profit (within "Administration, research and other expenses"). However, Pearson obviously thought that this exceptional operating expense warranted separate disclosure on the face of the profit and loss account. Along with many other major companies, Pearson does not report separately "Distribution costs", 'Administrative expenses" and "Other operating income" on the face of the profit and loss account; these items are amalgamated as "Net operating expenses". Pearson analyses "Net operating expenses" between "normal" and "exceptional" on the face of the profit and loss account; no total is provided, but none is required because "Net operating expenses" is not one of the statutory format headings. The statutory information is disclosed in the notes to the accounts.

Example 3
Pearson plc *31 December 1993*
Extract from the consolidated profit and loss account

	NOTES	1993 £m	1992 £m
Sales turnover			
Continuing operations		1,277.8	1,145.0
Acquisitions		41.8	
Discontinued operations		550.5	490.7
	2	1,807.1	1,635.7
Cost of sales	3	(1,005.6)	(919.7)
Gross profit		864.5	716.0
Net operating expenses — normal	3	(628.4)	(560.4)
exceptional	3	(20.0)	—
Operating profit			
Continuing operations		183.2	144.4
Acquisitions		7.1	
Discontinued operations		25.8	11.2
	2	216.1	155.6

Extract from note 3 to the accounts

3 Analysis of Consolidated Profit and Loss Account

	Continuing 1993 £m	Discontinued 1993 £m	Total 1993 £m	Continuing 1992 £m	Discontinued 1992 £m	Total 1992 £m
Cost of sales	(656.0)	(349.6)	(1,005.6)	(593.4)	(326.3)	(919.7)
Distribution costs	(103.9)	(54.8)	(158.7)	(95.7)	(48.2)	(143.9)
Administration, research and other expenses	(469.0)	(119.0)	(588.0)	(384.4)	(105.2)	(489.6)
Other operating income (note 6)	99.6	(1.3)	98.3	72.9	0.2	73.1
Net operating expenses	(473.3)	(175.1)	(648.4)	(407.2)	(153.2)	(560.4)
Analysed as:						
Net operating expenses						
— normal	(453.3)	(175.1)	(628.4)	(407.2)	(153.2)	(560.4)
— exceptional	(20.0)	–	(20.0)	–	–	–

The total figures for continuing operations in 1993 include the following amounts relating to acquisitions: cost of sales £28.9 million and net operating expenses of £5.8 million (being administrative expenses of £6.3 million and other operating income of £0.5 million).

The exceptional net operating expense of £20 million is a provision for permanent diminution in value of Number One Southwark Bridge Road, the head office of The Financial Times, and is included above in administration, research and other expenses.

Not all exceptional items that fall within operating profit are disclosed within one of the statutory format headings. **Example 4 British Aerospace plc** in its 31 December 1993 financial statements charged £250 million in respect of exceptional "recourse provisions". This amount was regarded as exceptional because it related to deliveries of turboprop aircraft prior to 1993; provisions had not previously been set up in respect of these aircraft, but had in respect of other commercial aircraft.

Example 4
British Aerospace plc *31 December 1993*
Extract from the financial review

Since the beginning of 1993, the sale of regional aircraft, other than for cash, has been accompanied by the making of a systematic lifetime recourse provision. This provision is calculated using precisely defined risk protocols which, based on experience, are intended to produce neither profit nor loss on the future results from leasing. At the end of the year, this approach was extended to the pre-1993 turboprop fleet through the making of a £250m exceptional charge, the regional jet fleet having been provided for as part of the 1992 reorganisation. The protocols demand very close co-operation between Group treasury managers and the aircraft manufacturing businesses in assessing risk.

Extract from the consolidated profit and loss account

		1993 £m	1992 £m Restated
	for the year ended 31st December		
	Sales		
	Continuing operations	**10,146**	9,411
	Discontinued operations	**614**	566
Note 2		**10,760**	9,977
Note 3	Cost of sales	**(10,531)**	(10,043)
Note 7	Exceptional recourse provision for continuing operations	**(250)**	—
	Operating profit/(loss)		
	Continuing operations	**(50)**	(80)
	Discontinued operations	**29**	14
		(21)	(66)

Extract from note 7 to the accounts

7 Exceptional items

The **exceptional recourse provision** of £250 million represents an additional provision at net present value for the expected level of financial exposure arising over the lifetime of aircraft finance arranged by the Group or by third parties in respect of turboprop aircraft. A deferred tax asset of £30 million has been established in respect of this provision.

8 Tax

	1993 £m	1992 £m
UK corporation tax at 33% (1992 33%)		
Current year	(1)	–
Prior year	12	50
Deferred tax	33	235
Advance corporation tax	(28)	(4)
Overseas tax	(7)	(9)
Associated undertakings	(3)	–
	6	272

Included above is a deferred tax credit of £30 million (1992 £250 million) arising in respect of exceptional items (note 7).

Included within interest on exceptional provision (note 4) is a credit of £17 million (1992 £nil) which represents the sum required to maintain the net present value of the deferred tax asset established for reorganisation of the Group's Regional Aircraft activities which was created in 1992 on a net present value basis.

The Financial Reporting Review Panel (Review Panel) discussed the accounts of **Example 5 BET plc** for the year ended 27 March 1993 with the directors. The statement issued by the Review Panel stated that "the Panel welcomed the decision of the company to adopt the provisions of Financial Reporting Standard (FRS) 3 in the 1993 accounts ahead of its mandatory commencement date but was concerned about the company's treatment of exceptional items". BET's 1993 profit and loss account disclosed £76.0 million of "operating exceptional items" (£42 million in respect of permanent diminutions in asset values and £34 million in respect of reorganisation costs). However, these costs were not allocated to statutory format headings but amalgamated and shown separately after a sub total entitled "Operating profit/(loss) before exceptional items".

Example 5
BET plc *27 March 1993*
Extract from the 1993 consolidated profit and loss account

for the year ended 27th March 1993	Notes	Continuing operations £m	Discontinued operations £m	1993 Total £m	1992 Total £m
TURNOVER 1		2,003.2	173.0	2,176.2	2,344.8
Cost of sales		(1,533.2)	(125.8)	(1,659.0)	(1,731.5)
Gross profit		470.0	47.2	517.2	613.3
Distribution costs		(187.5)	(32.2)	(219.7)	(218.9)
Administrative expenses		(231.0)	(20.9)	(251.9)	(276.3)
Other operating income		19.3	1.2	20.5	17.7
Income from interests in associated undertakings 4		8.1	—	8.1	2.5
OPERATING PROFIT/(LOSS) BEFORE EXCEPTIONAL ITEMS ....1 & 2		78.9	(4.7)	74.2	138.3
Permanent diminution in asset values		(42.0)	—	(42.0)	(59.7)
Reorganisation costs		(34.0)	—	(34.0)	(20.6)
Deferred costs		—	—	—	(14.5)
OPERATING EXCEPTIONAL ITEMS 3		(76.0)	—	(76.0)	(94.8)
OPERATING PROFIT/(LOSS)		2.9	(4.7)	(1.8)	43.5

BET's 1994 Annual Report referred to the discussions with the Review Panel and took into account the Panel's comments; the comparative figures were restated. The restatement did not involve any change to the operating loss (£1.8 million) for the year ended 27 March 1993.

Even though this Review Panel action did not cause BET to reissue its 1993 Annual Report, it is now clear that exceptional items that fall within operating activities must be included under one of the statutory format headings unless none of the format headings is appropriate.

Extract from the 1994 accounting policies

The financial statements have been prepared on a consistent basis in accordance with applicable Accounting Standards in the United Kingdom. The 1993 comparatives have been restated to show operating exceptional items of £76.0 million within the statutory format headings to which they relate (£60.2 million in cost of sales and £15.8 million in administrative expenses) in recognition of developing practice in the application of FRS 3 and after a recent discussion with the Financial Reporting Review Panel. The restatement of the previously disclosed operating exceptional items is highlighted in Note 1(c) on page 39.

Extract from the 1994 consolidated profit and loss account

for the year ended 2nd April 1994

	Notes	Continuing operations £m	Discontinued operations £m	1994 Total £m	1993 Restated Total (see page 36) £m
TURNOVER	1	1,785.1	188.9	1,974.0	2,176.2
Cost of sales		(1,318.7)	(154.7)	(1,473.4)	(1,719.2)
Gross profit		466.4	34.2	500.6	457.0
Distribution costs		(170.1)	(14.5)	(184.6)	(219.7)
Administrative expenses		(202.6)	(23.2)	(225.8)	(267.7)
Other operating income/(expense)		(0.5)	1.1	0.6	20.5
Income from interests in associated undertakings	4	5.6	0.2	5.8	8.1
OPERATING PROFIT/(LOSS)	1	98.8	(2.2)	96.6	(1.8)

Exceptional items that fall outside operating profit

Although FRS 3 requires most exceptional items to be reported within the appropriate statutory format heading, it requires three special categories of item to be shown separately on the face of the profit and loss account after operating profit and before interest. The three special categories are:

- profits or losses on the sale or termination of an operation;
- costs of a fundamental reorganisation or restructuring having a material effect on the nature and focus of the reporting entity's operations; and
- profits or losses on the disposal of fixed assets.

For each item it should be indicated whether it relates to continuing or discontinued operations.

Any tax or minority interest related to these items should be shown in a note to the profit and loss account. As a minimum, aggregate figures should be given for the related tax and for the related minority interest. If the impact differs for the various categories further information should be given.

Profits or losses on the sale or termination of an operation

FRS 3 recognises that although profits and losses on the sales and terminations of businesses form part of a company's ordinary activities, they can result in significant fluctuations in results from year to year. Accordingly, as stated above, the FRS requires such profits and losses to be reported separately from operating profits. **Example 6 Chrysalis Group plc** illustrates such fluctuations. In 1992 the group disposed of its interests in joint venture record companies which resulted in a profit of nearly £11 million; in 1993 the group closed a number of operations incurring losses of £11 million.

FRS 3 does not identify which items should be included within "profits or losses on the sale or termination of an operation". However, the standard requires the results of a discontinued operation to be shown under the relevant statutory format headings with the result that profits and losses from such operations up to the date of sale or termination do not form part of the profit or loss on sale or termination and thus should be included as part of the ordinary operating activities of the business. This is illustrated clearly by the Chrysalis Group which uses the columnar format disclosure of continuing and discontinued businesses.

FRS 3 includes a strict definition of what constitutes a discontinued operation; many sales and terminations do not meet this definition. Operations may only be treated as discontinued if they are sold or terminated and meet all of the following conditions:

- The sale or termination is completed either in the period or before the earlier of three months after the commencement of the subsequent period and the date on which the financial statements are approved.
- If a termination, the former activities have ceased permanently.
- The sale or termination has a material effect on the nature and focus of the reporting entity's operations and represents a material reduction in its operating facilities resulting either from its withdrawal from a particular market (whether class of business or geographical) or from a material reduction in turnover in the reporting entity's continuing markets.
- The assets, liabilities, results of operations and activities are clearly distinguishable, physically, operationally and for financial reporting purposes.
- The sale or termination must have resulted from a strategic decision by the reporting entity to withdraw from a market or to curtail its presence in a continuing market.

Operations that fail to meet all these criteria must be treated as continuing even if they have been discontinued by the time the financial statements are finalised or if it is public knowledge that they are in the process of being discontinued. Thus, it may not be possible to treat operations with long decommissioning periods as discontinued until the decommissioning is completed. In recognition of this, the standard suggests that the results of sold or terminated operations (or operations in the process of being sold or terminated) which do not meet FRS 3's definition of discontinued be disclosed by way of note. Chrysalis Group makes such disclosures at the foot of the profit and loss account.

Example 6
Chrysalis Group plc *31 August 1993*
Extract from the consolidated profit and loss account

		Continuing operations £000	Discontinued operations £000	1993 Total £000	1992 Total £000
	Note				
Turnover	2	**58,986**	**14,564**	**73,550**	65,968
Cost of sales		**(45,722)**	**(13,936)**	**(59,658)**	(53,679)
Gross profit		**13,264**	**628**	**13,892**	12,289
Net operating expenses		**(15,556)**	**(3,718)**	**(19,274)**	(17,330)
Operating loss	3	**(2,292)**	**(3,090)**	**(5,382)**	(5,041)
Income from interests in associated undertakings	4	**59**	–	**59**	(697)
(Loss)/profit on disposal and closure of discontinued operations	7	**(180)**	**(10,908)**	**(11,088)**	10,783
	*	**(2,413)**	**(13,998)**	**(16,411)**	5,045

* The loss before interest for continuing operations for the year to 31st August 1993 of £2,413,000 includes a loss of £1,535,000 relating to businesses which have been sold or otherwise discontinued but which do not fall within the FRS 3 definition of "discontinued operations" (see note 2B).

The heading "Profits or losses on the sale or termination of an operation" should also include provisions for losses in respect of the sale or termination of an operation. The rules for making provisions for the consequences of a decision to sell or terminate an operation are different under FRS 3 from what they were under SSAP 6. Under FRS 3, provision should be made for the losses arising as a consequence of a decision to sell or terminate an operation where the entity is "demonstrably committed" to the sale or termination. This requirement applies irrespective of whether the operation falls to be treated as discontinued in the current period. SSAP 6 stated that in considering the provision required where a decision had been made to discontinue a business segment, the provision should include "all debits and credits arising from trading after the commencement of implementation". Thus, provisions are likely to be made later under FRS 3 than under SSAP 6.

The term "demonstrably committed" is not defined by the FRS but it does indicate that for a termination evidence is given by:

- a detailed formal termination plan from which withdrawal is not realistic;
- public announcement of plans;
- commencement of implementation; or
- other circumstances obliging the entity to complete the termination.

Similarly for a sale, evidence is given by a binding sale agreement (possibly entered into after the period end, provided the decision to sell was clearly taken before the period end) or other circumstances obliging the entity to complete the sale.

Such provisions should be disclosed separately on the face of the profit and loss account. In subsequent periods the provisions should be used to offset the results of the operation. The related disclosure in subsequent periods should be to show the results of the operation under each of the statutory format headings with the utilisation of the provision analysed as necessary between the operating loss and the loss on sale or termination of the operation and disclosed on the face of the profit and loss account immediately below the relevant items.

Example 7 Richards plc, a group engaged predominantly in the manufacture of carpets and carpet yarns, illustrates the setting up and utilisation of such provisions. In 1992 the group took the decision to sell or close the group's linen interests. The weaving and fabric merchandising operations were sold in August 1992 and a loss of £389,000 in respect of this sale was recorded in the 1992 financial statements (shown as a non-operating exceptional item in the 1993 comparative figures that have been restated to comply with FRS 3). The linen bleaching and dying plant continued to operate into the 1993 financial year, but the directors recognised that further costs were likely to be incurred and made a provision of £800,000 in the 1992 financial statements for these costs and the losses that were likely to arise. During the 1993 financial year the linen bleaching and dying plant was shut, the employees made redundant and the plant and buildings sold. The total losses actually incurred in 1993 were £600,000. This comprised £463,000 of operating losses which included costs of redundancies, running down production and stock clearance and £137,000 of losses on the sale of fixed assets. The remaining £200,000 provision which was no longer required was released to the profit and loss account. In addition to the disclosure in the financial statements the transaction was described clearly in the company's "Operating and financial review".

Note 5 to Richards plc's accounts discloses only those exceptional costs that are not covered by provisions brought forward from the previous year. The note also illustrates the disclosure of an item (repositioning of shirt brands in 1992 – £250,000) that the directors decided was exceptional, but not so significant that it required disclosure on the face of the profit and loss account.

Example 7
Richards plc *30 September 1993*
Extract from the consolidated profit and loss account

	Note	1993 £000	1993 £000	1992 £000
Turnover	1			
Continuing operations		**65,877**		68,604
Acquisitions		**1,748**		
		67,625		68,604
Discontinued operations		**144**		3,343
			67,769	71,947
Cost of sales	2		**(61,209)**	(64,727)
Gross profit			**6,560**	7,220
Net operating expenses	2		**(6,707)**	(7,585)
Operating (loss)/profit	3			
Continuing operations		**(398)**		314
Acquisitions		**51**		
		(347)		314
Discontinued operations		**(463)**		(679)
Less 1992 provision		**663**		
			(147)	(365)
Profit on sale of properties in continuing operations	5		**362**	
Provision for loss on discontinued operations	5			(800)
Loss on disposal of discontinued operations	5	**(137)**		(389)
Less 1992 provision	5	**137**		
Profit/(Loss) on ordinary activities before interest			**215**	(1,554)

Extract from note 2 to the accounts

2 Operating costs	1993 Continuing £000	1993 Discontinued £000	1993 Total £000	1992 Continuing £000	1992 Discontinued £000	1992 Total £000
Cost of sales	**60,998**	**211**	**61,209**	61,304	3,423	64,727
Net operating expenses						
Distribution costs	**4,123**	**66**	**4,189**	4,009	66	4,075
Administrative expenses	**2,926**	**216**	**3,142**	3,039	541	3,580
Other operating income	**(75)**	**114**	**39**	(62)	(8)	(70)
	6,974	**396**	**7,370**	6,986	599	7,585
Less 1992 provision		**(663)**	**(663)**			
	6,974	**(267)**	**6,707**			

The total figures for continuing operations in 1993 include the following amounts relating to acquisitions: cost of sales £1,412,000, administrative expenses £285,000.

The discontinued operations referred to are the group's linen interests.

Extract from note 5 to the accounts

	1993 £000	1992 £000
5 Exceptional items		
Recognised in arriving at operating profit on continuing operations:		
Re-positioning of shirt brands		(250)
Recognised below operating profit:		
Gain on sale of property	**362**	
Provision for loss on discontinued operations		(800)
Loss on disposal of discontinued operations		(389)
	362	(1,189)

The Urgent Issues Task Force's third Abstract, UITF 3 "Treatment of goodwill on disposal of a business" (now incorporated into FRS 2), states that the profit or loss on disposal of a previously acquired business should be determined by including the attributable amount of purchased goodwill where it has not previously been charged in the profit and loss account. The effect of this Abstract in conjunction with FRS 3's requirement that the results of business disposals be taken into account in arriving at profit before tax is having a dramatic adverse effect on the profits of some groups.

Example 8 Racal Electronics plc sold or terminated a number of the group's operations including the 'Redac' computer-aided engineering activities, during the 1994 financial year. This gave rise to a loss of £19,594,000, of which £13,155,000 related to goodwill on acquisition which had previously been eliminated against reserves in accordance with the group's accounting policy. Prior to the introduction of FRS 3 and UITF 3 the group would have charged £6,439,000 (i.e., the loss prior to taking into account the goodwill) to the profit and loss account as an extraordinary item; no adjustment would have been made for the goodwill. The combination of UITF 3 and FRS 3 has, therefore, reduced Racal Electronics' profit on ordinary activities before taxation by nearly £20 million.

Example 8
Racal Electronics plc *31 March 1994*
Extract from the consolidated profit and loss account

	1994 Continuing operations £000	1994 Discontinued operations £000	1994 Total £000
2 & 3 Operating profit/(loss)			
Total	49,746	(5,728)	44,018
Profit on sale of properties	372	–	372
Losses on disposal or closure of operations including goodwill written off on acquisition in prior years (£13,155,000)	–	(19,594)	(19,594)
Provision for losses on discontinued operations	–	–	–
Cost of demerger of Chubb Security	–	(49)	(49)
Trading profit/(loss)	50,118	(25,371)	24,747

To mitigate the effect of UITF 3, some groups have written off goodwill by way of prior period adjustment. The argument normally put forward for this treatment is that the issue of UITF 3 caused management to reflect on the value of goodwill. Often the result of these reflections were a realisation that a permanent diminution in the value of the goodwill actually occurred a number of years ago and thus it should not be charged to a current period profit and loss account.

Writing off goodwill using a prior period adjustment appears to comply (individually) with the prudence concept, UITF 3 and FRS 3 provided it was only adopted in the first year in which UITF 3 became effective for the company. However, such a treatment should be used only in those situations where the overall result is not open to challenge. This is because the goodwill "cost" will never pass through a "current year" profit and loss account even on the ultimate disposal of the business and some people argue that this is against the spirit of UITF 3. The UITF have already issued a document clarifying the application of UITF abstracts as they believed that UITF 3 was being abused. Although the abuse did not relate to the use of prior period adjustments, the clarification emphasised that it is important to follow the spirit of the statements.

Example 9 Blue Circle Industries plc illustrates two disposals: one treats goodwill as a charge in the year under UITF 3; the other uses a prior period adjustment to write off the goodwill. The argument for using the prior period adjustment route in the latter case is that the group has been trying to sell the operation concerned for a substantial period of time; had UITF 3 been in force in 1990, presumably full provision would have been made at that time.

Example 9
Blue Circle Industries plc *31 December 1992*
Extract from the group profit and loss account

		Continuing Operations	Acquisitions	Discontinued Operations	Total	Total
		1992	1992	1992	1992	1991 as restated
	Notes	£m	£m	£m	£m	£m
TURNOVER	3 & 4	1,122.4	208.4	39.3	1,370.1	1,149.4
Cost of sales	4	804.7	156.7	27.1	988.5	794.2
GROSS PROFIT		317.7	51.7	12.2	381.6	355.2
Net operating expenses	4	(236.9)	(39.5)	(11.1)	(287.5)	(240.5)
Share of profits of related companies	4	36.5	—	1.9	38.4	42.0
Previous provision		—	—	(1.1)	(1.1)	6.8
OPERATING PROFIT	3 & 4	117.3	12.2	1.9	131.4	163.5
EXCEPTIONAL ITEMS						
Net profit/(loss) on disposal of discontinued operations	5	—	—	39.3	39.3	(1.1)
Provisions against losses on discontinued operations	5	—	—	20.4	20.4	(24.5)
Fundamental reorganisation costs	5	(62.1)	—	—	(62.1)	(16.5)
Write down in group premises	5	(9.4)	—	—	(9.4)	—
PROFIT ON ORDINARY ACTIVITIES BEFORE INTEREST	6	45.8	12.2	61.6	119.6	121.4

Extract from note 5 to the accounts

5 EXCEPTIONAL ITEMS

(i) Discontinued operations	1992 Profit/ (loss) £m	1992 Provision released in year £m	1991 Profit/ (loss) £m	1991 Provision created in year £m
Profit on sale of Blue Circle Limited (South Africa) and Croxton + Garry Limited (UK)	43.8	—	—	—
Disposal of Atco Qualcast Limited (UK)	(4.5)	20.4	—	(24.5)
Further costs in respect of disposal of other business segments	—	—	(1.1)	—
	39.3	20.4	(1.1)	(24.5)

The original goodwill attributable to Croxton + Garry Limited (UK) was £0.8m and has been taken into account in arriving at the above profit. There was no goodwill relating to Blue Circle Limited (South Africa) as the investment was originally purchased in 1912.

The Group decided to dispose of Atco Qualcast Limited in May 1990 and made provisions for expected losses on sale in both the 1990 and 1991 accounts. As the decision to sell the company was taken in 1990, the profits for that year in the Five Year Statement have been restated to include the write-off of the goodwill of £44.7m attributed to the business. This treatment ensures that the prior period figures are consistent with the requirements of UITF 3.

The disposals in the year have increased the group tax charge by approximately £3.4m.

Profits or losses on the disposal of fixed assets

This heading comprises profits or losses on the disposal of fixed assets, and provisions in respect of such items. However, such profits and losses are to be included under this heading only to the extent that they do not represent marginal adjustments to depreciation previously charged. The FRS does not specify the treatment of profits and losses that are such adjustments, but it is most appropriate to recognise them under the same statutory format heading as the normal depreciation charge.

Example 10 Anglian Water plc illustrates a common form of disclosure in such areas. The face of the profit and loss account shows "Profit on sales of assets in continuing operations" of £3.3 million, but there is no note disclosure or any evidence that operating profit includes the profits and losses that represent marginal adjustments to depreciation. However, there seems little need for such disclosures.

Example 10
Anglian Water plc *31 March 1993*
Extract from the group profit and loss account

For the year ended 31 March 1993	Notes	1993 £m	1992 £m
Turnover			
Continuing operations		**567.9**	523.1
Acquisitions		**15.3**	
Total turnover	2	**583.2**	523.1
Operating costs	3	**(371.6)**	(329.1)
Operating profit			
Continuing operations		**212.7**	194.0
Acquisitions		**(1.1)**	–
Total operating profit	2, 4	211.6	194.0
Profit on sales of assets in continuing operations		3.3	0.2
Profit on ordinary activities before interest		**214.9**	194.2

FRS 3 has narrowed the options available for accounting for the disposal of assets by requiring the profit or loss on disposal of an asset to be accounted for in the profit and loss account by reference to the net carrying amount of the asset, whether carried at historical cost or a valuation. Any past revaluation surpluses or deficits (for example, those representing temporary diminutions in value passed through the revaluation reserve) in the revaluation reserve relating to such an asset must be dealt with as a reserve transfer and cannot be taken through the face of the profit and loss account. For those companies that have revalued their fixed assets, this change has resulted in a reduction in the number of exceptional items because the amounts are now less likely to be material.

It has been suggested that an adverse impact on the profit and loss account can be avoided by changing valuation policy prior to disposal and restating the asset to be sold at its historical cost. This is obviously a device to avoid the provision of FRS 3. Changing policies (and thus using a prior period adjustment) to change back to the historical cost basis cannot be justified because it cannot realistically be argued that a policy of carrying assets at historical cost is preferable to carrying assets at valuation. Also it is not acceptable to carry out a "revaluation" back to historical cost as this would not be a legitimate revaluation and thus such a transfer from the revaluation reserve is prohibited by paragraph 34 of Schedule 4 to the Act.

It has also been suggested that the asset to be sold could be revalued (at sales proceeds in most case) immediately prior to the sale. The FRS does not appear to prevent such a revaluation. The revaluation surplus or deficit would then be taken to the revaluation reserve, but in the case of a deficit only to the extent that the revaluation reserve contains earlier revaluation surpluses in respect of that asset. This would result in the profit and loss account showing neither profit nor loss in those circumstances where the asset is sold for more than its historical cost. This treatment is consistent with the spirit of the ASB's discussion paper advocating more frequent valuations of assets that are likely to be disposed of; it will give the same result as continuous revaluations. Also, the treatment is not inconsistent with the principle set out in FRS 3 that individual gains or losses should be recognised only once, either in the profit and loss account or in the statement of total recognised gains and losses. However, whatever the technical merits of this treatment, some have suggested that it is against the spirit of FRS 3, notwithstanding the fact that it is not clear what the spirit of FRS 3 is meant to be in this area. This is a developing area and if companies are using this treatment it is not clear from their published accounts. As the ASB develops its framework for financial reporting we may well see further developments.

Costs of a fundamental reorganisation or restructuring
Costs included under this heading should be restricted to those relating to fundamental reorganisation or restructuring having a material effect on the nature and focus of operations. FRS 3 does not define what "having a material effect on the nature and focus of operations" means. However, it appears that the heading should cover only strategic restructurings; normal on-going reorganisation costs should be charged in arriving at operating profit. It is likely in many cases that companies that include charges under this heading will also have other exceptional items to disclose, for example, those resulting from sales or disposals of operations and assets.

This is illustrated by **Example 11 Thorn EMI plc**, a group which is undergoing considerable restructuring. Note 6 to Thorn EMI's accounts gives a great deal of information on the exceptional items, including information on the tax effects of the various items.

Example 11
Thorn EMI plc *31 December 1992*
Extract from the consolidated profit and loss account

	Notes	1993 £m	1993 £m	£m	1992 £m
Operating profit	1&3				
Continuing operations		319.1		277.8	
Acquisitions		58.1		–	
		377.2		277.8	
Discontinued operations		2.1		3.3	
			379.3		281.1
Exceptional items:	6				
Profits (losses) on businesses disposed of or terminated					
– continuing operations			(40.7)		–
– discontinued operations			10.4		(15.3)
Cost of fundamental reorganisations and restructuring					
– continuing operations			(23.4)		(91.9)
Profits (losses) on disposal of fixed assets					
– continuing operations			1.8		19.1
Profit before finance charges			327.4		193.0

Extract from note 6 to the accounts

6. Exceptional items	1993			1992		
	Gross	Tax	Net	Gross	Tax	Net
	£m	£m	£m	£m	£m	£m
Profits (losses) on businesses disposed of or terminated						
Fire Appliances Division	25.5	–	25.5	–	–	–
– goodwill written off	(4.4)	–	(4.4)	–	–	–
Thames Television Inc. (Reeves)*	(22.8)	–	(22.8)	–	–	–
– goodwill written off*	(17.9)	–	(17.9)	–	–	–
THORN EMI Software	–	–	–	42.5	1.3	43.8
– goodwill written off	–	–	–	(9.5)	–	(9.5)
Lamp business	(10.0)	1.5	(8.5)	(6.3)	2.1	(4.2)
Interest in Unitel	–	–	–	(14.9)	–	(14.9)
Other	(0.7)	(0.2)	(0.9)	(24.8)	4.5	(20.3)
– goodwill written off	–	–	–	(2.3)	–	(2.3)
	(30.3)	1.3	(29.0)	(15.3)	7.9	(7.4)
Advance corporation tax written off	–	(1.0)	(1.0)	–	(5.1)	(5.1)
	(30.3)	0.3	(30.0)	(15.3)	2.8	(12.5)
Cost of fundamental reorganisations and restructuring*						
Restructuring of Thames Television	(21.9)	1.0	(20.9)	(34.3)	9.7	(24.6)
Withdrawal from general electrical retailing	(1.6)	1.0	(0.6)	(57.6)	15.1	(42.5)
– goodwill written off	(3.4)	–	(3.4)	–	–	–
Other	3.5	(1.9)	1.6	–	–	–
	(23.4)	0.1	(23.3)	(91.9)	24.8	(67.1)
Advance corporation tax written off	–	(0.2)	(0.2)	–	(18.7)	(18.7)
	(23.4)	(0.1)	(23.5)	(91.9)	6.1	(85.8)
Profits (losses) on the disposal of fixed assets and investments*						
Disposal of part of Edmonton site	–	–	–	14.8	–	14.8
Other	1.8	–	1.8	4.3	–	4.3
	1.8	–	1.8	19.1	–	19.1
Total before minority interests	(51.9)	0.2	(51.7)	(88.1)	8.9	(79.2)
Minority interests in Thames	18.4	(0.4)	18.0	13.5	(1.0)	12.5
	(33.5)	(0.2)	(33.7)	(74.6)	7.9	(66.7)

*Continuing operations.

Columnar disclosure of exceptional items

In 1992 **Example 12 Imperial Chemical Industries plc** undertook substantial restructuring with the result that the group incurred exceptional items that in total amounted to £644 million. To disclose the effects of this clearly, ICI adopted a columnar approach which involved reporting four columns of figures: before exceptional items; exceptional items; discontinued operations; and total. This approach allowed the group to report the total for each of the statutory line items on the face of the profit and loss account as well as giving prominence to the results before exceptional items and discontinued activities. ICI has continued to use this presentation in its 1993 accounts even though the effect of exceptional items is less significant.

Example 12
Imperial Chemical Industries plc *31 December 1993*
Extract from the group profit and loss account

	1992			*For the year ended 31 December*		1993		
Continuing operations		Discontinued operations	Total			Continuing operations		Discontinued operations	Total
Before exceptional items	Exceptional items					Before exceptional items	Exceptional items		
£m	£m	£m	£m		Notes	£m	£m	£m	£m
7,557	–	4,504	12,061	Turnover	9	8,430	–	2,202	10,632
(7,458)	(346)	(4,311)	(12,115)	Operating costs	3, 4	(8,218)	–	(1,937)	(10,155)
74	–	51	125	Other operating income	4	123	–	33	156
173	(346)	244	71	**Trading profit (loss)**	3, 4, 9	335	–	298	633
				Share of profits less losses of					
41	(19)	5	27	associated undertakings	6	45	–	2	47
–	(207)	16	(191)	Losses less profits on sale or		–	(94)	(59)	(153)
				closure of operations	3				
–	(23)	(52)	(75)	Provisions for costs of reor-		–	–	–	–
				ganisation	3				
214	(595)	213	(168)	**Profit (loss) on ordinary activities before interest**	9	380	(94)	241	527
(51)	–	(165)	(216)	Net interest payable	7	(90)	–	(63)	(153)
163	(595)	48	(384)	**Profit (loss) on ordinary activities before taxation**		290	(94)	178	374
(124)	(63)	4	(183)	Tax on profit (loss) on ordinary activities	8	(105)	(18)	(71)	(194)
39	(658)	52	(567)	**Profit (loss) on ordinary activities after taxation**		185	(112)	107	180
(16)	14	(1)	(3)	Attributable to minorities		(38)	(4)	–	(42)
23	(644)	51	(570)	**Net profit (loss) for the financial year**		147	(116)	107	138
				Dividends	10				
			(393)	Cash					(199)
				Demerger					(363)
			(393)						(562)
			(963)	Loss retained for year					(424)
3.2p	(90.3)p	7.2p	(79.9)p	**Earnings (loss) per £1 Ordinary Share**	11	20.4p	(16.1)p	14.9p	19.2P

Results of associated companies

Although not strictly exceptional items, the results of associated companies are often reported alongside such items. FRS 3 allows some flexibility in the presentation of the results of associated companies in the profit and loss account. This is necessary because some groups carry out parts of their core business through associated companies while others have holdings in associates that are essentially that non-operating in nature.

Example 13 Blue Circle plc has investments in a number of associated companies, mainly overseas. These companies operate in the same business sectors as the remainder of the group, i.e., cement production and sale. Accordingly, Blue Circle treats the results of its associated companies as part of operating profit.

Example 13
Blue Circle plc *31 December 1993*
Extract from the consolidated profit and loss account

	Notes	1993 £m	1992 £m
Turnover	2 & 3	1,678.8	1,370.1
Cost of sales	3	1,173.7	988.5
Gross profit		505.1	381.6
Net operating expenses	3	(347.1)	(288.6)
Share of profits of related companies	3	40.4	38.4
Operating profit	2 & 3	198.4	131.4

On the other hand, **Example 14 Laura Ashley Holdings plc** reports its share of results of associated companies immediately after operating profit. Laura Ashley group companies are involved in the design, manufacturing, sourcing, distribution and sale of Laura Ashley products. The principal associated company, Revman Industries Inc., which contributes a substantial proportion of the group's profits, is a distributor of branded bed linen (including Laura Ashley products) to the retail market.

Example 14
Laura Ashley Holdings plc *29 January 1994*
Extract from the consolidated profit and loss account

	Notes	1994 £000	1993 £000
Turnover	1	300,387	247,793
Cost of sales		(142,000)	(109,835)
Gross profit		158,387	137,958
Other operating expenses	2	(156,086)	(136,892)
Operating profit	4	2,301	1,066
Income from interests in associated undertakings	10	1,823	1,473
Net interest payable	5	(1,096)	(753)
Profit on ordinary activities before taxation		3,028	1,786

Example 15 Guinness plc illustrates a more complicated presentation in the profit and loss account of the contribution from associated companies. Guinness divides its interests in associated companies into two categories for the purposes of reporting their contribution to the group's results in the profit and loss account: LVMH; and others. The reason for this split is, presumably, the significance of the contribution by LVMH. At 31 December 1993 Guinness had a cross shareholding and LVMH whereby Guinness held approximately 24 per cent. of LVMH's share capital and LVMH held a similar proportion of Guinness' share capital. LVMH contributed £125 million to the group's pre interest profit of £890 million. Other associated companies, in aggregate, contributed £44 million; these results are not reported separately on the face of the profit and loss account, but are included with "Net trading costs".

After the end of the financial year the Guinness board decided to restructure its investment in LVMH. This restructuring involved, *inter alia*, the sale of the investment in LVMH. This decision resulted in a provision of £173 million (before tax) being recognised in the 1993 financial statements. This provision was charged as an exceptional item shown in the profit and loss account immediately below the share of profit of LVMH.

Example 15
Guinness plc *31 December 1993*
Extract from the group profit and loss account

For the year ended 31 December 1993	Notes	1993 £m	1992 £m	Growth %
TURNOVER	1	**4,663**	**4,363**	**7**
Net trading costs	2	(3,725)	(3,340)	
Reorganisation costs	3	–	(125)	
Total operating costs	2	(3,725)	(3,465)	
PROFIT BEFORE INTEREST AND TAXATION (EXCLUDING LVMH)	1	**938**	**898**	**4**
Share of profit before taxation of LVMH	4	125	101	
Provision against investment in LVMH	5	(173)	–	
PROFIT BEFORE INTEREST AND TAXATION		**890**	**999**	**(11)**

Extract from note 2 to the accounts

2. TOTAL OPERATING COSTS

	1993 £m	1992 £m
Raw materials and consumables	941	843
Increase in stocks of finished goods and work in progress	(27)	(97)
Excise duties	1,224	1,184
Staff costs (Note 6)	568	514
Depreciation	138	127
Other operating charges	925	815
Share of profits of associated undertakings (other than LVMH)	(44)	(46)
Net trading costs	3,725	3,340
Reorganisation costs (Note 3)	–	125
	3,725	**3,465**

EARNINGS PER SHARE

The introduction to this chapter referred to past obsessions with earnings per share and trends in earnings per share; it is clear that the ASB thought that there should be significantly less emphasis on such figures. However, the proper use of such figures can aid a fuller understanding of a company's performance, provided the figures used are tailored to the use to which they are to be put. It is not possible for an accounting standard setter to determine one "magic number" that is correct for all occasions so the ASB decided that FRS 3 should require disclosure of a range of financial information. As far as exceptional items are concerned the FRS requires that sufficient information be disclosed to enable the informed reader of the financial statements to be in a position to make his own evaluation of how each item should be treated and to make any necessary adjustment to earnings per share for his own purposes if the treatment of any item is different from the one which he prefers.

Statement of Standard Accounting Practice No 3 "Earnings per share" (SSAP 3) requires companies listed on a recognised stock exchange for any class of equity capital (except banking and insurance companies claiming exemption from disclosure requirements) to disclose earnings per share on the face of the profit and loss account together with comparative figures for the previous year. Both "basic" earnings per share and "fully diluted" earnings per share (i.e., after taking account of conversion of convertible loan stock, exercising of options, etc.) should be shown. It is not necessary to show fully diluted earnings per share if the dilution is less than 5 per cent of the basic earnings per share.

Following FRS 3's amendment to SSAP 3, the basic earnings per share to be disclosed is: profit after tax, minority interests and extraordinary items and after deducting preference dividends and other appropriations in respect of preference shares (i.e., profit attributable to equity shareholders) divided by the weighted average number of equity shares in issue and ranking for dividend.

In addition to the earnings per share figures required by SSAP 3, FRS 3 allows additional earnings per share figures calculated at other levels of profit to be given provided that:

- they are presented on a consistent basis over a period of time;
- they are reconciled to the "basic" earnings per share figure. (The reconciliation should list the items for which adjustment is being made and disclose their individual effect on the calculation);
- the "basic" earnings per share figure is at least as prominent as any additional earnings per share figures;
- the reasons for the additional figures are explained; and
- the reconciliations and explanations appear adjacent to the earnings per share disclosure or a reference is given there as to where they may be found.

A measure that directors could consider presenting is the "headline earnings" measure set out in Statement of Investment Practice No 1 "The Definition of Headline Earnings" (SoIP 1), issued by the Institute of Investment Management and Research (IIMR). IIMR "headline earnings" is intended to provide accounts users, the press and statistical companies with an unambiguous reference point for the reporting of trading profit. It follows that this figure should be capable of precise determination based on information disclosed in financial statements that comply with FRS 3. *The Financial Times* and *Extel* have both announced their intention to publish earnings per share and price earnings ratios based on IIMR headline earnings.

SoIP 1 includes both a detailed definition and explanation. In summary, IIMR headline earnings will be calculated to remove the following items from FRS 3 based profit after tax and extraordinary items:

- profit (loss) on the sale or termination of an operation (but no adjustment for the operating results of discontinued operations);
- profit (loss) on the sale of fixed assets or business, or their permanent diminution in value (includes trade investments, but excludes assets acquired for resale, such as marketable securities);

- profit (loss) arising from reorganisation of long-term debt (such as under UITF 8);
- profit (loss) from prior period adjustments to the extent these are included in earnings;
- provision for exceptional items listed in FRS 3 paragraph 20 (which should be allocated to the period in which the expense occurs, rather than the period when provision is made);
- bid defence costs;
- goodwill written off;
- extraordinary profits (losses) as defined by FRS 3; and
- tax and minority interest effects related to the above adjustments.

It follows that no adjustment should be made for the following items:

- notional interest on any of the above items;
- exceptional items (for example, reorganisation or restructuring) other than those listed above;
- acquisitions or discontinued operations to the extent included in operating profit;
- pension (and other post-retirement benefit) charges and credits including one-off items;
- foreign currency items (unless attaching to an excluded item);
- abortive bid costs;
- one-off costs of complying with major new legislation;
- litigation costs (whether normal or abnormal); and
- diminution in value of current assets.

Example 16 Coats Viyella plc chose to report the IIMR measure in its 1993 Annual Report and Accounts. Note 11 to the accounts discloses the reconciliation to the FRS 3 basic earnings per share. Both measures are presented on the face of the profit and loss account with equal prominence.

Example 16
Coats Viyella plc *31 December 1993*
Extract from the consolidated profit and loss account

| | | Continuing operations | | | |
| | | | Acquisitions | Total | Total |
For the year ended 31 December 1993	Notes	1993 £m	1993 £m	1993 £m	1992 £m
Turnover	1 & 2	**2,243.8**	**200.0**	**2,443.8**	2,109.8
Cost of sales	1	(1,566.5)	(136.1)	(1,702.6)	(1,469.5)
Gross profit		**677.3**	**63.9**	**741.2**	640.3
Distribution costs	1	(375.9)	(22.1)	(398.0)	(351.2)
Administrative expenses	1	(166.3)	(13.5)	(179.8)	(151.8)
Other operating income	1 & 3	8.2	0.1	8.3	8.9
Operating profit	1, 2 & 3	**143.3**	**28.4**	**171.7**	146.2
Profit on sale of fixed assets	1	14.7	0.1	14.8	10.1
Gains/(losses) on sale or termination of operations	1	6.4	–	6.4	(0.4)
Profit on ordinary activities before interest	2	**164.4**	**28.5**	**192.9**	155.9
Share of profits of associated companies				1.3	3.3
Interest receivable and similar income	6			21.5	13.4
Interest payable and similar charges	7			(65.4)	(63.5)
Profit on ordinary activities before taxation				**150.3**	109.1
Tax on profit on ordinary activities	8			(49.5)	(43.8)
Profit on ordinary activities after taxation				**100.8**	65.3
Equity minority interests				(9.5)	(5.3)
Non-equity minority interests				(0.6)	(0.7)
Profit for the financial year	9			**90.7**	59.3
Preference dividends on non-equity shares				(0.7)	(0.7)
Profit attributable to ordinary shareholders				**90.0**	58.6
Ordinary dividends on equity shares	10			(53.2)	(41.9)
Transferred to reserves	24			**36.8**	16.7
Earnings per ordinary share of 20p	11			**14.6p**	10.0p
Headline earnings per ordinary share of 20p	11			**11.4p**	8.4p

DISCLOSURE OF EXCEPTIONAL AND EXTRAORDINARY ITEMS UNDER FRS 3

Extract from note 11 to the accounts

	1993	1992 Restated	1993 £m	1992 £m
11 Earnings per share				
Earnings per share are based on profit available for ordinary shareholders of:			**90.0**	58.6
and on average number of shares of:	**616.6m**	584.1m		
resulting in earnings per share of:	**14.6p**	10.0p		
Less:				
profit on sale of fixed assets	**(2.4)p**	(1.8)p	**(14.8)**	(10.1)
(gains)/losses on sale or termination of operations	**(1.1)p**	0.1p	**(6.4)**	0.4
taxation relating to these items	**0.1p**	–	**0.6**	–
minority interests relating to these items	**0.2p**	0.1p	**1.2**	0.2
Headline earnings per share	**11.4p**	8.4p	**70.6**	49.1

Headline earnings per share has been calculated in accordance with Statement of Investment Practice Number 1 issued by The Institute of Investment Management and Research and is provided in order to assist users of accounts to identify earnings derived from trading activities.

The number of shares in issue for 1992 and 1993 have been adjusted so as to treat the shares issued in respect of the enhanced share dividends as though they were rights issues at less than full market price in accordance with SSAP 3.

Exercise in full of all outstanding share options and conversion of all the £75.625m 6.25% Senior Convertible Bonds of Coats Viyella Plc would not result in any material dilution of earnings per share for 1993.

Example 17 Williams Holdings plc has chosen to report an adjusted earnings per share based on the results before acquisition reorganisation costs and exceptional items.

Example 17
Williams Holdings plc   *31 December 1993*
Extract from the consolidated profit and loss account

	Notes	1993 £m		1992 £m Restated
Turnover	2			
Continuing operations		**1,097.3**		985.9
Acquisitions		**66.9**		
		1,164.2		
Discontinued operations		**48.4**		49.5
		1,212.6		1,035.4
Cost of sales	3	(703.5)		(604.3)
Gross profit		509.1		431.1
Net operating expenses:	3			
Acquisition reorganisation costs		**(3.1)**		–
Other operating costs		**(314.4)**	(261.4)	
		(317.5)		(261.4)
Operating profit	4			
Continuing operations		**179.4**		160.9
Acquisitions		**6.3**		
		185.7		
Discontinued operations		**5.9**		8.8
		191.6		169.7
Loss on disposal of discontinued operations	5	(17.1)		(5.0)
Profit on share disposal	5	–		11.1
Profit on ordinary activities before interest		174.5		175.8
Interest payable less interest and other income receivable	6	(21.3)		(18.4)
Profit on ordinary activities before tax		153.2		157.4
Tax on profit on ordinary shares	7	(52.8)		(45.2)
Profit on ordinary activities after tax		100.4		112.2
Dividends	8	(86.7)		(84.3)
Retained profit for the financial year		13.7		27.9
Earnings per share	9			
Basic		15.7p		18.6p
Adjusted		19.7p		17.3p

DISCLOSURE OF EXCEPTIONAL AND EXTRAORDINARY ITEMS UNDER FRS 3

Extract from note 9 to the accounts

9 Earnings per share

Basic earnings per share in accordance with FRS 3 have been calculated on an adjusted profit of £76.3m (1992 £87.8m) and a weighted average number of shares in issue during the year of 485.8m (1992 471.9m).

An adjusted earnings per share calculation based upon the results before acquisition reorganisation costs and exceptional items is set out below to facilitate comparison of the underlying performance of the group:

Earnings adjustments	1993 FRS 3 £m	Adjusted £m	1992 FRS 3 £m	Adjusted £m
Profit on ordinary activities before tax	153.2	153.2	157.4	157.4
Acquisition reorganisation costs	–	3.1	–	–
Profit on share disposal	–	–	–	(11.1)
Loss on disposal of discontinued operations	–	17.1	–	5.0
	153.2	173.4	157.4	151.3
Tax charge	(52.8)	(52.8)	(45.2)	(45.2)
Tax on acquisition reorganisation costs	–	(1.0)	–	–
Preference dividends	(24.1)	(24.1)	(24.4)	(24.4)
	76.3	95.5	87.8	81.7
Earnings per share	15.7p	19.7p	18.6p	17.3p

Reconciliation to adjusted earnings per share	pence	pence
Earnings per share per FRS 3	15.7	18.6
Profit on share disposal	–	(2.4)
Loss on disposal of discontinued operations	3.5	1.1
Acquisition reorganisation costs	0.7	–
Tax on acquisition reorganisation costs	(0.2)	–
Adjusted earnings per share	19.7	17.3

Example 18 Racal Electronics plc has also chosen to report an adjusted earnings per share. The purpose of this adjusted earnings per share figure is "to give an understanding of the base for the future".

Example 18
Racal Electronics plc *31 December 1993*
Extract from the consolidated profit and loss acccount

Note		1994 Continuing operations £000	1994 Discont'd operations £000	1994 Total £000	1993 Adjusted Continuing operations £000	1993 Adjusted Discont'd operations £000	1993 Adjusted Total £000	1993 Statutory Total £000
2	Turnover							
	Existing	885,879	–	885,879	908,941	–	908,941	908,297
	Acquisitions	1,089	–	1,089	–	–	–	–
	Discontinued	–	29,123	29,123	–	37,978	37,978	375,803
	Total	886,968	29,123	916,091	908,941	37,978	946,919	1,284,100
2 & 3	Operating profit/(loss)							
	Existing	49,159	–	49,159	54,196	–	54,196	54,196
	Acquisitions	587	–	587	–	–	–	–
	Discontinued	–	(5,856)	(5,856)	–	(18,297)	(18,297)	3,633
	Prior year provisions utilised	–	128	128	–	11,100	11,100	16,425
	Total	49,746	(5,728)	44,018	54,196	(7,197)	46,999	74,254
	Profit on sale of properties	372	–	372	118	–	118	143
	Losses on disposal or closure of operations including goodwill written off on acquisition in prior years (£13,155,000)	–	(19,594)	(19,594)	–	–	–	–
	Provision for losses on discontinued operations	–	–	–	–	–	–	(750)
	Cost of demerger of Chubb Security	–	(49)	(49)	–	(3,719)	(3,719)	(3,719)
	Trading profit/(loss)	50,118	(25,371)	24,747	54,314	(10,916)	43,398	69,928
5	Net interest receivable			1,633			4,297	2,849
	Profit on ordinary activities before taxation			26,380			47,695	72,777
8	Tax on profit on ordinary activities			11,323			19,183	30,103
	Profit on ordinary activities after taxation			15,057			28,512	42,674
	Loss/(profit) attributable to minority interests			240			57	(755)
	Profit on ordinary activities attributable to members of the parent company			15,297			28,569	41,919
9	Dividends			11,890				172,846
23	Retained profit/(loss) for the year			3,407				(130,927)
10	Earnings per share			5.47p			10.24p	15.02p
10	Adjusted earnings per share			11.86p			13.15p	

DISCLOSURE OF EXCEPTIONAL AND EXTRAORDINARY ITEMS UNDER FRS 3

Extract from note 10 to the accounts

10 EARNINGS PER SHARE

i) Earnings per share has been calculated by reference to the average of 279,489,466 (1993: 279,036,965) ordinary shares of 25p each in issue during the year based on the consolidated profits of £15,297,000 (1993 adjusted: £28,569,000, 1993 statutory: £41,919,000) after deducting taxation and profits attributable to minority interests.

The average numbers of shares stated reflect the capital reorganisation in October 1992.

There would be no material dilution of earnings per share if the outstanding share options were exercised.

ii) Adjusted earnings per share has been calculated as follows:

	1994 Attributable Profits £000	1994 Earnings Per Share p	1993 Attributable Profits £000	1993 Earnings Per Share p
Consolidated profits/earnings per share	15,297	5.47	28,569	10.24
Adjustments:-				
Cost of demerger of Chubb Security	49		3,719	
Taxation recovered on demerger and bid defence costs	(5,333)		(83)	
Discontinued operations	25,322		7,197	
Taxation on discontinued operations	(2,178)		(2,697)	
Adjusted consolidated profits/earnings per share	33,157	11.86	36,705	13.15

The adjusted earnings per share has been shown for the continuing operations to give an understanding of the base for the future.

RESTATEMENT OF COMPARATIVE FIGURES

The introductionof FRS 3 has resulted in companies having to restate the presentation of the results of earlier years. The areas in which most changes have occurred relate to exceptional and extraordinary items.

In its 1992 accounts **Example 19 Redland plc** reported a loss on disposal of its interest in an associated company as an extraordinary item. No exceptional items were reported on the face of the profit and loss account. In the 1993 accounts the extraordinary item was reclassified as an exceptional item, shown separately after operating profit. The 1992 comparative figures in the 1993 accounts also showed profits on the disposal of properties on the face of the profit and loss account. This information was not previously disclosed separately in a primary financial statement.

Example 19
Redland plc   *31 December 1993*
Extract from the group profit and loss account

Notes		1993 £ million	1992 £ million
2	**Turnover including share of sales of associates**	**2,473.7**	2,089.9
	Group share of sales of associates	**(257.4)**	(199.7)
	Turnover	**2,216.3**	1,890.2
	Cost of sales	**(1,543.9)**	(1,300.6)
	Distribution costs	**(255.1)**	(230.1)
	Gross profit	**417.3**	359.5
	Administrative expenses	**(147.2)**	(140.1)
	Group share of profits of associates	**34.0**	14.8
2	Operating profit	**304.1**	234.2
	Profits on the disposal of properties	**8.9**	13.7
	Profits on the disposal of businesses	**2.7**	–
	Loss on the disposal of an investment in an associate	**–**	(22.5)
3	Interest payable, net	**(36.8)**	(26.4)
3	**Profit on ordinary activities before taxation**	**278.9**	199.0
4	Tax on profit on ordinary activities	**(85.0)**	(62.4)
	Profit on ordinary activities after taxation	**193.9**	136.6
	Minority interests	**(59.3)**	(48.4)
	Preferred stock dividends	**(5.9)**	(5.7)
	Profit for the financial year attributable to Redland plc	**128.7**	82.5
5	Dividends	**(128.1)**	(111.2)
6	Retained profit/(loss)	**0.6**	(28.7)
7	**Basic earnings per share**	**26.1p**	18.6p
	Adjustment for the loss on the disposal of an investment in an associate	**–**	5.1p
	Adjusted earnings per share	**26.1p**	23.7p
5	Dividends per share	**25.0p**	25.0p

DISCLOSURE OF EXCEPTIONAL AND EXTRAORDINARY ITEMS UNDER FRS 3

Extract from the 1992 group profit and loss account

Notes		1992 £ million	1991 £ million
2	**Turnover including share of sales of associates**	**2,089.9**	1,503.6
	Group share of sales of associates	**(199.7)**	(204.4)
	Turnover	**1,890.2**	1,299.2
	Cost of sales	**(1,296.1)**	(885.2)
	Distribution costs	**(230.1)**	(137.8)
	Gross profit	**364.0**	276.2
	Administrative expenses	**(130.9)**	(104.6)
	Group share of profits of associates	**14.8**	14.7
2	Operating profit	**247.9**	186.3
3	Interest payable, net	**(26.4)**	(0.3)
3	**Profit on ordinary activities before taxation**	**221.5**	186.0
4	Tax on profit on ordinary activities	**(62.4)**	(51.1)
	Profit on ordinary activities after taxation	**159.1**	134.9
	Minority interests	**(48.4)**	(29.8)
	Preferred stock dividends	**(5.7)**	(8.1)
	Profit attributable to Redland plc before extraordinary items	**105.0**	97.0
5	Extraordinary item	**(22.5)**	–
	Net profit for the financial year	**82.5**	97.0
6	Dividends	**(111.2)**	(84.9)
7 & 15	Retained (loss)/profit transferred to reserves	**(28.7)**	12.1
8	**Earnings per share**	**23.7p**	30.0p
6	Dividends per share	**25.0p**	25.0p

Investment property companies have experienced particular problems implementing FRS 3. Under SSAP 6 investment property companies accounted for profits or losses on disposal of investment properties in one of three ways:

- exceptional items;
- extraordinary items; or
- reserve movements.

In its 1994 accounts **Example 20 Land Securities plc** re-presented its 1993 profit and loss account to comply with FRS 3. The effect of this was to combine the "revenue profit and loss account" with the "capital profit and loss account".

Example 20
Land Securities plc *31 March 1994*
Extract from the consolidted profit and loss account

	Notes	£m	1994 £m	£m	1993 £m
GROSS PROPERTY INCOME	3		448.9		436.9
NET RENTAL INCOME	3		389.4		380.7
Property management and administrative expenses	4		(22.2)		(24.6)
PROFIT ON ORDINARY ACTIVITIES BEFORE PROPERTY SALES AND INTEREST			367.2		356.1
Profit/(loss) on sales of properties			2.3		(4.3)
PROFIT ON ORDINARY ACTIVITIES BEFORE INTEREST AND TAXATION			369.5		351.8
Interest receivable	5		14.9		21.0
Interest payable	5		(147.3)		(143.7)
Revenue profit		234.8		233.4	
Profit/(loss) on sales of properties		2.3		(4.3)	
PROFIT ON ORDINARY ACTIVITIES BEFORE TAXATION			237.1		229.1
Taxation on:					
Revenue profit		(56.5)		(63.4)	
Profit/(loss) on sales of properties		–		–	
Taxation	9		(56.5)		(63.4)
PROFIT ON ORDINARY ACTIVITIES AFTER TAXATION			180.6		165.7
Dividends	11		(122.2)		(115.3)
RETAINED PROFIT FOR THE FINANCIAL YEAR	23		58.4		50.4
Earnings per share	12		35.66p		32.83p
Adjustment for (profit)/loss on sales of properties after taxation			(.46)p		.85p
Adjusted earnings per share	12		35.20p		33.68p
DIVIDEND COVER (times)					
Profit after taxation			1.48		1.44
Profit excluding profit/loss on sales of properties after taxation			1.46		1.47

The 1993 Consolidated Profit and Loss Account has been re-presented to comply with FRS 3.

DISCLOSURE OF EXCEPTIONAL AND EXTRAORDINARY ITEMS UNDER FRS 3

Extracts from the 1993 revenue profit and loss account and capital profit and loss account

REVENUE PROFIT AND LOSS ACCOUNT	Notes	1993 £m	1992 £m
GROSS PROPERTY INCOME	2	436.9	406.7
NET RENTAL INCOME	2	380.7	353.6
Property management and administrative expenses	3	(24.6)	(23.6)
PROFIT ON ORDINARY ACTIVITIES BEFORE INTEREST AND TAXATION		356.1	330.0
Interest receivable	4	21.0	29.3
Interest payable	4	(143.7)	(131.8)
PROFIT ON ORDINARY ACTIVITIES BEFORE TAXATION		233.4	227.5
Taxation	7	(63.4)	(62.9)
PROFIT ON ORDINARY ACTIVITIES AFTER TAXATION		170.0	164.6
Dividends	9	(115.3)	(109.8)
RETAINED REVENUE PROFIT FOR THE YEAR	23	54.7	54.8
EARNINGS PER SHARE	10	33.68p	32.62p
DIVIDEND COVER (times)		1.47	1.50
CAPITAL PROFIT AND LOSS ACCOUNT			
(Deficit)/surplus realised on sales of properties over book value	11	(4.3)	.6
Costs of raising loan capital		–	(8.1)
Other items		–	(.4)
CAPITAL LOSS BEFORE TAXATION		(4.3)	(7.9)
Taxation		–	2.7
RETAINED CAPITAL LOSS FOR THE YEAR		(4.3)	(5.2)
RETAINED REVENUE PROFIT AND CAPITAL LOSS FOR THE YEAR		50.4	49.6

CONCLUSION

FRS 3 was a response to demands from users of financial statements for improvements in the quality of information in the profit and loss account. The ASB decided that the performance of a complex organisation could not be summarised in a single number (e.g., earnings per share) and therefore decided to adopt an "information set" approach that highlights a range of important components of performance. The solution was probably more radical than was expected by many. The Board believed that, although the approach adopted would mean that financial statements would sometimes appear more complex than under the former standard, the presentation and disclosure requirements of the FRS should provide a framework that will better facilitate the analysis and interpretation of the various aspects of performance.

FRS 3 is not without its critics, however. Some people argue that financial statements have become too complex for "ordinary shareholders" to understand; some would like listed companies to produce a high level "glossy" review of activities and a separate report along the lines of the US Form 10-K. Others argue that the basic earnings per share figure now required by SSAP 3, following its amendment by FRS 3, is of no use whatsoever for analysis purposes. This latter view is not out of line with the ASB's own view but the earnings per share figure has been retained to provide an unambiguous starting point for alternative measures such as those put forward by the Institute of Investment Management and Research (IIMR).

As far as the disclosure of exceptional and extraordinary items is concerned, the ASB seems to have achieved its aim of better presented information. The fact that third parties, such as *The Financial Times* and *Extel* can calculate IIMR measures of earnings per share from financial statements that comply with FRS 3 is testimony to this.

Future developments
Further changes are likely, however, but these will have to wait until the ASB is in a position to finalise its views on certain aspects of its statement of principles. Potential changes include:

- how assets should be accounted for and, in particular, how the disposals of assets should be dealt with; and
- accounting for associates and joint ventures.

Asset accounting
The current position whereby the profit or loss on the disposal of an asset is based on the balance sheet carrying amount (cost or valuation), but companies have the choice of whether or not they revalue assets, is a "half-way house", with the result that gains may appear either in the profit and loss account or in the statement of total recognised gains and losses or part in each. It could be argued that the statement of total recognised gains and losses should report the entire gain on holding fixed assets, but a move to this position will have to await a review of the purpose of depreciation and how it should be accounted for.

Associates and joint ventures
The discussion paper issued by the ASB in July 1994 "Associates and joint ventures" proposes substantial changes to the accounting for associates and joint ventures. The paper proposes that associates and joint ventures be confined to "strategic alliances", i.e., there will be a reduction in the number of such entities. It is proposed that such entities should be included in group accounts using an "expanded equity method" of accounting. The proposals will also increase substantially the amount of information disclosed in the notes to the accounts.

Quality of financial reporting
The quality of financial reporting has increased significantly as a result of the ASB's efforts over the last four years. On the whole companies have taken the ASB's new accounting standards, including FRS 3, and applied them sensibly to their particular situations. The examples included within this chapter demonstrate that a variety of presentations are still possible within the framework of FRS 3 and that companies can

still present the performance measures that they believe will be of most use to their shareholders. Also users of accounts have woken up to the fact that analysis of a company's financial position and future prospects involves much more than simply looking at the earnings per share figures.

LIFE PROFIT REPORTING

James Dean and Nic Nicandrou

INTRODUCTION

1. The development of life assurance accounting

A unique feature of life assurance is its long operating cycle. The duration from policy commencement to final termination can span a number of decades. In view of the difficulties inherent in predicting events that may take place over this operating cycle, the industry developed a basis of accounting which ensured that life offices were able to meet their future potential liabilities to policyholders. Traditionally, insurers have followed a cash flow basis of accounting, with the emphasis on solvency as opposed to profitability. The supervisory authorities wholeheartedly endorsed this approach and these traditional accounting practices are also used in preparing the annual returns to the Department of Trade and Industry. However, as the concept of solvency is far removed from that of profitability, shareholders and their advisors who are more interested in the earning power of the business, are unable to glean much information from financial reports drawn up on this basis.

There is currently an acceptance by the life assurance industry that the existing solvency based approach of reporting profits is deficient. This perception was driven by:

(a) two major acquisition battles during the 1980's; that of Allianz and BAT for Eagle Star and that of Australian Mutual Provident for Pearl Assurance. In the case of Eagle Star, the value of its life assurance business was conservatively stated in its financial statements at £100,000. In its bid defence document, however, it published an appraisal value of approximately £375 million. Similar disparities were also highlighted in the case of Pearl Assurance, where its appraisal value was quoted in the defence document at £1.2 billion compared to that shown in the financial statements of £184 million. In view of their unfamiliarity with appraisal values, markets were not fully influenced by them and industry insiders consider that Eagle Star and Pearl were both acquired on the cheap.

(b) the diversification of banks into life operations; under the solvency based approach banks were faced with the unhelpful prospect of reporting losses on business that they were developing rapidly and considered to be highly profitable.

The pressures that were put on the solvency based approach as a result of these two factors, encouraged the search for alternative approaches to life profit reporting. The late 1980's and early 1990's saw the gradual emergence of other bases which were used by an increasing number of groups incorporating life assurance companies.

Banks were the main drivers behind the quest for an alternative basis which would have enabled them to demonstrate that their life operations represented a sensible investment and were profitable. This led to the development of the embedded value method, which is adopted by most banks and now building societies in their group accounts in reporting the financial performance of their life assurance subsidiaries.

A number of proprietary life offices have also published embedded value information or have made supplementary disclosures using another alternative method developed by the Association of British Insurers ("ABI"), known as the accruals basis.

The chapter considers the bases adopted by various groups in reporting the 1993 results of their life operations and looks forward at the changes that will take place in 1995 as a result of the European Insurance Accounts Directive and the recent initiative by listed proprietary life companies to obtain agreement on a single method to be used as an alternative basis of reporting life profits.

2. Framework for reporting

Framework

The framework for financial reporting of proprietary life assurance companies is derived from the following sources:

(a) statutory requirements as regards basis of preparation of the financial statements derived from the Companies Act 1985 and the Insurance Companies Act 1982. It is the Insurance Companies Act 1982 which imposes the prudential requirements which seek to ensure that sufficient assets are maintained to meet liabilities to policyholders; the cash flow basis of accounting, commonly referred to as the statutory solvency basis, has been developed as a result of this requirement. Until 1995, insurance companies are exempted from the true and fair requirements of the 1985 Companies Act and are permitted to carry hidden reserves.

(b) Statements of Standard Accounting Practice ("SSAP's") and Financial Reporting Standards ("FRS's") prescribe the accounting practices and bases that need to be followed in preparing the financial statements. Clearly not all of these are applicable to life assurance business and furthermore they have not overridden the Companies Act exemptions.

(c) Statement of Recommended Practice – Accounting for Insurance Business ("SORP"); this was issued by the ABI and prescribes the basis of accounting for life assurance business, outlining best practice relating to accounting policies adopted and disclosures for premium income, claims and expenses.

(d) Insurance industry practice; the adoption of a consistent approach over a period of time has led to certain practices becoming accepted as industry best practice.

Statutory solvency basis

The Insurance Companies Act 1982 provides the legal framework for the preparation of regulatory returns. Explicit guidance is provided as regards the bases of valuation of assets and liabilities, and although these bases are in some instances different from those adopted for financial reporting, the legal framework outlined by this Act has influenced financial reporting to the extent that, historically, reporting practice has revolved around statutory solvency requirements. In addition, Schedule 9A to the Companies Act 1985, permits certain disclosure exemptions and allows considerable flexibility in the utilisation of reserves to support solvency and the distribution of surplus. The precise requirements of the statutory solvency basis and the manner by which they influence life profit reporting are outlined in more detail in Section 3.

Other adopted accounting bases

As mentioned in the introduction, the inadequacies of the statutory solvency basis have led to the development of other bases, mainly the embedded value and the accruals profit methods. Guidance as to the mechanics of these bases is available in two draft documents, an Institute of Actuaries Working Party report on "Recognition of Life Assurance Profits – The Embedded Value Approach" (October 1988) and an ABI draft prosposal on "Accounting for shareholders' profits in long-term insurance business" (July 1992). The ABI method is known as the accruals basis.

Whilst the industry has been unable to unanimously endorse either of these two bases, a number of life companies, have adopted them in reporting their results. To this effect, reporting on these bases is gradually becoming an accepted industry practice for listed companies. Later in this chapter, these two bases are considered in more detail, and examples of their adoption in practice are reviewed. Furthermore, the steps taken by the industry in developing a single basis of life profit reporting designed to be acceptable to both embedded value and accruals profit users, are also considered.

Looking forward

The European Insurance Accounts Directive introduces the requirement for life assurance accounts to show a true and fair view for the first time from 1995 with a prescribed accounting format. The ABI has issued proposals on how the requirements of the Directive will be implemented on financial reporting. Section 4 considers these proposals for a "modified statutory" basis of accounting.

3. Statutory solvency basis

Guidance

The statutory solvency basis of accounting for life profits is heavily influenced by:

(i)   the statutory valuation rules prescribed in the Insurance Companies Act 1982;
(ii) the contractual obligations of the life assurer; and
(iii) the relationship with the policyholder.

Section 18 of the Insurance Companies Act 1982 requires the appointed actuary to carry out, on an annual basis, an investigation into the financial condition of the long term business and to test the long term fund for adequacy by comparison with the actuarial valuation of the long term liabilities. Any surplus, subject to certain prescribed levels of minimum solvency, is available for distribution to policyholders (if the company writes participating business) and to shareholders or may be carried undistributed within the long term fund.

It is at the discretion of management to decide upon the final distribution policy on the basis of the advice offered by the appointed actuary. The element of the surplus transferred to the shareholders is commonly referred to as the "profit and loss account transfer" and represents the profits of the life assurance undertaking which are available for distribution to shareholders as dividends. The factors underlying this basis, which are outlined below, are inconsistent with accounting practices adopted in other industries and the "true and fair" concept because they result in hidden reserves.

Factors affecting statutory solvency profits

A number of factors can affect the emergence of profits under the statutory solvency basis.

(a) It is common practice to value long term liabilities on the bases prescribed by legislation for the regulatory returns; these tend to be more cautious than under conventional accounting practices applying to other industries.

(b) Selling profitable new business contracts has the effect of depressing surplus because the existing Regulations effectively prohibit the carrying forward of acquisition expenses, which can be significant; this effect is commonly referred to as new business strain.

(c) For with-profit business (i.e., business where the policyholder participates in the surplus of the fund) the transfers to the profit and loss account are directly related to bonuses declared for the relevant period; as bonuses are commonly loaded towards the end of the term of the policy, for with-profit contracts, a substantial proportion of surplus is often released when the policy matures.

(d) Long established life offices writing with-profit business may have accumulated substantial capital gains on their investments; these gains are a source of surplus which is intended to fund future terminal bonuses which, being non-contractual, is excluded from the statutory actuarial valuation and affords the life office an element of flexibility in its surplus distribution strategy.

(e) There is a general requirement for proprietary companies writing with-profit business to meet the reasonable expectations of the policyholders, which are deemed to preclude instability or excessive volatility of benefits; companies declare bonuses in a way which reflects the smooth trends over time of investment returns of long-term fund assets which in turn necessitates the carrying of surplus/investment gains to finance bonuses in periods where investment performance is below expectations.

All these factors result in the disclosure of annual statutory solvency profits which, in most cases, are entirely unrelated to management's actual performance in running the life operations during the period.

Statutory solvency basis in practice

The large majority of life assurance undertakings in the UK report their life profits on the statutory solvency basis. As required by the SORP, the basis of accounting is explained in the accounting policy note of the financial statements. The precise wording used varies and can be detailed or brief. **Example 1 Sun Life Corporation plc** and **Example 2 Guardian** demonstrate the disparity in the information disclosed, albeit reflecting the different commercial focus of these companies.

Example 1
Sun Life Corporation plc   *31 December 1993*
Extract from accounting policies

ACCOUNTING FOR LONG-TERM INSURANCE BUSINESS Surpluses on the long-term insurance business fund of Sun Life Assurance Society plc ("the Society") are ascertained on the basis of annual actuarial valuations of the Society's assets and liabilities. The directors make appropriations from surpluses:

– to with-profit policyholders by way of bonuses, and
– to shareholders by way of transfer to the profit and loss account,

in accordance with the requirements of the Insurance Companies Act 1982 and the laws and regulations of the Society. Any unappropriated surplus is carried forward in the fund. Accordingly, the results shown in the profit and loss account reflect the transfers from the Society's revenue account for the year.

In the case of unit-linked companies there are no participating policyholders and transfers to the profit and loss account are determined by the directors having regard to the actuarial valuations of assets and liabilities.

Example 2
Guardian   *31 December 1993*
Extract from accounting policies

c) Operating results
Operating results represent that part of the life fund surplus attributable and released to shareholders as a result of annual actuarial valuations. Valuations are made in accordance with local regulations and practice.

Profit transfers are normally shown in the revenue account which otherwise provides the reader with little additional information regarding the source of these profits. **Example 3 Legal & General Group plc** shows a typical illustration of a revenue account. This depicts the revenue transactions (effectively cash flows) which have occurred during the period and arrives at a global profit amount, which is further analysed by geographical segment to comply with the requirements of SSAP 25.

Example 3
Legal & General Group plc *31 December 1993*
Extract from notes to Financial Statements

		1993 £m	1992 £m
1.	LIFE AND PENSIONS BUSINESS		
	Premium income – gross	2,414.1	2,058.8)
	– reinsurance	(56.2)	(51.9)
	– net	2,357.9	2,006.9
	Corporate pensions income	1,898.2	526.2
	Investment incomes less interest expense	1,281.1	1,213.8
	Transfer from investment reserves	1,136.1	202.7
	Investment appreciation – linked business	1,667.9	649.6
		8,341.2	**4,599.2**
	Payable to policyholders – gross	2,059.9	1,792.0
	– reinsurance	(33.7)	(37.0)
	– net	2,026.2	1,755.0
	Commission	185.1	168.8
	Expenses	277.7	288.3
	Taxation	78.3	43.5
		2,567.3	**2,255.6**
		5,773.9	**2,343.6**
	Increase in provision for liabilities to policyholders	5,214.6	1,817.8
		559.3	**525.8**
	Allocation of bonuses to policyholders	450.1	417.1
	Profit after taxation	**109.2**	**108.7**
	Taxation attributable to shareholders	42.3	43.3
	Profit before taxation	**151.5**	**152.0**
	Less profit reported as fund management business	—	1.1
	Life and pensions business profit	**151.5**	**150.9**
	Attributable to:		
	UK	119.6	109.1
	Australia	9.6	10.2
	USA	20.8	30.3
	France	1.7	1.7
	Netherlands	(0.2)	(0.4)
	WORLDWIDE TOTAL	**151.5**	**150.9**

Some life offices also analyse profits by class of business, although the ABI have issued guidance to members suggesting that, for reporting purposes, UK life business can be treated as one single segment. In **Example 4 United Friendly Group plc**, a sub-analysis of the profits of its two UK business segments by class of business is provided in the notes to the accounts.

Example 4
United Friendly Group plc *31 December 1993*
Extracts from notes to the accounts

1(d)	CONTINUING OPERATIONS		
	ANALYSIS OF TRANSFER TO	**1993**	1992
	PROFIT AND LOSS ACCOUNT	**£000**	£000
	Industrial branch		
	Life: non-linked	**8,463**	9,166
	Ordinary branch		
	Life: non-linked	**1,916**	1,972
	linked	**509**	(1,243)
	Pensions:		
	non-linked	**1,757**	1,378
	linked	**(136)**	(103)
		12,509	11,170

No further information is typically available within the financial statements to enable the reader to evaluate the true profitability of the life office and the impact thereon of the decisions taken by management in the accounting period. Whilst information relating to the volume of new business written, investment return and bonus rates are indicators of profitability, the reader is left unclear as to how these three factors have combined to produce the reported profits.

In particular, bonus rates payable to participating policyholders can act as an indicator of current and future profitability of the business, given that shareholders receive a proportion of surpluses on participating business. However, bonus rates are only indicative of trends and should not be relied upon in isolation as indicators of performance. In **Example 5 Legal & General Group plc**, we observe that despite fluctuations in value of new business written, investment return and allocation of bonuses to policyholders, reported profits increase at a relatively steadier rate.

Example 5
Legal & General Group plc *31 December 1993*
Extract from Five Year Financial Review

Five Year Financial Review

	1993	1992	1991	1990	1989
LIFE AND PENSIONS BUSINESS	**£m**	£m	£m	£m	£m
NEW BUSINESS PREMIUMS					
Annual	**199.2**	196.3	223.2	290.1	314.9
Single	**1,196.3**	874.6	1,030.8	584.2	511.9
REVENUE					
Premium income – continuing operations	**2,357.9**	2,006.9	2,101.4	1,637.6	1,408.3
– discontinued operations	**—**	—	—	83.9	104.2
	2,357.9	2,006.9	2,101.4	1,721.5	1,512.5
Corporate pensions income	**1,898.2**	526.2	649.0	878.6	801.4
Investment incomes less interest expense	**1,281.1**	1,213.8	1,098.0	997.8	916.5
Appropriation from investment reserves	**1,136.1**	202.7	430.2	264.0	152.0
Investment appreciation – linked business	**1,667.9**	649.6	384.5	(605.1)	620.4
	8,341.2	4,599.2	4,663.1	3,256.8	4,002.8
Payable to policyholders	**2,026.2**	1,755.0	1,184.4	1,282.2	1,571.3
Commission and expenses	**462.8**	457.1	450.9	454.9	405.0
Taxation	**78.3**	43.5	66.9	59.6	37.5
	2,567.3	2,255.6	1,702.2	1,796.7	2,013.8
	5,773.9	2,343.6	2,960.9	1,460.1	1,989.0
Increase in provision for liabilities to policyholders	**5,214.6**	1,817.8	2,437.9	913.2	1,496.9
Allocation of bonuses to policyholders	**450.1**	417.1	432.0	460.1	418.0
Profit after taxation	**109.2**	108.7	91.0	86.8	74.1
Taxation attributable to shareholders	**42.3**	43.3	36.9	36.2	30.8
	151.5	152.0	127.9	123.0	104.9
Less profit reported as fund management business	**—**	1.1	1.5	0.5	0.9
Life and pensions business profit	**151.5**	150.9	126.4	122.5	104.0

Deficiencies in the methodology
As a result of the regulatory, contractual and legal requirements outlined in section 3(2), the statutory solvency basis has a number of shortcomings:

(a) shareholder profits are taken as cash transfers of surplus from the fund rather than being calculated as they accrue; the fundamental accounting concept which is normally used for profit measurement;

(b) the financial statements do not fairly reflect management performance or sales effort during that accounting period nor do they provide shareholders with a reliable indication of the underlying value of the operation;

(c) as the current method tends to understate profits where business is growing, there is a danger that the position may not be widely understood by investors with the end result of shares being valued on an inappropriate basis; this is of particular concern to listed companies;

(d) due to the existence of hidden reserves, the financial statements do not provide a true and fair view.

4. Other adopted bases

Forces of change

Over the last few years, a number of listed groups with life assurance subsidiaries have sought to report the results of these subsidiaries in a way which would reflect their true profitability and their true worth. Banks have led the way, in their quest to demonstrate that their life operations represented a sensible and a profitable investment. Large proprietary life offices have followed suit, in an effort to satisfy demands for realistic profitability information from shareholders and their advisors.

The form and content of profit reporting on these alternative bases has varied greatly. The section that follows outlines the treatment adopted and the disclosures made by the majority of UK groups who have adopted an alternative approach.

Embedded value

The embedded value method was the first alternative basis to be adopted by banks (initially) and by proprietary life companies (subsequently). Before considering some examples in practice, it may be useful to briefly outline the terminology and the mechanics of the method.

The embedded value method works by placing a value on the business already sold. This value is taken to be the net present value of future profits recognised (and normally distributed to shareholders) on a statutory solvency basis which are projected to arise from the policies currently "in-force".

The value of the business "in-force" together with the net worth (the sum of shareholders' capital and reserves and the shareholders' element of the surplus carried forward in the long term fund) is referred to as the embedded value of the company.

Another commonly used term is the appraisal value. The appraisal value is the sum of the embedded value and the goodwill. The goodwill is quantified as the net present value of profits arising from business not yet written (reflecting a life office's ability to write new business).

In arriving at the embedded value of a life office, the projected profits need to make allowance for prudent best estimates of mortality, investment return, lapses and expenses; overall prudence is built into the calculation by using a risk rate of return to discount future profits.

Once the embedded value is calculated at the end of each period and established on the balance sheet as a shareholders' asset, the progression of the business can be measured by the movement in the embedded value over the accounting period, giving the embedded value profits.

Embedded value reporting by banks

Three major UK banks with substantial life assurance operations (TSB Group plc, Lloyds Bank plc and Barclays plc) have adopted the embedded value approach since the late 1980's by incorporating the embedded value results of these operations in their consolidated financial statements. However, the embedded value method has never been appropriately codified and the form and content of the disclosures made in the financial statements of the three banks differ considerably. The difference in the level of disclosure principally reflects the materiality of the banks' various life assurance operations to their overall business.

(i) TSB Group plc

The most detailed of the embedded value approach is given in the TSB Group plc financial statements, reflecting the fact that the TSB Group plc has substantial life operations, with policyholder assets exceeding £6 billion at 31 October 1993 compared with total assets of £31 billion and profits from life assurance representing 51% of pre-taxation group profits. The accounting policy note, shown in **Example 6 TSB Group plc**, is sufficiently detailed to enable the reader to understand the distinction between statutory solvency profits (deemed as distributable) and profits calculated on the embedded value basis.

Example 6
TSB Group plc *31 October 1993*
Extract from the notes to the accounts

> **Life assurance and pension businesses** Actuarial valuations are prepared annually and the directors of the Group's assurance subsidiaries, with advice from actuaries, determine the proportion of the actuarial surpluses or deficits to be transferred between the funds and the profit and loss account. The balance of the actuarial surpluses is carried forward in the life assurance and pension business funds.
>
> The value to the Group of the long-term life assurance and pension businesses represents the net present value of the profits which are calculated to arise from business in force and retained surpluses in the funds. The value, which is included in the balance sheet, is determined in consultation with independent actuaries.
>
> The increase in the value of the Group's long-term businesses is credited to the profit and loss account in addition to the release of surplus from the funds. The increase in the value of long-term businesses is grossed up for tax at the corporation tax rate. The increase after tax in the value of long-term businesses included in the profit and loss account is transferred to non-distributable reserves.

Interestingly, TSB Group plc do not explicitly show the embedded balue of the life operations. Instead, only the retained surplus element of the net worth is aggregated with the present value of profits arising from the business in force, to arrive at what is referred to as the "value to the Group of the long-term life assurance and pension businesses". The remaining component of the net worth, representing the life business' shareholder assets, appears to have been included within the various other shareholder asset categories in the group balance sheet. Sufficient disclosure is made to enable the reader to understand the treatment, but this treatment emphasises the lack of standardisation in industry approach and the care which must be taken when making comparisons between companies.

The value of the long-term assurance business of £460 million features prominently on the face of the consolidated balance sheet as shown in **Example 7 TSB Group plc**. The aggregate value of the long-term fund assets (net of the retained surplus) is also shown on the face of the balance sheet. Liabilities include an amount relating to the "long-term life assurance and pension business funds" which represents the assets attributable to policyholders net of retained surpluses.

Example 7
TSB Group plc   *31 October 1993*
Extract from the consolidated Balance Sheet

			1993	1992 restated (note 1)
			£m	£m
Assets	19	Assets of long-term life assurance and pension business funds	**6,033**	4,593
	20	Value of long-term life assurance and pension businesses	**460**	409
Liabilities		Long-term life assurance and pension business funds	**6,033**	4,593

In view of the non-distributable nature of the movement in the value of the long-term business amount, much of this value is held as a revaluation reserve as shown in **Example 8 TSB Group plc**.

Example 8
TSB Group plc   *31 October 1993*
Extract from notes to the accounts

The Group's reserves at 31 October 1993 include surpluses on the valuation of long-term life assurance and pension business in force of £399m (1992 £348m) and on the revaluation of premises of £5m (1992 £5m), and a share premium account of £11m (1992 £7m).

The reserve note records £399 million in the revaluation reserve; the balance of £61 million presumably reflects the pre-acquisition element of the value of long-term life and pension businesses.

Information pertaining to the movement in the value of the long-term businesses is disclosed in note 20 to the TSB financial statements as shown in **Example 9 TSB Group plc**. This analyses the movement in the value of the long-term businesses between the distributable element relating to statutory solvency profits (£53 million net of tax) and the non-distributable element (£51 million in total net of tax). It also provides an insight into the key assumptions used in the calculation.

Example 9
TSB Group plc *31 October 1993*
Extract from notes to the accounts

Note 20
Value of long-term
life assurance and
pension businesses

The value of the long-term life assurance and pensions businesses is analysed as follows:

	1993 **£m**	1992 £m
Gross increase in value of long-term businesses	**155**	166
Taxation	**(51)**	(56)
	104	110
Surplus released from the funds	**(53)**	(46)
Net increase in value of long-term businesses	**51**	64
Balance at beginning of year	**409**	345
Balance at 31 October	**460**	409

The gross increase in the value of the long-term businesses is included in the consolidated profit and loss account. In the year ended 31 October 1992 the gross increase included £30m in respect of the commission adjustment (note 7).

The major actuarial assumptions used in the calculation of the value of the long-term life assurance and pension business in force and unchanged from 1992 and are as follows:
- future distributable profits after taxation have been discounted at a rate of 15% per annum;
- future gross investment returns have been assumed at rates varying from 9% to 11% per annum depending on the type of asset;
- long-term inflation rate of 6.5% per annum;
- tax has been provided in full at the rates applicable to investment income, capital gains and annuity profits under the relevant tax legislation; and
- future mortality rates, lapse rates and expense levels have been derived from analysis of the recent experience of the funds.

Finally, the gross increase in the value of the long-term business is not explicitly disclosed on the face of the consolidated profit and loss account shown as **Example 10 TSB Group plc**; instead it is included within the insurance result. However, the net increase in the value of the long-term business which is deemed to be non-distributable is shown on the face of the profit and loss account as being transferred to reserves.

Example 10
TSB Group plc *31 October 1993*
Extracts from the consolidated profit and loss account

		1993	1992
			restated
			(note 1)
		£m	£m
4	Profit before taxation:		
	TSB Insurance	**194**	129
	Retained profit/(loss for the year)	**73**	(118)
	Transfer to non-distributable reserves	**51**	64
	Transfer to/(from) distributable reserves	**22**	(118)

(ii) Lloyds Bank plc

Lloyds Bank plc also utilise the embedded value method in reporting the results of its life assurance subsidiaries. The information disclosed in the Lloyd's Bank financial statements is, in some respects, less detailed than that included in the TSB Group plc accounts, reflecting the lower materiality of life assurance operations to the group's other operations and results (life profits accounted for 22% of profits attributable to shareholders in 1993). More detailed disclosure of the embedded value approach is also given in the accounts of Lloyds Bank plc's publicly listed subsidiary, Lloyds Abbey Life plc, further details of which are given below.

The accounting policy note, shown as **Example 11 Lloyds Bank plc**, explains the basis of accounting used.

Example 11
Lloyds Bank plc *31 December 1993*
Extract from notes to the accounts

m Long-term assurance business

The value placed on the Group's long-term assurance business attributable to shareholders represents a prudent valuation of future earnings of policies in force, together with the net worth of the business, being the net tangible assets and the surplus retained within the long-term insurance funds. This value is determined annually in consultation with independent actuaries and is included separately in the balance sheet.
Changes in the value placed on long-term assurance business attributable to shareholders, which are determined on a post-tax basis, are included in the profit and loss account. For the purpose of presentation, the change in this value is grossed-up at the underlying rates of tax in the long-term assurance funds.

The reserves note shown as **Example 12 Lloyds Bank plc**, show the amount of non-distributable reserves relating to the value of the long-term assurance business in force included within reserves.

Example 12
Lloyds Bank plc   *31 December 1993*
Extract from notes to the accounts

> The Group profit and loss account reserves at 31 December include £261 million (*1992: £216 million*) not presently available for distribution representing the Group's share of the value of long-term assurance business in force and the surplus retained within the long-term assurance funds.

The consolidated balance sheet separately discloses the assets relating to the value of the long term assurance business attributable of shareholders. As shown in **Example 13 Lloyds Bank plc**, this is shown separately from the long-term assets attributable to policyholders reflecting the different nature of the shareholders' and policyholders' interests in the long term assurance business.

Example 13
Lloyds Bank plc   *31 December 1993*
Extract from the balance sheets

	Group	
	1993	*1992 restated (note 2)*
	£ million	*£ million*
Assets		
Long-term assurance business attributable to shareholders	997	*912*
Long-term assurance assets attributable to policyholders	8,121	*6,095*

	Group	
	1993	*1992 restated (note 2)*
	£ million	*£ million*
Liabilities		
Long-term assurance liabilities to shareholders	8,121	*6,095*

Unlike TSB Group plc, Lloyds Bank plc's "long term assurance business attributable to shareholders" reflects the embedded value asset, being the sum of net worth (shareholders' life assurance business net assets and retained surplus in the fund) and the value of business in force. In this respect, Lloyds Bank plc adopts a different approach to reporting embedded values compared to TSB Group plc. The notes to the Lloyds Bank plc accounts, relevant extracts of which are included as **Example 14 Lloyds Bank plc**, provide the reader with the relevant analysis, between the various embedded value components.

Example 14
Lloyds Bank plc *31 December 1993*
Extract from the notes to the accounts

26 Long-term assurance business	1993 £m	1992 £m
The value of long-term assurance business attributable to shareholders included in the consolidated balance sheet comprises:		
Net tangible assets of life companies	74	75
Suplace retained within the long-term assurance funds	169	150
Net worth of life companies	243	225
Value of policies in force	754	687
	997	912
The long-term assurance assets attributable to policyholders are:		
Investments	8,401	6,377
Value of policies in force	754	687
Premises and equipment	26	28
Net current liabiities	(63)	(85)
	9,118	7,007
Long-term assurance business attributable to shareholders	(997)	(912)
	8,121	6,096
Investments shown above comprise:		
Fixed interest securities	1,440	1,143
Stocks, shares and unit trusts	5,569	3,828
Investment properties	423	385
Other properties	22	22
Mortgages and loans	93	110
Deposits	854	889
	8,401	6,377

The increase in the value of the long-term assurance business included in the consolidated profit and loss account for the year ended 31 December 1993 amounted to £225 million before tax; £152 million after tax (*1992: £245 million before tax; £163 million after tax*).

In determining the value of long-term assurance business in force, assumptions relating to future mortality, persistence and levels of expenses are based on experience of the type of business concerned. Gross investment returns assumed vary depending upon the type of asset to which they relate. Profits expected to arise in the future from business currently in force are discounted at 12.5 per cent per annum after provision has been made for tax.

Finally, Lloyds Bank plc do not separately disclose the life assurance result on the face of the consolidated profit and loss account but rather incorporate it within the "other operating income" line, and disclose the amount in the notes to the accounts, as shown in **Example 15 Lloyds Bank plc.**

105

Example 15
Lloyds Bank plc *31 December 1993*
Extract from the notes to the accounts

5 Profit on ordinary activities before tax	1993	*1992*
	£m	*£m*
Profit on ordinary activities before tax is stated after taking account of:		
Income from:		
Increase in value of long-term assurance business	225	*245*

As illustrated by the extracts from the report and accounts referred to above, there are a number of differences in embedded value accounting between Lloyds Bank plc and TSB Group plc. Lloyds Bank plc provide the reader with a more conventional breakdown of the assets representing the long-term assurance business attributable to shareholders, analysing between life business shareholders' assets, retained surplus and value of policies in-force. TSB Group plc exclude the shareholders' net assets from its "value of long-term life assurance and pensions businesses" which is in turn not analysed between its two other components. On the other hand, TSB Group plc provide the reader with an analysis in its gross movement in the value of the long-term life assurance and pensions businesses, breaking it down between statutory solvency profits and profits arising from the movement in the value of the in-force business and the movement in shareholder surplus retained within the fund post profit transfer. Lloyds Bank plc only disclose the total movement in the value of long-term business attributable to shareholders. The analysis between statutory solvency profits and other profits is not made explicitly being disclosed in the accounts of Lloyds Abbey Life plc.

One other difference is in the level of disclosure relating to the assumptions. Lloyds Bank plc disclose key assumption (the risk discount rate used in calculating the value of the in-force business), whilst TSB Group plc also discloses the expense inflation rate and the investment return rates for various assets.

(iii) Barclays plc
Barclays plc have also adopted the embedded value methodology in reporting life profits. Reflecting the fact that Barclays plc's life operations are much less significant in overall group terms than those of the other two bancassurers considered above, (approximately £3 billion out of total assets of £166 billion at 31 December 1993) the level of information disclosed in the Barclays plc report and accounts is not extensive.

The accounting policy note shown as **Example 16 Barclays plc** is relatively concise. The key assumption relating to the risk discount rate used in the embedded value calculation is disclosed in the note.

Example 16
Barclays plc *31 December 1993*
Extract from Accounting Policies

(e) Value of long-term life assurance and pensions policies
A value is placed on the shareholders' interest in the in-force policies of the long-term assurance fund of Barclays Life Assurance Company Limited. This value is a prudent

estimate, based on the advice of a qualified actuary, of the net present value of the profits inherent in such policies, using a discount rate of 12.5% per annum. Changes in the value are included in the profit and loss account, grossed up for notional taxation.

The shareholders' interest in the long term assurance fund and the movement thereon, are not separately disclosed in the primary financial statements. The shareholders' interest in the life fund is included within other assets and the movement thereon forms part of other operating income. Other assets and other operating income are analysed in the notes to the accounts as shown in **Example 17 Barclays plc** below.

Example 17
Barclays plc *31 December 1993*
Extracts from the notes to the accounts

4 Other operating income

	1993	1992
	£m	£m
Profits on disposal of investment securities	17	18
Increase in value of long-term assurance policies	107	67
Other income	153	166
	277	251

28 Other assets

	1993	1992
	£m	£m
Balances arising from off-balance sheet financial instruments	6,725	9,645
Items in transit	435	379
Purchased mortgage servicing rights	180	372
Shareholders' interest in the long-term assurance fund	361	289
London Metal Exchange warrants and other metals trading positions	1,649	537
Sundry debtors	1,210	1,701
	10,560	12,923

The report and accounts provide no further embedded value information.

Embedded value reporting by life undertakings

Insurance groups with significant life operations have in recent years emulated the trend set by the banks and presented the results of their life operations on the embedded value basis. The approach that has generally been adopted is either to consolidate the embedded value results of life subsidiaries in the main report and accounts (Lloyds Abbey Life plc and Royal Insurance) or to disclose the embedded value profits in the form of supplemental information (Legal & General Group plc, Commercial Union plc and Sun Alliance Group plc). This section considers the form and content of embedded value reporting for these companies.

(i) Lloyds Abbey Life plc

Lloyds Abbey Life plc utilises the embedded value method and gives comprehensive disclosure. The basis of accounting for life assurance operations is explained in some detail by the accounting policy note as shown below:

Example 18
Lloyds Abbey Life plc *31 December 1993*
Extract from Accounting policies

Recognition of profits arising on long term assurance business
The surplus arising during the year from long term assurance business is determined by the appointed actuaries following their annual investigations of the long term assurance business.

The value of the long term assurance business in force represents the present value of profits expected to emerge in the future from business currently in force. In determining this value assumptions relating to future mortality, persistence and levels of expenses are based on experience of the type of business concerned. Gross investment returns assumed vary depending upon the type of asset to which they relate. For UK operations future profits are discounted at 12.5% per annum after provision has been made for taxation. For German operations the discount rate of 11.0% is used as this rate more reasonably reflects the underlying economic factors in that market. The valuation is determined in consultation with independent actuaries on an annual basis.

The surplus arising and the increase in the value of the long term assurance business in force are credited to the profit and loss account, together grossed up at the underlying rates of taxation in the long term assurance funds. The after tax increase in value of business in force reflected in the profit and loss account is transferred to a non-distributable reserve. This increase is treated as non-distributable until it emerges as part of the surplus arising during the year.

The risk discount rates used in the calculation are disclosed in the accounting policy note. It is interesting to note that different risk rates are used in the discounting of UK and German embedded value profits. As reported, this reflects the underlying economic factors in the two markets. However, as in the case of the banks (except for TSB Group plc), the risk discount rate is the only assumption which is disclosed.

Lloyds Abbey Life plc's consolidated profit and loss account (shown as **Example 19 Lloyds Abbey Life plc**) clearly analyses the components of the life profits and demonstrates the distinction between the distributable and non distributable element of the net life profits.

Example 19
Lloyds Abbey Life plc *31 December 1993*
Consolidated profit and loss account

	Note	1993 £m	1992 £m
Surplus arising from long term assurance business		**134.6**	146.4
Increase in value of long term assurance business in force		**90.1**	98.9
Profit arising from life business		**224.7**	245.3
Profit arising from non-life business	3	**98.9**	52.3
Group operating profit before taxation	4	**323.6**	297.6
Taxation	5	**(103.6)**	(100.8)
Group profit after taxation	6	**220.0**	196.8
Minority interests		**(4.1)**	(3.3)
Group profit after minority interests		**215.9**	193.5
Retained within the long term assurance fund		**(18.3)**	(10.9)
Transfer to non-distributable reserves		**(59.6)**	(58.1)
Profit available for distribution		**138.0**	124.5
Dividends	7	**(125.0)**	(119.8)
Transfer to retained profits for the year		**13.0**	4.7

The value of the long-term assurance business in force attributable to shareholders is shown on the face of the balance sheet (**Example 20 Lloyds Abbey Life plc**). The long-term fund is analysed between the element which represents the long-term liabilities to policyholder and the element which relates to shareholder surplus. This highlights the fact that there is an amount of surplus retained within the long-term fund which is attributable to shareholders. Unlike the presentation adopted by the banks, which adopt a one line consolidation approach to reflect the different nature of banking and insurance business, long-term fund assets are aggregated with the other non-long-term assets on the face of the balance sheet.

Example 20
Lloyds Abbey Life plc *31 December 1993*
Extract from the Consolidated balance sheet

	Note	1993 £m	1992 £m
Assets			
Value of long term assurance business in force	11	**754.4**	687.5
Long term assurance fund			
Valuation of liabilities		**8,121.2**	6,095.2
Surplus retained within the fund	1	**168.7**	150.4

In the notes to the accounts, further embedded value information is disclosed. As shown in **Example 21 Lloyds Abbey Life plc**, the analysis of the movement in surplus retained within the fund makes the distinction between statutory solvency profits (£74.4 million for 1993) and surplus retained.

Example 21
Lloyds Abbey Life plc *31 December 1993*
Extract from Notes to the Accounts

	1993 £m	1992 £m
Statement of surplus		
Surplus at the beginning of the year	**150.4**	139.5
Surplus arising in the year	**92.7**	104.5
Transfer to profit and loss account	**(74.4)**	(93.6)
Surplus retained at the end of the year	**168.7**	150.4

The amount relating to surplus arising in the year of £92.7 million, grossed up for taxation, gives £134.6 million of surplus as shown in the consolidated profit and loss account. Given that only £74.4 million net of tax has been transferred from the long-term funding to the profit and loss account, thus becoming available for distribution, the non-distributable balance of £18.3 million is transferred out of the profit and loss account (**Example 19 Lloyds Abbey Life plc**) and is included within the surplus retained within the fund caption on the consolidated balance sheet (**Example 20 Lloyds Abbey Life plc**).

The value of the long-term assurance business in force is also shown in the embedded value note to the accounts (**Example 22 Lloyds Abbey Life plc**). As shown in this note, the movement for the period of £66.9 million grossed up for tax to give £90.1 million, is taken to the profit and loss account.

Example 22
Lloyds Abbey Life plc *31 December 1993*
Extract from Notes to the Accounts

11 Embedded value

The embedded value of long term assurance business comprises:

	1993 £m	1992 £m
Net tangible assets of life companies	**74.3**	74.4
Surplus retained within the long term assurance fund	**168.7**	150.4
Net worth of life companies	**243.0**	224.8
Value of long term assurance business in force	**754.4**	687.5
	997.4	912.3

Finally, the movement in shareholders' reserves note, extracts of which are shown as **Example 23 Lloyds Abbey Life plc**, shows the movement in the reserve relating to the value of the business in-force. These accumulated reserves differ from the value of business in-force as, presumably, only the post acquisition element of this amount is included in reserves.

Example 23
Lloyds Abbey Life plc *31 December 1993*
Extract from Notes to the Accounts

	Value of long term assurance business in force £m
17 Reserves – Group	
At the beginning of the year	641.4
Transfer from profit and loss account for the year	59.6
Translation of overseas subsidiaries	(4.5)
At the end of the year	696.5

This extensive level of disclosure, makes the financial statements of Lloyds Abbey Life plc a good illustrative example of life profit reporting under the embedded value method.

(ii) Royal Insurance

Royal Insurance also adopted an alternative approach for valuing its shareholders' interest in the long-term fund following the embedded value methodology. However, only the statutory solvency profits are taken to the profit and loss account. The movement in the value of the long-term insurance business, as explained in the accounting policy note (**Example 24 Royal Insurance**), is taken directly to a long-term insurance business reserve. This compares with the approach adopted by Lloyds Abbey Life plc where the total amount of embedded value profits is initially included within reported profits and the non-distributable element is transferred to reserve.

Example 24
Royal Insurance *31 December 1993*
Extract from Accounting Policies

Long-term Insurance Profit
Other than for US business, Long-term Insurance Profit represents a proportion of the total distributed surplus, as determined annually on Actuarial Valuation of the long-term insurance funds, in which shareholders have a proprietary interest. In the Profit & Loss Account the profit is grossed up by the estimated UK and Overseas Taxation referable to it and is net of an appropriate allocation of Group administration expenses. For business transacted in the United States, results have been included under US Generally Accepted Accounting Principles.

Value of Long-term Insurance Business
This item represents the amounts which the Directors consider to be a prudent value of the Group's existing long-term business: a corresponding amount, other than the element thereof relating to subsidiaries at date of acquisition, is credited to Long-term Insurance Business Reserve.

The assumptions used in the embedded value calculation are not disclosed in the financial statements. By contrast to the examples considered so far, the level of disclosure is relatively limited as Royal Insurance is predominantly a general business insurer.

(iii) *Legal & General Group plc*

A number of life offices have continued to adopt the statutory solvency basis for reporting profits in their financial statements, but have considered it appropriate to disclose information in the form of supplements to their accounts showing what the profits would have been on an alternative approach. Legal & General Group plc, first disclosed profits on an embedded value basis within the Review of Operations section of the 1990 financial statements. This practice was continued in subsequent accounting periods and the relevant extracts from their 1993 report and accounts are shown as **Example 25 Legal & General Group plc**.

Example 25
Legal & General Group plc *31 December 1993*
Extract from Operating and Financial Review

UK long term fund

The Group's Life & Pensions business in the UK is written in the UK Long Term Fund. This statutory Fund comprises separately identified assets and liabilities. Transfers out of the Fund from the surplus of assets over liabilities are only possible following an actuarial investigation, including an actuarial valuation of the liabilities, which must be prepared on prudent principles prescribed in statutory regulations.

Distributions to shareholders from the Fund are net of tax. These transfers, grossed up at an attributable tax rate, are reported in the Group's financial statements as profits from its UK Life & Pensions business.

Shareholders' profits retained within the Fund are not reflected either in the Group's reported earnings or in the shareholders' funds shown in the Group's balance sheet. The retention of such profits within the Fund provides the financial strength to support both existing business and the Group's marketing strategy to generate new business. The distribution of these profits to the shareholders is governed by UK insurance regulations and the Society's Articles of Association.

At the end of 1993, the Group's estimate of the value to shareholders (excluding goodwill) of their interest in the UK Long Term Fund was at least £2.30 billion, after tax, based on stated assumptions (see alongside). The value reported at the end of 1992 was at least £1.84 billion, after tax. These values have been reviewed by Tillinghast, independent actuaries, and our auditors, Price Waterhouse, who agree that they are reasonable.

The assumptions used to report the value of the shareholders' interest in the Fund are reviewed each year and reflect recent operating experience and current economic conditions. As for 1992, the principal changes for 1993 related to the assumptions for future rates of investment return, inflation and bonus. Taken together with a corresponding reduction in the discount rate, the aggregate effect on the opening 1993 value was an increase of £20 million.

The increase in the value to shareholders after tax during 1993, on the revised assumptions, was £520 million (1992, £230 million), before the distribution of £82 million (1992, £75 million). This distribution is reflected in the Group's consolidated profit and loss account for 1993, as pre-tax life and pensions profits of £120 million.

The increase in the value includes approximately £40 million of value attributed to new business written during 1993 (1992, £30 million). The increase of £480 million (1992, £200 million) in the value relating to the management of the business in force, particularly reflects the exceptional investment returns achieved in 1993. In addition, we have benefited from the continued improvements in our operational performance.

The methodology and key assumptions we have used are outlined below:

i) The value of the shareholders' interest in the Fund represents the aggregate of the discounted value of potential transfers to shareholders related to the portfolio of in-force business, and the value of the shareholders' capital retained in the Fund.

ii) This value is net of tax at current rates, including the present value of tax which would become payable if the shareholders' capital retained in the Long Term Fund were eventually to be distributed.

iii) The assumed future pre-tax return on fixed interest securities is set by reference to redemption yields available in the market at the end of each year. The corresponding returns on equities and property are set by reference to this fixed interest assumption. These assumptions, which are shown below, are therefore not intended to represent the Group's view of future investment returns.

	1993	1992
Fixed interest	6.75% p.a.	9.0% p.a.
Equities & property	9.25% p.a.	11.5% p.a.

Investments which are regarded as matched to contractual non-linked liabilities are effectively valued on an amortised basis.

iv) The disk discount rate, which has been set by reference to the assumed future investment returns, is 9.0% p.a., net of tax, (1992, 11.0% p.a.).

v) The assumed expense and earnings inflation rates are 4.5% p.a. (1992, 6.0% p.a.). RPI inflation is used for indexation purposes and has been set at 3.5% p.a. (1992, 5.0% p.a.).

vi) The value of new business has been calculated using actual 1993 acquisition costs.

vii) Future bonus rates have been set at levels which would fully utilise the assets associated with the with profits business.

viii) Subsidiaries have been included at net asset value, other than Legal & General Investment Management Holdings Ltd. which is included at cost.

ix) The value reflects a prudent provision for possible compensation in relation to pensions transfers and opt-outs.

x) Other assumptions, including those relating to mortality, lapses and renewal expenses have been set at levels no more favourable than those currently being experienced. These levels are assumed to remain constant subject, where appropriate, to expense inflation.

There will be changes in the presentation of our Life & Pensions operations as a result of the EC Directive on insurance company accounting. The 1995 accounts will be the first which will have to be prepared in the new format.

Discussions continue within the insurance industry on the interpretation of the requirment for true and fair reporting. We believe, however, that the permitted accounting basis will accommodate the methodology we employ to report the shareholders' interest in the Long Term Fund, although there may be minor changes.

The information disclosed in the Legal & General Group plc report and accounts differs from that disclosed in the examples considered so far in that Legal & General Group plc explain to the reader how life profits are recognised in their financial statements and go on to explain why it is that the reported profits do not reflect the true shareholder earnings and the real worth of the life business. Legal & General Group plc are careful not to describe the after tax movement in the shareholders' interest in the UK Long Term fund of £520 million as profits. Instead this is simply referred to as "an increase in the value". This increase is compared against the reported after tax profit of £82 million, demonstrating the significant restriction of the statutory solvency basis on profit emergence. The most interesting aspect of the supplemental information provided by Legal & General Group plc is the broad breakdown of the source of the increase in the value, £40 million of which is attributed to new business and the remainder to in force business. This analysis allows the readers to assess current management's performance and the effectiveness of the selling process. Finally, recognising the significance of the assumptions used in the calculation, Legal & General Group plc provide a relatively detailed description of the key assumptions and the methodology used and quantify the impact of assumption changes.

(iv) Commercial Union plc

Commercial Union plc have for a number of years commented on the shortcomings of the statutory solvency basis in reporting life profits. In the 1989 Financial Review, Commercial Union plc announced for the first time:

Example 26
Commercial Union plc   *31 December 1989*
Extract from Financial Review

Life business valuation

Existing accounting methods are not designed to show the value to shareholders of our life business and there is as yet no agreement between the various professional bodies involved as to how such a value should be shown. The calculation of embedded and appraisal values, which we have used for some time for purposes of management information, is a widely accepted means of valuing life businesses. The embedded value is an estimate of the value to the shareholders of the future profits from the existing life business together with the value of the shareholders' funds supporting this business. The appraisal value is the embedded value plus an estimate of the value of the new business which the management expect to undertake in the future. The directors, having taken the advice of consulting actuaries, can disclose that in their opinion the appraisal value at the balance sheet date of the Group's worldwide life business is in excess of £1,500m. Of this amount, life shareholders' funds of £395m and a value for the Northern Non-Participation Life fund of £90m are already included in the balance sheet.

Commercial Union plc did not disclose any appraisal value information in the 1990 and 1991 report and accounts. In 1992, in his statement, the chairman further highlighted the shortcomings of the existing statutory solvency method by stating:

Example 27
Commercial Union plc   *31 December 1992*
Extract from Chairman's statement

Life assurance

Continued progress was made in the Group's life operations. Not only was an excellent level of new business achieved overall, a 46% increase at comparable rates of exchange, but it was spread throughout the Group's territories. Under our conservative accounting practices this new business led to a slight reduction in life profits, when adjusted for exchange rate movements, against which shareholder value has been enhanced and future profits will increase. The appraisal value of the Group's life operations continued to grow and the directors believe, on the basis of independent actuarial advice, that it is in excess of £2 billion (of which £678m is included in the balance sheet), compared with £1.5 billion disclosed in 1989. Growth in life business remains a key element of our strategy.

Despite the limitations surrounding the statutory solvency basis as outlined by its chairman in 1992, Commercial Union plc continued to report life profits on this basis. This practice was adopted for the 1993 financial statements, but in his statement the chairman disclosed:

Example 28
Commercial Union plc   *31 December 1993*
Extract from Chairman's statement

Contemporaneously with this report we are publishing a supplement setting out an alternative approach to the way in which we have historically shown those profits in our accounts. This alternative approach to calculating profits is based on embedded value methodology. In our own case it has to take account of the spread of the Group's life business, which is wider than with most United Kingdom companies, and variations in local conditions; further modification may be called for.

The "Commercial Union – 1993: An alternative method of reporting profits" supplemental information (the full text of which is included as Appendix I, page 126) is similar in form and content to the Legal & General Group plc disclosure. Commercial Union plc did not continue with the practice of disclosing appraisal value information reverting to publishing embedded value information. The impact on the 1993 results and shareholders' funds is summarised in **Example 29 Commercial Union plc**. This table also describes the impact of the alternative basis on the earnings per share and the net asset value per ordinary share.

Example 29
Commercial Union plc   31 December 1993
Extract from the supplement: An alternative method of reporting life profits

	Existing basis (as per published accounts)	Alternative basis (unaudited)
Life profits	£119m	£280m
Non-life operating profit	£99m	£99m
Operating profit before taxation and less on termination of activities	£218m	£379m
Profit attributable to shareholders	£321m	£426m
Operating earnings per ordinary share	31.4p	50.6p
Shareholders funds	£2.5bn	£3.5bn
Net asset value per ordinary share	418p	596p

The supplement also explain in some detail the methodology and assumptions. Key assumptions are also disclosed. It is interesting to note that Commercial Union plc have utilised different risk discount rates for traditional and unit linked business, recognising the different risks attaching to each type of business.

(v) Sun Alliance Group plc

Sun Alliance Group plc were one of the other few major insurers to provide a brief comment on the embedded value of its life operations (Sun Alliance Life) in the Group Chief Executive's Review which accompanied the 1993 financial statements (**Example 30 Sun Alliance Group plc**). This only revealed the amount of the embedded value. No further disclosure of assumptions or an analysis of the movement was provided.

Example 30
Sun Alliance Group plc *31 December 1993*
Extract from Group Chief Executive Review

SUN ALLIANCE LIFE

Shareholders' profits from our UK life and pensions business rose by 11% compared with 1992. The embedded value of the business increased to £668m at the end of the year. This takes account only of business in force, with no allowance for profits from future new business and no part of the value is included in the Group's shareholders' funds.

Overall assessment of the adoption of embedded value reporting

One feature of embedded value reporting is the marked diversity of the form and content of the reporting. Commentators have attributed this diversity to the fact that the methodology was initially developed by the actuarial profession. Whilst the methodology has evolved with the passage of time, it has never been codified and has consequently not been endorsed by an accounting standard setting body or the ABI. The inconsistency of accounting treatment and disclosure has left the methodology open to considerable criticism within the accounting profession in particular. Investors also view the results with some scepticism, which is partly a reflection of their unfamiliarity with the language and the expressions used.

The perceived drawback of the embedded value methodology for profit recognition is that reported earnings are calculated as the difference between the opening and closing value of the long-term fund business. This essentially represents a balance sheet approach. It has not always been easy to analyse the movement caused by the various factors such as experience variations, new business growth and investment return. Furthermore it is not normal UK practice to treat changes in the value of assets as earnings for reporting purposes.

Another criticism of the methodology is that embedded value profits can be sensitive to fluctuations in market rates of interest and changes in asset values. There is a school of thought that advocates the smoothing of these fluctuations. Others believe that if the owners of life assurance companies have a further insight into their investment, then they should be prepared to accept the volatile nature of results. However it is generally believed that there is virtue in allowing some element of smoothing in the calculations.

The valuation background to the method is reflected in the use of a risk discount rate. It has no counterpart in any other area of accountancy. The actual rate of discount used can alter the profit emergence. Low rates of interest produce higher profits for new business but lower profits on business already in force. Thus a lower discount rate produces better profits for a small, rapidly expanding office.

Profit and loss accounts designed to provide a true and fair view should of course be based on prudent best estimates for mortality, lapses, surrenders, etc. The use of a risk rate of return to discount projected profit transfers based on such prudent best estimates, however, is regarded by many accountants as a rather blunt instrument for allocating profit to accounting periods. It is normally the function of investors to allow for risk when they value a company as reflected by differing P/E ratios for companies and industries. Accordingly conceptual problems exist in utilising embedded value accounting in its current form.

In other industries the price earnings ratio compares the earnings of a company, calculated in accordance with generally accepted accounting policies that have no regard to the risk of those earnings, with a market price which reflects investors perception of risk. The use of risk discount rates to arrive at embedded value profits means that profits represent risk adjusted earnings. Risk therefore features in embedded value earnings figures and the use of P/E ratios is arguably not appropriate.

The accruals profit approach

The industry and the accounting profession have sought to develop a methodology which would overcome the limitations of the embedded value method.

In 1990, the ABI established a Steering Group comprising finance directors from various insurance companies to devise a possible "accounting" solution. The solution which was published in a Consultative Document in July 1991 was the accruals profit method. This method:

- applies UK accounting practice on long-term contracts;
- considers each contract individually and recognises profit earned rather than cash transferred; and
- utilises a profit recognition pattern which matches work performed (i.e., services provided) and risk borne (i.e., degree of risk attaching at different stages of the contract). This is consistent with the philosophy that the life assurer takes risks and that the earnings profile should match the risk taken as well as the services provided (risk reflecting the work performed by the business).

This method of accounting for shareholders' interest in the long-term business has been embraced by a section of the UK life insurers. Two companies, The Prudential Corporation plc and BAT Industries, which have publicly reported accruals basis profits are considered below:

(i) The Prudential Corporation plc

The Prudential Corporation plc is the pre-eminent example of accruals profit reporting. The Prudential proclaimed its support for the accrual basis by pubishing accruals profits in the form of supplementary documents.

The first supplement was published in November 1992. In it the Prudential explained the implications of a move from the simple cash basis of accounting for surpluses currently used, to the accruals method. In the document, the 1990 and 1991 results were restated on an accruals basis. Full disclosure was given of the methods and assumptions used.

A further supplement was also published during 1993 which disclosed the 1992 accruals profits results. These results included a more comprehensive analysis of profits than had previously been attempted by other UK insurers and were audited.

The reporting of the 1993 results under the accruals basis was incorporated within the Prudential Corporation plc Annual Report but still in the form of supplementary information. This remains the most comprehensive illustration of the accruals profits approach in practice. The full text of the Prudential's Supplementary information is included as Appendix II, page 129. The level of disclosure is impressive. Life accruals profits are analysed between those arising from new business, business in-force and investment return on the shareholders' accrued interest.

A separate analysis is also provided for each of the major life operations reflecting the difference in type of business written and the risks attaching to each type. For example, Prudential Assurance in the UK predominantly sells life and pension products which have a high savings and low risk content and are intended to be held for the long term. The nature of these products is such that the majority of profits can be recognised in the year of sale, hence the higher proportion of new business profits. The US subsidiary Jackson National Life, sells savings and protection products with the majority of the sales being single premium annuites. Consequently, recognising the different risk characteristics of the business, profit emergence of this division is less weighted towards new business than Prudential Assurance and a larger proportion of profits arises from business in force.

In addition, restated financial statements of Prudential Corporation are also disclosed, showing the impact of the methodology on results and shareholders' capital and reserves. Finally, there is extensive disclosure of assumptions and the effect on profits of changes to the assumptions from the previous accounting period.

A separate auditors' opinion covers the supplementary information confirming that it has been "properly prepared in conformity with the methodology and disclosure requirements contained in the 'Draft Proposals on Accounting for Shareholders' Profits in Long-Term Insurance Business' issued by the Association of British Insurers in July 1992".

(ii) BAT Industries
BAT Industries have also endorsed the accruals profit methodology. Whilst the consolidated financial statements incorporate the profits of Allied Dunbar and Eagle Star which emerge on a statutory solvency basis, the notes to the accounts (Example 30 BAT Industries) incorporate supplemental information on accruals accounting.

Example 31
BAT Industries   *31 December 1993*
Extract from notes on the accounts

41 Accruals accounting – financial services life business

The way life profits are currently reported does not fully reflect performance and the Group has been active in the industry-wide effort to resolve this issue. On 2 July 1992 the Association of British Insurers issued proposals for the "accruals" method as a way of recognising shareholder profits from life insurance business in published financial statements. Companies were encouraged to experiment in applying these proposals so that, at a later date, an acceptable method could be agreed and used in published reporting and the Group is supportive of these proposals. The effect of applying the accruals method for the Group life companies is set out below and the principles adopted and calculations performed have been confirmed by the Company's Auditors, Coopers & Lybrand, as being consistent with the ABI proposals.

	"Accruals" method		As published	
	1993 **£m**	1992 £m	**1993** **£m**	1992 £m
Profit from:				
New business	**73**	55		
In-force business	**280**	262		
Investment return not related to in-force business	**244**	92		
	597	409	**321**	274
Taxation *page 41 note (d)*	**(181)**	(100)	**(80)**	(56)
Profit after taxation	**416**	309	**241**	218
Group's equity interest	**3,548**	3,137	**2,348**	2,144

(a) The principal assumptions have taken account of current and expected future experience. It has been assumed that future investment returns, claims experience, policy lapses and expenditure will prudently reflect this experience, while bonuses on "with profit" policies are adjusted accordingly. Future investment returns of 6·5 to 11 per cent, gross of tax, have been assumed reflecting the mix of the investment portfolios in each life company. Investment returns have been smoothed, using a five year averaging, where it is appropriate to moderate short term fluctuations.

(b) The planned margins have been selected to give reasonable weight to the ongoing operations of the life business resulting in prudent recognition for current activities. The principal margins are as follows:

Investment	25%	Mortality	10%
Policy lapses	10-30%	Expenses	15-20%
Investment spread (US universal life products)			25%

Planned margins have been restricted for products where their application would result in a loss being shown on new business which is ultimately expected to be profitable.

The information is less explicit than in the case of the Prudential Corporation reflecting the relatively smaller significance of life operations to the BAT Group.

Overall assessment of accruals profit reporting
The accruals profit approach, as adopted in practice, provides a relatively detailed analysis of the sources of profit. In this respect, it is more comprehensive than the approach to embedded value profits used by the banks, which merely focuses on movements in the balance sheet amounts.

The codification of the accruals profit methodology in the form of a draft ABI statement of recommended practice, has made it more readily understandable by investors. The methodology is expressed in more conventional accounting terms as it broadly follows the principles of SSAP 9 "Accounting for long term work in progress".

Another perceived advantage of the methodology is the ability, via the use of planned margins, to attach different levels of prudence to each assumption, reflecting differing levels of uncertainty. No overall risk discount rate needs to be applied, with the result that earnings calculated on an accruals basis are essentially unadjusted for risk. Price to earnings ratios are consequently more meaningful.

5. Looking forward to 1994–1995

EC accounts directive
The implementation of the European Insurance Accounts Directive in the UK has been actively debated over recent years fuelled in 1992 by the DTI's Consultation Document on the new Regulations and more recently by ABI working parties.

The ABI has sought to provide guidance on implementing the new regulations of the Companies Act 1985 (Insurance Companies Accounts) Regulations 1993 which bring the European Insurance Accounts Directive into UK law. The Regulations apply to insurance companies and groups for accounting periods commencing on or after 23 December 1994. To this effect the ABI issued a Consultation Document on 2 June 1994.

The principal objectives of the ABI as outlined in the Consultation Document are as follows:

(a) to set out recommended accounting practice for insurance undertakings (other than Lloyds' syndicates) within the framework of the Regulations in order to narrow the areas of difference and variation in accounting treatment and to enhance the usefulness of published accounting information.

(b) to revisit some of the areas covered in the previous statement with a view to either amending the recommended practice or improving the wording to facilitate a clearer understanding.

(c) to provide extra statutory guidance on the provisions of the Regulations where the working of those provisions requires clarification, or is insufficient in itself to ensure a uniform interpretation of the requirements, or would result in an inappropriate diversity of accounting practices".

One of the most important changes is the new requirement for insurance accounts to show a true and fair view. Previous legal exemptions, which in particular allowed insurers to carry hidden reserves, have been swept away. All insurance enterprises will also be expected to follow Financial Reporting Standards (FRS's) and Statements of Standard Accounting Practice (SSAP's) issued by the Accounting Standards Board and its predecessor and Urgent Issues Task Force (UITF) Abstracts. A second major change concerns the format of accounts which is heavily prescribed by the new Regulations.

It is intended that the implementation of the European Insurance Accounts Directive will harmonise financial reporting ensuring greater comparability between insurance company results.

Modified statutory solvency basis

The Regulations require the statutory accounts of a life insurer to give a "true and fair" view. In the DTI's 1992 Consultation Document it was noted that this requirement:

"is given content by the requirements of the Directive and the Act. Under normal circumstances, treatment which is required or permitted by the Directive and which will be required or permitted under the new Schedule 9A will not be incompatible with the requirement to show a true and fair view".

The Regulations also introduce the new concept of the "Fund for future appropriations" which it defines as comprising:

"all funds, the allocation of which either to policy holders or to shareholders has not been determined by the end of the financial year."

The Fund for future appropriations is a liability account in the prescribed formats. Under the guidance, this account will effectively comprise a mixture of provisions and reserves, presenting a particular interpretational challenge to UK accountants brought up in an accounting environment which seeks to distinguish between provisions and reserves.

Interpretation of the "true and fair" requirement has been extensively debated by the industry. In particular, a difficulty exists as to how to accommodate long term fund surplus and the accumulated investment reserves within the framework prescribed by the Directive in a manner which would support the true and fair requirement. The solution that is prescribed within the ABI's Consultation Document could result in an interpretation of the "true and fair" concept under the new Regulations which differs from that applied to UK companies other than insurance companies.

Having adopted this approach to the interpretation of the Regulations "true and fair" requirements, the ABI sought to minimise the changes in accounting practice that are necessary. In order to give a true and fair view and comply with the new regulations, a "modified statutory solvency basis" is recommended by the ABI's Consultation Document. This method required two significant adjustments to be made to the "statutory solvency basis":

(a) deferral of new business acquisition costs incurred but relating to subsequent periods:
(b) inclusion within shareholders' funds or the Fund for future appropriations of certain reserves previously included within the long term business fund such as investment, resilience and similar reserves or reserves in respect of general contingencies or the specific contingency that the fund will be closed to new business.

In all other respects, the Regulations are not expected to substantially alter the basis of accounting.

The Regulations do not change the requirements of the Insurance Companies Act 1982. In particular, life companies will still have to maintain a separate long term business fund and transfers to shareholders will continue to be permitted only out of surplus ascertained after carrying out an actuarial valuation.

Similarly, the Regulations maintain the status quo under section 268 of the Companies Act 1985; only amounts properly transferred to shareholders from a surplus of the long term business fund are to be treated as distributable profits.

The DTI have confirmed that they will continue to monitor compliance with the Insurance Companies Act 1982 through the annual DTI return, although the content of these returns is separately under review as part of the Government's deregulation initiative.

Implications for profit reporting

It is not anticipated that profits declared by most with-profits companies will be altered under the "modified statutory solvency" basis. Similarly, mutual life companies will continue not to recognise any free reserves. This reflects use of the Fund for future appropriations by with-profits and mutual companies to finance acquisition costs and carry "reserves" which can no longer be included as part of policyholder provisions.

By contrast, in the case of proprietary offices where the life business is 100% owned by shareholders, which includes most linked offices, deferral of acquisition costs and inclusion of "reserves" as part of shareholders' funds will fundamentally change the basis of reporting profits. This situation arises because, following the ABI's guidance, these offices will not be permitted to use the Fund for future appropriations.

The ABI's guidance is not yet finalised and the possibility remains that significant changes may yet be made. The profit reporting framework for 1995 remains uncertain and it is therefore unlikely that companies will wish to implement the requirements of the Directive early.

Alternative methods the "converged" basis

Accounts prepared on a modified statutory solvency basis will continue to be heavily influenced by the regulatory requirements under the Insurance Companies Act 1982 and its associated regulations and by the contractual and statutory relationship with the policy holder. In the ABI Consultation Document, the following limitations in the method are noted:

"(a) expected future cash transfers to shareholders out of the long term fund from business which has already been written will not normally be recognised beyond any element relating to deferred acquisition expenses;

(b) liabilities are calculated on a conservative basis generally incorporating many of the margins of prudence required for regulatory purposes; and

(c) for with-profits business the profits attributable to shareholders will be dependent upon bonus policy."

Recognising these limitations, the ABI goes on to say that:

"In consequence the usefulness of the modified statutory solvency method for proprietary, companies is restricted."

The ABI has continued to seek the development of an alternative accounting method similar to embedded value or accruals profit. The ABI's Consultation Document recognises the efforts made by the industry to develop an alternative basis and acknowledges that certain companies may wish to report to shareholders on both the modified statutory solvency and on an alternative basis.

Under the initiative of listed proprietary life companies, the industry set up a Steering Committee in 1993 to arrive at an agreed alternative for accounting for shareholders' interest in long term funds. Whilst the life assurance industry was divided on whether the embedded value or the accrual profit basis is the more appropriate, the Steering Committee came to the conclusion that, in practice, there are many more similarities between the two methodologies than differences.

In particular, both bases recognise that the shareholders has an interest in the long-term fund and seek to quantify this interest. In practical terms, both use essentially the same modelling process and recognise risk; embedded value through the risk discount rate and accruals profit through the planned margins. Indeed, depending on the choice of risk discount rates and planned margins, the results of the two bases can be very similar. In fact, some commentators view the accruals profit method as a refinement of embedded value. This point was demonstrated by Commercial Union plc, who utilised different risk discount rates in the embedded value calculation for traditional and unit linked business, matching the flexibility of approach in different circumstances which the accruals profit method achieves through the use of planned margins.

In developing a third alternative, the Steering Committee took the view that the broad framework needed already existed and sought to draw on the best aspects of the two existing bases. Recognising the similarities between the two methods previously adopted, the Steering Committee proposed a "converged" method which is essentially a synthesis of the accruals profit and the embedded value methods.

To converge the two methods, it is being accepted that the two mechanisms for deferring profits (risk discount rates for embedded values and planned margins for accruals) provide similar results. In the draft proposals which have now been put forward to the ABI for its approval, the steering committee proposes the use of "risk margins" reflecting the risk attached to each assumption. However it allows the option of utilising different "risk margins" for each assumption or combining these "risk margins" in an overall discount rate. The draft proposals also specify disclosure requirements, recognising that it is difficult to compare information currently, published by the life industry because the bases of calculation are not normally adequately disclosed.

CONCLUSION

Financial reporting for life assurance business profits has been in a state of transition in recent years. It is recognised that the existing statutory solvency basis of arriving at profits understates net assets in an effort to safeguard solvency. Whilst this represents an adequate basis for ensuring policyholder protection, it is also generally regarded as inappropriate for financial reporting purposes in that it does not provide the shareholder with information on the financial position, performance and financial stability of the long-term business. The fact that the financial statements do not show a true and fair view re-enforces the shortcomings of the existing basis of accounting.

Banks and other large groups incorporating substantial life operations have experimented in the use of alternative bases for reporting life profits, namely the embedded value and the accruals profit methods. We have also seen a wide diversity in accounting treatment and level of disclosure relating to methodology and assumptions. Though many commentators regard the development of these methodologies as a step in the right direction, the current practices diverge so widely that their usefulness is restricted. The fact remains that, in the current climate of limited and varied disclosure, investors will continue to treat the results of such methodologies with an element of suspicion. The emergence of these alternative bases of accounting and the arrival of the European Insurance Accounts Directive, precipitated a re-think of the basis of accounting and reporting for long term business. Through various working parties and committees the ABI, the insurance industry, the accounting and the actuarial profession have sought to develop guidance.

Out of this process, the "modified statutory solvency basis" was developed by the ABI, intended to be used solely for financial reporting as opposed to regulatory control purposes. It is currently undergoing consultation and this way result in significant changes to the Final Consultation Document. The new method has to meet the requirement for a "true and fair" view and will provide the framework for consistency in the form and content of financial statements. However, it will not represent a radical new method of recognising life profits.

Acknowledging this fact, the industry has continued to work towards an acceptable new basis of recognising profits along the lines of embedded value and accruals profit. The "converged" basis has emerged as the likely successor, drawing upon the best aspects of these two methodologies. The "converged" basis is currently in the draft proposal stage and has yet to be accepted by the ABI. Even if it is endorsed it is widely accepted that this alternative basis of reporting will need to undergo a further period of experimentation and evolution before it can come to be regarded as industry practice.

In conclusion, the current state of transition is expected to continue for a while longer. Whilst there is little doubt that the implementation of the European Insurance Accounts Directive will improve comparability of accounting information disclosed in the financial statements of life assurance companies, there is still some way to go in moving towards a basis which sensibly supports annual financial reporting whilst genuinely reflecting the longer term emergence of profits on this unique and complex business.

APPENDIX I

Commercial Union 1993

An alternative method of reporting life profits

28 February 1994

Dear Shareholders,

I am writing about the progress of work on the reporting of life profits within Commercial Union. As you may be aware, this is a subject to which the United Kingdom life insurance industry has been devoting considerable attention.

Commercial Union is outstanding among the major composite insurance companies based in the United Kingdom for the spread of its life assurance operations where total assets exceed £15 billion. Apart from its United Kingdom life business, the Group has acquired or developed significant operations in a number of Continental European countries, and in North America. Practice regarding recognition of life profits and the valuation of shareholders' interest in such businesses varies from country to country; it is principally for this reason that it has taken time for us to reach a point at which we can provide more complete information to you about the profiitability of our life business and the significant contribution it makes to the underlying financial strength of the Group as a whole.

The traditional accounting methods for life business, which we use in our audited Report and Accounts are based on statutory reporting standards designed to protect the security of policyholders and, as such, are very conservatively calculated. These methods tend to understate the economic value of our life business to shareholders; they imply a significant deferral in the recognition of profits if we take account of the time when these profits are effectively earned; finally they are increasingly out of line with the objectives and the measures of performance which we apply in the management of our life businesses.

This is the background to the statement in the 1992 Report and Accounts that we would provide shareholders with supplementary information derived from an alternative basis of arriving at the annual profits arising from the Group's life business and the value of shareholders' interest in that business. Using this alternative method, life profits in 1993 were £280m and the accumulated shareholders' interest some £1.7 billion. The report with this letter sets out the way in which these figures are arrived at and compares them with the statutory equivalent shown in our audited Report and Accounts.

Those of you who are also life policyholders should be aware that your interests will continue to be safeguarded by the regulatory requirements which govern dividend transfers to shareholders and the amount of capital which must be retained in the life business. Thus the high level of security enjoyed by our policyholders and the financial strength of our life business will not be affected by any new approach to profit reporting.

It may be some time before an industry consensus emerges on the most realistic way of showing life profits. In publishing this information, as a supplement to our formal Report and Accounts, we aim to show where our own thinking stands; I hope we have given you a useful insight into the value of our life business and a better appreciation of its overall importance to the Group.

Yours faithfully

N H Baring
Chairman

Commercial Union plc, PO Box 420, St. Helen's, 1 Undershaft, London EC3P 3DQ
Registered in England No. 2468686

Introduction

Commercial Union, in common with most other United Kingdom life insurers, has reported in its published accounts the profits of its life businesses on bases which in the main are used to satisfy local regulatory requirements. These requirements are principally concerned with demonstrating the solvency of life business and very conservative assumptions are, therefore, used for the valuation of assets and liabilities. For many types of contract, this results in a substantial deferment in the recognition of profits, compared with when the profit is effectively earned. This existing basis of accounting, therefore, does not provide a complete picture of the underlying performance in the period of review.

As a consequence, the industry under the auspices of the Association of British Insurers has encouraged life companies to consider and experiment with alternative methods of reporting life profits. The group has played a full role in industry discussions and has carried out its own work on an alternative method of reporting life profits.

In view of the importance to shareholders of the Group's substantial life businesses, we have decided to publish an estimate of our life profits on an alternative basis. However, it should be emphasised that we have produced our audited accounts for 1993 on the existing basis of accounting. The results of the alternative method set out in this document have not been audited and may be subject to further modification.

Should this alternative method or a variant of it become our main basis of reporting, we would continue additionally to disclose the surpluses released from the life funds on the existing basis of accounting since these determine the amount of profit legally distributable to shareholders.

An alternative method of reporting life profits

The alternative method set out in this report uses embedded value methodology to calculate profits. Profits after tax are determined by the change in shareholders' interest in the life businesses during the year, adjusted for transfers to or from shareholders. The shareholders' interest represents the value of the shareholders' assets employed in the life businesses and the present value of projected future cashflows from business in force calculated on a prudent risk discount basis.

Set out below are the results of calculating life profits for 1993 on this alternative method, together with details of the methodology and assumptions used.

1993 Results

Published life profits for 1993 on our existing basis of accounting amounted to £119m before taxation and shareholders' funds included in the published balance sheet amounted to £713m.

Using the alternative method of calculation, life profits for 1993 amounted to £280m before taxation, which includes £60m arising from the change in economic conditions during the year mainly related to the substantial fall in interest rates. The value of new business written in 1993, and included in this result, was £25m over and above the required risk discount return to shareholders. The shareholders' interest in our life business using this method amounted to £1,700m at the end of 1993.

Extensive external advice has been taken in determining the results on the alternative method. Bacon & Woodrow, independent actuaries, advised the Group on the choice of methodology and assumptions and on the calculation of the shareholders' interest. On the basis of the date provided by the Group and the application of such methodology and assumptions, Bacon & Woodrow consider that the results are reasonable.

For comparison, key features of our audited 1993 results on the existing basis of accounting and using the alternative method, on consistent tax assumptions, are as follows:–

	Existing basis (as per published accounts)	Alternative basis (unaudited)
Life profits	£119m	£280m
Non-life operating profit	£99m	£99m
Operating profit before taxation and loss on termination of activities	£218m	£379m
Profit attributable to shareholders	£321m	£426m
Operating earnings per ordinary share	31.4p	50.6p
Shareholders' funds	£2.5bn	£3.5bn
Net asset value per ordinary share	418p	596p

Methodology and assumptions

The alternative method of calculating life profits represents the increase in shareholders' interest in the life businesses during the year, adjusted for transfers to or from shareholders.

The shareholders' interest represents the value, discounted at risk rates of return, of projected future transfers to shareholders from profits related to the in force business and to associated shareholders' funds. The shareholders' interest is calculated on a going concern basis but nothing is included for the value of future new business.

Profits are determined by applying the economic factors and assumptions at the start of the year to the opening and closing liabilities and corresponding assets, and then adjusting for the change in economic factors and assumptions at the end of the year. These adjustments are applied to the assets as well as to the liabilities.

The principal economic assumptions used in calculating the shareholders' interest are consistent with the methodology used and reflect current economic conditions. The change in economic conditions increased the shareholders' interest at the end of 1993 as the use of lower discount rates increased the value of future cashflows.

The Group's international spread of life businesses is much wider than most United Kingdom companies and local circumstances vary considerably. The Group has taken care to seek consistency between territories in the assumptions used whilst properly reflecting local conditions and in reporting the results under the alternative method.

PRINCIPAL UNITED KINGDOM ECONOMIC ASSUMPTIONS

	1993	1992
Risk discount rate:		
Traditional business	8.5%	10.5%
Unit linked business	9.5%	11.5%
Pre-tax investment returns: Government fixed interest securities	6.7%	9.1%
Equities and property	7.7%	10.1%
Future expense inflation	4.25%	5.50%

Other assumptions such as mortality and expenses were chosen with regard to recent experience.

In the United Kingdom, the shareholders' interest in with profits business is calculated using revisionary and terminal bonus assumptions consistent with the assumed investment returns. It also reflects our bonus philosophy which incorporates a high degree of smoothing of investment returns and a relatively high proportion of the surplus being distributed through revisionary bonuses. The profit recognised in respect of new with profits business is calculated consistently on a self-supporting basis. For the purpose of assessing the shareholders' interest, any remaining investment reserves or undistributed surplus are deemed to be distributed to existing business by way of a terminal bonus.

Capital allocated to meet local requirements, including solvency margins, is assumed to earn interest at the investment rate until it can be released to shareholders.

Realised and unrealised capital gains and losses on non-linked equities and properties in the United Kingdom and the Netherlands, after adjustment to reflect the effect of interest changes, are reduced by a precautionary margin and then smoothed by averaging over five years.

The shareholders' interest on the alternative basis is calculated and shown net of tax, and accordingly profits are also determined net of tax. These after tax profits have been grossed up for tax at the overall notional rate of 30.5% to obtain the figures shown above.

All figures in this document are based on currency exchange rates as at 31 December 1993.

APPENDIX II

Prudential Corporation plc

Supplementary information

Long-term Business Results—Accruals Basis

Financial Overview	1993 £m	1992 £m
Operating profit		
Long-term business	**887**	807
General Insurance and shareholders' other income	**167**	13
	1,054	820
Interest payable	**(59)**	(51)
Profit on ordinary activities before tax	**995**	769
Earnings per share	**35.1p**	28.5p
	1993 £m	1992 £m
Shareholders' capital and reserves		
Statutory basis	**788**	504
Profits retained in long-term funds	**3,386**	2,796
Accruals basis	**4,174**	3,300

Review of Results

As I explained earlier, we believe that the accruals basis of reporting provides a better insight into the performance and underlying profitability of our business than the statutory basis. However, the method is still at an experimental stage and results on this basis are therefore shown as supplementary information rather than as the principal financial statements. An explanation of the accruals basis of reporting is set out on page 56.

On the accruals basis our long-term business contributed profits of £887 million in 1993, up 10 per cent. Taken together with the significant improvement in the general insurance results, our total pre-tax profits were close to £1 billion, with earnings per share on the accruals basis increasing by 23 per cent to 35.1 pence.

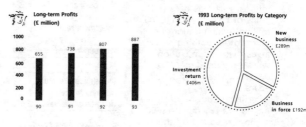

Accruals profits arise from three sources – new business, business in force and the investment return on the shareholders' accrued interest in the long-term funds.

Profits from new business fell by 12 per cent to £289 million primarily as a result of a one-third fall in sales of single premium annuity products on Jackson National Life.

Profits from business in force have been reduced by a charge of £170 million resulting from a reassessment of the expected rate of future investment returns on our main UK in force portfolio. The anticipated pre-tax return has been reduced to 10 per cent per annum from the 11 per cent applied in 1992. Nevertheless good investment returns around the world in 1993, an increase in realised gains in Jackson National Life, and the benefit of expense reductions in our Home Service division helped profits from business in force to increase by 54 per cent to £192 million.

Business Area Review

The third element of the accruals profits, the investment return on the shareholders' accrued interest in the long-term business, grew by 15 per cent to £406 million.

The accruals basis of reporting also shows the profits retained in the long-term business of our operations. The shareholders' accrued interest in the Group's long-term funds rose by 21 per cent to £3.4 billion during 1993 reflecting the growth in retained profits which we are achieving from sales of new policies, the management of the business in force and particularly in 1993, strong investment performance. The shareholders' accrued interest includes deferred gains of £530 million (£206 million) which under our policy of smoothing investment appreciation will be included in operating results in future years.

After including the net assets of £788 million (£504 million) reported on the statutory basis, total shareholders' funds on the accruals basis at the end of 1993 were £4.2 billion (£3.3 billion). In my review on pages 8 to 25 I dealt in some detail with the progress in each of our main businesses. In presenting accruals information, the results of Home Service, Prudential Financial Services and our overseas retail operations (other than in the USA) are reported under Prudential Assurance, their principal operating company.

Long-term profits of the Group in 1993 were as follows:

1993 Long-term Profits by Business Area (£ million)

- M&G £164m
- Prudential Assurance £536m
- Jackson National Life £187m

Prudential Assurance

	1993 £m	1992 £m
New business		
Annual premiums	411	458
Single premiums	3,178	2,620
Operating profit		
New business	223	226
Business in force	41	36
Investment return on the shareholders' accrued interest	272	225
	536	487
Shareholders' accrued interest in the long-term business	2,153	1,753

Prudential Assurance and its subsidiaries are responsible for all of the Group's retail operations outside the USA and sell life and pensions products to both the individual and corporate markets. These products generally have high savings and low risk content and are designed to be held for the long term. The nature of the products allows recognition in the year of sale of a high proportion of the total shareholders' profits which will ultimately emerge from new business. The other main constituent of Prudential Assurance's profits is investment

return on the shareholders' accrued interest in the long-term funds, which represents profits retained in the funds primarily to meet valuation and solvency requirements.

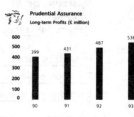

Prudential Assurance Long-term Profits (£ million)

90	91	92	93
399	431	487	536

Sales of single premium policies were up by 21 per cent with strong growth in most of our major markets. However, annual premium sales fell in most areas, reflecting the continued reluctance of consumers to enter into regular financial commitments. Also, profitability of individual contracts sold in the year was slightly lower than in 1992 due to our expectation of lower future investment returns. Taken together, these factors resulted in 1993 new business profits of £223 million, similar to the 1992 level.

However, there were encouraging features within the 1993 new business results. In the UK, profits from Prudence Bond, our successful single premium with profits investment contract, rose by 15 per cent to £54 million, whilst overseas, our Asian and Australian operations together contributed £35 million of new business profit in 1993. Unit linked business in Australia is now financed wholly by shareholders' funds and consequently shareholders receive all of the profit previously shared with the life fund.

Profits from business in force increased by 14 per cent to £41 million. In the UK, smoothed investment returns were some £90 million higher than in 1992 but this was outweighed by the charge of £170 million for the effect of lower anticipated UK investment returns. The benefits already delivered from our cost reduction programme in the Home Service division allowed us to recognise a one-off reduction in our expected future expenses. Overseas, profits from business in force improved slightly, mainly due to much improved investment returns in Australia. However, the results of our Canadian operations were again disappointing due to the need for further provisions for investment default losses.

The investment return on the shareholders' accrued interest in the long-term funds increased by 21 per cent between 1992 and 1993 to reach £272 million reflecting both the increase in retained profits and good investment performance.

Investment return was the major contributor to

the growth in the shareholders' interest in the long-term business of Prudential Assurance which rose by 23 per cent during 1993 and stood at £2,153 million at the end of the year.

Jackson National Life

	1993 £m	1992 £m
New business		
Annual premiums	64	73
Single premiums	1,068	1,575
Operating profit		
New business	39	68
Business in force	97	40
Investment return on the shareholders' accrued interest	51	49
	187	157
Shareholders' accrued interest in the long-term business	470	410

Jackson National Life sells savings and protection products in the USA individual market, with the majority of its sales being single premium annuities. In recognition of the different risk characteristics of the USA annuity market, profit emergence on Jackson's products is less weighted towards new business than is the case for Prudential Assurance. A larger proportion of profits therefore tends to arise from business in force. As mentioned in my review, Jackson's rapid sales growth reversed in 1993. Single premium sales fell by a third and new business profits fell accordingly, from £68 million to £39 million. On the other hand, profits from business in force more than doubled to £97 million, mainly due to a £53 million increase to £62 million in realised

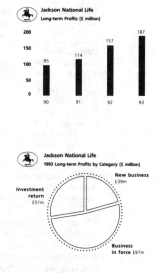

Jackson National Life
Long-term Profits (£ million)

Jackson National Life
1993 Long-term Profits by Category (£ million)

investment gains allocated to shareholders.

Investment returns on the shareholders' interest rose from £49 million to £51 million, the growth in the shareholders' interest being offset by lower interest rates. The shareholders' interest itself increased by 15 per cent to £470 million.

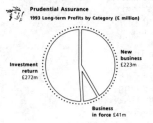

Prudential Assurance
1993 Long-term Profits by Category (£ million)

Conclusion

Mercantile & General

	1993 £m	1992 £m
New business		
Annual premiums	61	61
Single premiums	552	386
Operating profit		
New business	27	35
Business in force	54	49
Investment return on the shareholders' accrued interest	83	79
	164	163
Shareholders' accrued interest in the long-term business	763	633

Mercantile & General is a major participant in worldwide life and disability reassurance markets. Its business is more exposed to underwriting risk than the Group's retail businesses whose products are mainly orientated towards the medium- to long-term savings market. The pattern of accruals profit emergence reflects this characteristic by taking a lower proportion of the ultimate profit in the year of sale.

Investment return on the shareholders' accrued interest in the long-term business forms the largest constituent of M&G's accruals basis profits, reflecting the high level of profits and solvency capital retained within M&G's long-term funds. Since M&G does not have any

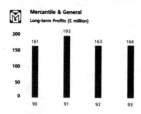

Mercantile & General
Long-term Profits (£ million)

participating policyholders the whole of the investment return on these retained funds is attributable to shareholders.

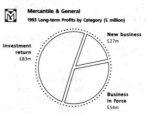

Mercantile & General
1993 Long-term Profits by Category (£ million)

Investment return £83m — New business £27m — Business in force £54m

In total, 1993 profits of £164 million were similar to the 1992 level. For new business, annual premium sales were virtually unchanged but single premiums increased by 43 per cent, mostly due to a higher level of medical expense business. However, the growth in new business profits that might be expected has been outweighed by he effects of a reassessment of the appropriate profile of accruals profit recognition for certain lines. In addition the results for UK disability business deteriorated in 1993; recent rises in premium rates in the primary market will not have significant effect for M&G until 1994.

Accordingly, profits from new business fell by £8 million to £27 million in 1993.

This reduction was offset by growth in profits from business in force, up 10 per cent to £54 million, due mainly to improved investment returns. The shareholders' accrued interest in M&G's long-term business rose during 1993 to £763 million, an increase of 21 per cent.

This is the third time that we have published our results on the accruals basis. We remain committed to the development of this method of reporting. I believe that the results once again demonstrate much more clearly to both management and shareholders the factors, both positive and negative, which have contributed to the underlying performance of our main businesses.

M G Newmarch
Group Chief Executive
18 April 1994

Consolidated Profit and Loss Account—Accruals Basis

Year ended 31 December 1993

	1993 £m	1992 £m
Operating profit (loss)		
Continuing operations:		
Long-term business		
New business	289	329
Business in force	192	125
Investment return on the shareholders' accrued interest	406	353
	887	807
General insurance	67	(110)
Shareholders' other income	100	134
	1,054	831
Discontinued operations	—	(11)
Total operating profit	1,054	820
Interest payable	(59)	(51)
Profit on ordinary activities before tax	995	769
Tax	(333)	(234)
Minority interests	—	(1)
Profit for the financial year	662	534
Dividends	(250)	(224)
Retained profits for the financial year	412	310
Earnings per share		
Based on earnings of £662m (£534m) and 1,884m (1,873m) shares.	35.1p	28.5p
Dividend per share	13.2p	11.9p

Statement of Total Recognised Gains and Losses—Accruals Basis

Year ended 31 December 1993

Note		1993 £m	1992 £m
	Profit for the financial year	662	534
	Other recognised gains (losses)		
5	Increase in investment gains not included in profit	434	12
8	Exchange (losses) gains	(3)	166
	Other movements	4	(20)
		435	158
	Total recognised gains	1,097	692

This supplementary information has been prepared on the accruals basis of financial reporting described on page 56.
Financial statements prepared on the statutory basis of financial reporting are provided on pages 30 to 46.

Summarised Consolidated Balance Sheet—Accruals Basis

31 December 1993

	1993 £m	1992 £m
Investments	**62,407**	50,017
Other assets	**2,420**	2,539
Total assets	**64,827**	52,556
Less **Liabilities**	**2,096**	2,082
Total assets less Liabilities	**62,731**	50,474
Less **Insurance funds and reserves**		
Long-term business	**60,247**	48,118
Less Shareholders' accrued interest in the long-term business	**3,386**	2,796
	56,861	45,322
General insurance	**1,696**	1,852
	58,557	47,174
	4,174	3,300
Shareholders' capital and reserves		
Share capital	**95**	94
Share premium	**119**	93
Retained profit and reserves (statutory basis)	**574**	317
Profit retained in long-term funds (accruals basis)	**3,386**	2,796
	4,174	3,300

Reconciliation of Movement in Shareholders' Capital and Reserves—Accruals Basis

Year ended 31 December 1993

	1993 £m	1992 £m
Total recognised gains	**1,097**	692
New share capital subscribed	**27**	20
Dividends	**(250)**	(224)
Net addition to shareholders' capital and reserves	**874**	488
Shareholders' capital and reserves at beginning of year	**3,300**	2,812
Shareholders' capital and reserves at end of year	**4,174**	3,300

This supplementary information has been prepared on the accruals basis of financial reporting described on page 56.
Financial statements prepared on the statutory basis of financial reporting are provided on pages 30 to 46.

The Accruals Basis of Financial Reporting

The accruals basis of financial reporting is based on conventional accounting principles and recognises profit as it accrues over the life of an insurance contract. Although total profits from long-term business calculated under this method are the same as under the statutory solvency method, the timing of recognition is different.

The timing difference can be illustrated by considering an individual contract. Using prudent assumptions of the main elements of future income and expenditure – investment return, death claims, lapses, surrenders and administration expenses – the total profit expected to be earned from the contract can be estimated at the time of its sale.

Under the statutory solvency basis of reporting, this profit will be recognised as it is released to shareholders as a series of cash flows from the long-term funds. Under the accruals method, however, the pattern of profit recognition is based on an assessment of work performed and risks borne by the insurer over the life of the contract. The total profit expected to be earned is allocated to indiviidual financial years by incorporating planned profit margins into the assumptions made at the time of sale about future income and expenditure. These margins are set by Prudential's board to reflect work done and risks borne in future financial years. Provided that the actual outcome is in line with the original assumptions, profits will be earned in each accounting period as these margins are released. Any anticipated losses are recognised immediately as are differences between actual and assumed income and expenditure.

Major elements of work performed are marketing, staff training and policy administration, all of which are concentrated to a large entent in the year of sale. Consequently, a significant proportion of the total profit from the contract will normally be recognised in the year of sale, reflecting the success of these efforts. This element of profit is known as the profit on new business. The release of planned margins and variances between actual and assumed experience during the remainder of the contract period produces the profit on business in force.

Under the accruals method, profits are recognised earlier than under the statutory solvency basis of reporting, which derives from statutory requirements designed to ensure and demonstrate solvency in the long-term funds. The additional profits recognised at an earlier stage under the accruals method are retained within the long-term funds, thus ensuring the solvency of those funds. These retained profits are known as the shareholders' accrued interest in the long-term business and the investment return on this amount forms part of the accruals profit for the year.

The total accruals basis profits reported for an accounting year can therefore be analysed into three separate components:
• profits from new business;
• profits from business in force; and
• the investment return on the shareholders' accrued interest in the long-term business.

The accruals basis is designed to report profits which reflect business performance during the year under review, particularly new business sales and investment performance. Both sales and investment returns can change significantly from period to period and so accruals basis profits are expected to show more variability than profits reported on the statutory solvency basis.

It is important to note that the use of the accruals basis does not affect the cash surpluses which are related to shareholders' funds from the long-term funds. These continue to be determined by post-tax profits recognised on the statutory solvency basis. It should also be noted that the accruals basis does not affect amounts available for dividend payments to shareholders, as the profits which are recognised earlier when using the accruals basis are not legally distributable.

The non-distributable element of retained profit is represented by the shareholders' accrued interest in the long-term business and, when combined with shareholders' funds reported on the statutory solvency basis, provides an improved measure of total shareholders' funds of the Group. It is important to realise, however, that the shareholders' accrued interest does not represent the value to shareholders of the business in force as, in future years, further profits will be earned on this business.

Notes on the Supplementary Information

1 Basis of Preparation
The accruals basis results have been prepared in accordance with the Draft Proposals on Accounting for Shareholders' Profits in Long-term Insurance Business issued by the Association of British Insurers in July 1992.
The information is supplementary to the financial statements on pages 30 to 46.

2 Assumptions
The accruals basis results have been prepared on the basis of prudent forecasts of future rates of investment return, policy discontinuances, mortality and morbidity, expenses, expense inflation and taxation. In preparing these forecasts, account has been taken of recent experience and general economic conditions, together with inherent uncertainty.
It has been assumed that the bases and rates of taxation, both direct and indirect, will not change materially in any of the countries in which the Group operates.
Assumed future rates of investment return reflect prevailing interest rates, the outlook for inflation and the mix of the investment portfolios. A pre-tax rate of 10% per annum, before applying planned margins, has been assumed for the UK with profits fund of Prudential Assurance, compared with a rate of 11% per annum assumed in 1992. The assumption in the current year of a lower future rate of return reduces the expected cash flows from business in force at the start of the year and has resulted in a charge to 1993 profits from business in force of £170m.
The proportion of surplus from the with profits business of Prudential Assurance allocated to shareholders has been based on the present level of 10% but with an allowance for the estimated future effects of taxation on UK pensions business.
In the UK, Department of Social Security rebate business has been treated as single premium business.

3 Planned Margins
Planned margins are designed to provide an appropriate return on risks borne and work done in future periods. The margins on the most important assumptions, expressed as proportions of those assumptions, are as follows:

Investment return	15–22%	Mortality and morbidity	8–18%
Proprietor's margin on investment returns		Policy discontinuance	20–50%
(USA annuity products)	25%	Expenses	20%

Planned margins have been restricted to below the levels shown above for products where their application would result in a loss being shown on new business which is expected to be profitable.
The planned margins used are the same as in 1992 with the exception of investment return where the margins in 1992 were 15% to 20%.

4 Investment Return
The accruals basis of accounting recognises the total investment return of the long-term business to the extent attributable to shareholders. The return comprises income and gains, both realised and unrealised, and includes expected future returns on existing contracts after providing for planned margins.
With the exception of fixed interest investments held by North American subsidiaries, investment gains during the period are included in the shareholders' accrued interest as they arise but are spread forward over five years for the purposes of calculating operating results. In the case of North American subsidiaries, it is assumed that fixed interest investments will normally be held until maturity. Therefore unrealised gains are not reflected in the accruals results and only income received and the amortisation of the difference between costs and maturity values, to the extent attributable to shareholders, are recognised in operating results. Some investments are realised before maturity, mainly through early redemption by issuers or mortgage holders. In the case of Jackson National Life, the directors have discretion over the allocation of resulting gains between shareholders and policyholders. The amount allocated to shareholders is consistent with assumed future policyholder interest crediting rates, and is recognised in the operating result and shareholders' accrued interest in the year of realisation. Realised gains on fixed interest investments arising in other North American subsidiaries are amortised to the original maturity date.

5 Deferred Investment Gains
Deferred gains included within the shareholders' accrued interest but not yet recognised in operating results amounted to £530m (£206m), net of tax.

Notes on the Supplementary Information

6 Discount Rates
The shareholders' interests in future cash flows within the long-term funds have been discounted to present value at the post-tax rates of return assumed to be earned by the relevant funds. The release of the discount is included in the investment return on the shareholders' accrued interest.

7 Tax
Under the accruals method, the profit for the year is calculated initially at the post-tax level. This profit has been grossed up for presentation purposes at the full rates of company tax applicable to the countries and periods concerned irrespective of the effective rates of tax actually allowed for in calculating the profit after tax.

8 Foreign Currency Translation
Foreign currency amounts have been translated at year end rates of exchange. Exchange gains on the opening shareholders' interest of nil (£130m) have been excluded from profits, but are included in the Statement of Total Recognised Gains and Losses.

Report of the Auditors on the Supplementary Information

to the members of Prudential Corporation plc

We have audited the supplementary information on pages 54 to 58, which has been prepared on the basis set out in Note 1 on page 57 and is limited to a restatement of the Group profit and the shareholders' interest in the Group's life funds to an accruals basis.

Respective responsibilities of directors and auditors
As noted in the Statement of Directors' Responsibilities on page 47, the Company's directors are responsible for the preparation of the supplementary information. It is our responsibility to form an independent opinion, based on our audit, on that supplementary information and to report our opinion to you.

Basis of opinion
We conducted our audit in accordance with Auditing Standards issued by the Auditing Practices Board. An audit includes an examination, on a test basis, of evidence relevant to the amounts and disclosures in the supplementary information. It also includes an assessment of the significant estimates and judgements made by the directors in the preparation of the supplementary information and of whether the accounting policies are appropriate to the circumstances of the Group, consistently applied and adequately disclosed.
We planned and performed our audit so as to obtain all the information and explanations which we considered necessary in order to provide us with sufficient evidence to give reasonable assurance that the supplementary information is free from material misstatement, whether caused by fraud or other irregularity or error. In forming our opinion we also evaluated the overall adequacy of the presentation of the supplementary information.

Opinion
In our opinion, the accruals basis Group profit for the year ended 31 December 1993 and shareholders' interest in the life funds at that date have been properly prepared in conformity with the methodology and disclosure requirements contained in the 'Draft Proposals on Accounting for Shareholders' Profits in Long-term Insurance Business' issued by the Association of British Insurers in July 1992.

Price Waterhouse
Chartered Accountants
London

18 April 1994

Part II

SURVEY TABLES AND EXAMPLES

by

David J. Tonkin

SURVEY TABLES AND EXAMPLES

David J. Tonkin

Table 1: Audit opinions: Incidence of qualifications and special comments

	FT-SE 100		Listed		Unlisted		Total	
Number of companies.......	100	(100)	150	(150)	50	(50)	300	(300)
Qualifications:	%	(%)	%	(%)	%	(%)	%	(%)
non-compliance...........	—	(—)	—	(1)	2	(4)	—	(1)
uncertainty	—	(—)	1	(1)	—	(2)	—	(1)
Fundamental uncertainty:								
reference to going concern basis	—	(2)	1	(1)	—	(—)	1	(1)
no reference to going concern basis...........	—	(1)	1	(—)	—	(—)	—	(—)
Special comments:								
cost convention...........	32	(2)	26	(1)	34	(—)	29	(1)
presentation & policies....	37	(2)	44	(1)	52	(—)	42	(1)
cca....................	1	(1)	2	(—)	—	(—)	1	(—)
special rules for insurance & banking	8	(8)	—	(—)	—	(2)	3	(3)
other....................	—	(—)	1	(—)	—	(—)	1	(—)
No qualifications or special comments...............	53	(89)	53	(97)	46	(92)	52	(94)

Notes:
1 The above percentages are based on the number of companies.
2 A special comment is taken to mean any piece of information which is not worded as a qualification and which is in some sense additional to the normal scope or opinion information.

Commentary

In May 1993 the Auditing Practices Board revised its guidance to auditors by publishing Statement of Auditing Standards 600 (SAS 600) "Auditors' report on financial statements". Prior to that the standard audit report had been distilled down to a very short statement indeed, with reference to cost convention and/or accounting policies, which appeared in one in three reports seven years previously, having become virtually extinct. From 30 September 1993, the effective date of the Standard, auditors' reports have been styled in the format prescribed by SAS 600, as illustrated in the following examples.

Examples

SAS 600 introduces a "fundamental uncertainty" clause, which bridges the division between qualification and non-qualification of the auditors' opinion. In **Example 1.1 Queens Moat Houses**, the fundamental uncertainty relates to the going concern basis of preparation, while that in **Example 1.2 Thorntons** relates to the provision for restructuring.

Example 1.1
Queens Moat Houses plc   *2 January 1994*
Extract from auditors' report:

> We have audited the accounts on pages 29 to 64.
>
> **Respective responsibilities of directors and auditors**
> As described on page 27 the company's directors are responsible for the preparation of accounts. It is our responsibility to form an independent opinion, based on our audit, on those accounts and to report our opinion to you.
>
> **Basis of opinion**
> We conducted our audit in accordance with Auditing Standards issued by the Auditing Practices Board. An audit includes examination, on a test basis, of evidence relevant to the amounts and disclosures in the accounts. It also includes an assessment of the significant estimates and judgements made by the directors in the preparation of the accounts, and of whether the accounting policies are appropriate to the company's circumstances, consistently applied and adequately disclosed.
> We planned and performed our audit so as to obtain all the information and explanations which we considered necessary in order to provide us with sufficient evidence to give reasonable assurance that the accounts are free from material misstatement, whether caused by fraud or other irregularity or error. In forming our opinion we also evaluated the overall adequacy of the presentation of information in the accounts.
>
> *Fundamental uncertainty*
> In forming our opinion, we have considered the adequacy of the disclosures made in the accounts concerning the basis of preparation. The accounts have been prepared on a going concern basis and the validity of this depends on the group's banks and other lenders continuing their support by providing adequate facilities pending the successful completion of a financial restructuring, on the successful completion of such a restructuring, and on the company's first mortgage debenture stockholders not seeking to enforce their security. The accounts do not include any adjustments that would result should the group be unable to continue in operational existence. Details of the circumstances relating to this fundamental uncertainty are described in the accounting policies (note (a)). Our opinion is not qualified in this respect.
>
> *Unlawful distributions*
> In forming our opinion, we have also considered the adequacy of the disclosures made in the accounts concerning certain dividend payments made by the company during the year and prior year which were in breach of the Companies Act 1985 as the company did not have sufficient distributable reserves at the time of payment. Details of the circumstances relating to these unlawful distributions are described in note 9. Our opinion is not qualified in this respect.
>
> **Opinion**
> In our opinion the accounts give a true and fair view of the state of affairs of the company and the group at 2 January 1994 and of the loss, total recognised gains and

cash flows of the group for the year then ended and have been properly prepared in accordance with the Companies Act 1985.

Coopers & Lybrand
Chartered Accountants and Registered Auditors
London
8 April 1994

Example 1.2
Thorntons plc *26 June 1993*
Extract from auditors' report:

To the Shareholders of Thorntons PLC

We have audited the financial statements on pages 27 to 50 which have been prepared under the accounting policies set out on pages 32 and 33.

Respective responsibilities of directors and auditors
As described on page 21, the company's directors are responsible for the preparation of financial statements. It is our responsibility to form an independent opinion, based on our audit, on those statements and to report our opinion to you.

Basis of opinion
We conducted our audit in accordance with Auditing Standards. An audit includes examination, on a test basis, of evidence relevant to the amounts and disclosures in the financial statements. It also includes an assessment of the significant estimates and judgements made by the directors in the preparation of the financial statements, and of whether the accounting policies are appropriate to the group's circumstances, consistently applied and adequately disclosed.
We planned and performed our audit so as to obtain all the information and explanations which we considered necessary in order to provide us with sufficient evidence to give reasonable assurance that the financial statements are free from material misstatement, whether caused by fraud or other irregularity or error. In forming our opinion we also evaluated the overall adequacy of the presentation of information in the financial statements.

Fundamental uncertainty
In forming our opinion, we have considered the adequacy of the disclosures made in the financial statements concerning the provision for restructuring the French business. The nature of the restructure, the progress on its implementation thus far and the uncertainties deriving from factors outside the management's control, are such that the losses resulting cannot be accurately determined at this time. However, we consider the amount included in the provision in respect of these uncertainties is a reasonable estimate. The basis of the provision and the uncertainties inherent therein are described in Note 4. Our opinion is not qualified in this respect.

Opinion
In our opinion the financial statements give a true and fair view of the state of affairs of the company and of the group at 26th June 1993 and of the group's loss for the period then ended and have been properly prepared in accordance with the Companies Act 1985.

PANNELL KERR FORSTER
Chartered Accountants
11th October 1993   *Registered Auditors*

The auditors of **Example 1.3 British Airways** adopt SAS600 in its full form and make reference to the cost convention and the accounting policies in the preamble to their report.

Example 1.3
British Airways plc   *31 March 1994*
Extract from auditors' report:

REPORT OF THE AUDITORS TO
THE MEMBERS OF BRITISH AIRWAYS plc

We have audited the accounts on Pages 12 to 38, which have been prepared under the historical cost convention as modified by the revaluation of certain fixed assets and on the basis of the accounting policies set out on Pages 16 and 17.

RESPECTIVE RESPONSIBILITIES OF DIRECTORS AND AUDITORS

As described above the Company's Directors are responsible for the preparation of the accounts. It is our responsibility to form an independent opinion, based on our audit, on those accounts and to report our opinion to you.

BASIS OF OPINION

We conducted our audit in accordance with Auditing Standards issued by the Auditing Practices Board. An audit includes examination, on a test basis, of evidence relevant to the amounts and disclosures in the accounts. It also includes an assessment of the significant estimates and judgements made by the Directors in the preparation of the accounts, and of whether the accounting policies are appropriate to the Group's circumstances, consistently applied and adequately disclosed.
We planned and performed our audit so as to obtain all the information and explanations which we considered necessary in order to provide us with sufficient evidence to give reasonable assurance that the accounts are free from material misstatement, whether caused by fraud or other irregularity or error. In forming our opinion we also evaluated the overall adequacy of the presentation of information in the accounts.
Investment in USAir Group, Inc.
In forming our opinion we have considered the information disclosed in the accounts concerning the Group's investment of £275.3 million in USAir. The value of the Group's investment is dependent upon the successful outcome of the restructuring initiatives proposed by USAir. The circumstances relating to this fundamental uncertainty are fully described in Note 17 to the accounts. Our opinion is not qualified in this respect.

OPINION

In our opinion the accounts give a true and fair view of the state of affairs of the Company and of the Group as at 31 March 1994 and of the profit of the Group for the year then ended and have been properly prepared in accordance with the Companies Act 1985.

Ernst & Young
Chartered Accountants
Registered Auditor
London
23 May 1994

A number of utilities require, for regulatory purposes, to publish current cost information in addition to their historical cost accounts. The auditors of **Example 1.4 Midlands Electricity** extend their report to embrace the current cost information contained in that company's accounts.

Example 1.4
Midlands Electricity plc   *31 March 1993*
Extract from auditors' report:

Report of the Auditors to the Members of Midlands Electricity plc

We have audited the financial statements on pages 8 to 27.

Respective responsibilities of Directors and Auditors
As described above, the Company's Directors are responsible for the preparation of financial statements. It is our responsibility to form an independent opinion, based on our audit, on those statements and to report our opinion to you.

Basis of opinion
We conducted our audit in accordance with Auditing Standards issued by the Auditing Practices Board. An audit includes examination, on a test basis, of evidence relevant to the amounts and disclosures in the financial statements. It also includes an assessment of the significant estimates and judgements made by the Directors in the preparation of the financial statements, and of whether the accounting policies are appropriate to the Group's circumstances, consistently applied and adequately disclosed.

We planned and performed our audit so as to obtain all the information and explanations which we considered necessary in order to provide us with sufficient evidence to give reasonable assurance that the financial statements are free from material misstatement, whether caused by fraud or other irregularity or error. In forming our opinion we also evaluated the overall adequacy of the presentation of information in the financial statements.

Opinion
In our opinion the financial statements give a true and fair view of the state of affairs of the Company and the Group at 31 March 1993 and of the profit, total recognised gains and cash flows of the Group for the year then ended and have been properly prepared in accordance with the Companies Act 1985.

In our opinion the summary current cost information set out on page 30 has been properly prepared in accordance with the accounting policies described on page 31.

Coopers & Lybrand
Chartered Accountants and Registered Auditors

Birmingham

6 July 1993

Although the accounts of banks no longer universally resort to the special provisions of the Companies Act, auditors' reports on the accounts of insurance companies continue to make reference to the fact that they are prepared in terms of the provisions of the Act which relate to insurance companies. Price Waterhouse so state in the accounts of **Example 1.5 Legal & General**.

Example 1.5
Legal & General Group plc   *31 December 1993*
Extract from auditors' report:

REPORT OF THE AUDITORS *to the members of Legal & General Group Plc. We have audited the financial statements on pages 38 to 63 which have been prepared in accordance with the accounting policies set out on pages 38 and 39.*

RESPECTIVE RESPONSIBILITIES OF DIRECTORS AND AUDITORS
As described on page 36 the Company's directors are responsible for the preparation of the financial statements. It is our responsibility to form an independent opinion, based on our audit, on those financial statements and to report our opinion to you.

BASIS OF OPINION
We conducted our audit in accordance with Auditing Standards issued by the Auditing Practices Board. An audit includes examination, on a test basis, of evidence relevant to the amounts and disclosures in the financial statements. It also includes an assessment of the significant estimates and judgements made by the directors in the preparation of the financial statements and of whether the accounting policies are appropriate to the circumstances of the Company and the Group, consistently applied and adequately disclosed.

We planned and performed our audit so as to obtain all the information and explanations which we consider necessary in order to provide us with sufficient evidence to give reasonable assurance that the financial statements are free from material misstatement, whether caused by fraud or other irregularity or error. In forming our opinion we also evaluated the overall adequacy of the presentation of information in the financial statements.

OPINION
In our opinion the balance sheet of the Company gives a true and fair view of the Company's state of affairs at 31 December 1993 and has been properly prepared in accordance with the Companies Act 1985, and the consolidated financial statements have been properly prepared in accordance with the provisions of the Companies Act 1985 applicable to insurance companies.

Price Waterhouse
*Chartered Accountants
and Registered Auditors
London
5 April 1994*

The auditors of **Example 1.6 MFI** extend their report to embrace pro forma figures, published by the company to show the notional effect of a flotation and renegotiation of borrowings as if they occurred at a date earlier than they did.

Example 1.6
MFI Furniture Group plc *24 April 1993*
Extract from auditors' report:

REPORT OF THE AUDITORS

To the members of MFI Furniture Group Plc

We have audited the financial statements set out on pages 21 to 48.

Respective responsibilities of directors and auditors
As described above, the Company's directors are responsible for the preparation of financial statements. It is our responsibility to form an independent opinion, based on our audit, on those statements and to report our opinion to you.

Basis of opinion
We conducted our audit in accordance with Auditing Standards issued by the Auditing Practices Board. An audit includes examination, on a test basis, of evidence relevant to the amounts and disclosures in the financial statements. It also includes an assessment of the significant estimates and judgements made by the directors in the preparation of the financial statements, and of whether the accounting policies are appropriate to the Group's circumstances, consistently applied and adequately disclosed.

We planned and performed our audit so as to obtain all the information and explanations which we considered necessary in order to provide us with sufficient evidence to give reasonable assurance that the financial statements are free from material misstatement, whether caused by fraud or other irregularity or error. In forming our opinion we also evaluated the overall adequacy of the presentation of information in the financial statements.

Opinion
In our opinion the financial statements give a true and fair view of the state of affairs of the Company and the Group as at 24 April 1993 and of the profit of the Group for the 52 week period then ended and have been properly prepared in accordance with the Companies Act 1985.

Pro forma profit and loss
A pro forma profit and loss account and related notes are set out on pages 14 and 15 to illustrate the effect on the results had the flotation and renegotiation of the Group's borrowing occurred before the beginning of each period rather than in July 1992. In our opinion, the pro forma profit and loss account, so far as the calculations are concerned, has been properly compiled on the basis set out in the notes thereto.

KPMG Peat Marwick   **London**
Chartered Accountants   **12 July 1993**
Registered Auditors

Finally we contrast the pre-SAS 600 style of audit report, as it appears in the accounts of **Example 1.7 Redrow**, with the SAS 600 format used by the auditors of **Example 1.8 Boots**. It is noteworthy that the latter makes no reference to cost convention or accounting policies – this is a trend which was beginning to emerge towards the end of the period under review.

Example 1.7
Redrow Group plc *30 June 1993*
Extract from auditors' report:

To the members of Redrow Group plc

We have audited the financial statements on pages 22 to 34 in accordance with Auditing Standards.

In our opinion the financial statements give a true and fair view of the state of affairs of the Company and the Group at 30 June 1993 and the profit, total recognised gains and losses and cash flows of the Group for the year then ended and have been properly prepared in accordance with the Companies Act 1985.

Coopers & Lybrand

Chartered Accountants and Registered Auditors
Manchester

3 September 1993

Example 1.8
The Boots Company plc *31 March 1994*
Extract from auditors' report:

Report of the Auditors to the members of The Boots Company PLC.

We have audited the financial statements on pages 40–65.

Respective responsibilities of directors and auditors
As described above, the company's directors are responsible for the preparation of the financial statements. It is our responsibility to form an independent opinion, based on our audit, on those financial statements and to report our opinion to you.

Basis of opinion
We conducted our audit in accordance with Auditing Standards issued by the Auditing Practices Board. An audit includes examination, on a test basis, of evidence relevant to the amounts and disclosures in the financial statements. It also includes an assessment of the significant estimates and judgements made by the directors in the preparation of the financial statements, and of whether the accounting policies are appropriate to the group's circumstances, consistently applied and adequately disclosed.

We planned and performed our audit so as to obtain all the information and explanations which we considered necessary in order to provide us with sufficient evidence to give reasonable assurance that the financial statements are free from material misstatement, whether caused by fraud or other irregularity or error. In forming our opinion we also evaluated the overall adequacy of the presentation of information in the financial statements.

Opinion
In our opinion the financial statements give a true and fair view of the state of affairs of the company and the group as at 31st March 1994 and of the profit of the group for the year then ended and have been properly prepared in accordance with the Companies Act 1985.

KPMG Peat Marwick
Chartered Accountants
Registered Auditors
Birmingham
1st June 1994

Table 2: Capital instruments

	FT-SE 100		Listed		Unlisted		Total	
Number of relevant companies.....	44	(44)	42	(43)	5	(8)	91	(95)
Number of companies.............	100	(100)	150	(150)	50	(50)	300	(300)
	%	(%)	%	(%)	%	(%)	%	(%)
Disclosure and classification of instruments:								
On balance sheet:								
Equity:								
convertibles.....................	12	(9)	18	(12)	40	(25)	17	(12)
redeemables...................	10	(11)	11	(9)	40	(38)	12	(13)
options/warrants...............	5	(2)	7	(5)	20	(—)	7	(3)
optionally convertible or								
redeemable..................	19	(21)	33	(47)	40	(25)	26	(33)
hybrids........................	—	(5)	2	(2)	—	(—)	1	(3)
Debt:								
variable interest................	2	(7)	—	(7)	—	(—)	1	(6)
deep discount..................	12	(11)	2	(2)	—	(—)	7	(6)
convertibles....................	55	(52)	33	(23)	—	(25)	42	(37)
hybrids........................	23	(14)	2	(7)	—	(—)	12	(10)
No disclosure	—	(—)	2	(—)	—	(—)	1	(—)
Disclosure of terminal liability on redemption and conversion price:								
Redeemables with no conversion:								
terminal liabiity disclosed........	19	(21)	14	(12)	20	(25)	17	(17)
Convertibles:								
terminal liability and								
conversion price disclosed.....	55	(48)	45	(56)	40	(—)	50	(47)
terminal liability only disclosed....	2	(2)	2	(2)	—	(13)	2	(3)
conversion price only disclosed ...	34	(34)	38	(33)	20	(13)	35	(32)
No disclosure of terminal liability								
or conversion price..............	10	(16)	7	(9)	33	(50)	10	(16)
Disclosure of income effect:								
Disclosed:								
charged to income	57	(52)	52	(70)	40	(50)	54	(60)

Note

The percentages are based on the number of relevant companies, that is, those with evidence of capital instruments.

Commentary

FRS 4 "Capital instruments", which became effective on 22 June 1994, set out *inter alia* to correct some of the sillier treatments of capital instruments accorded by companies, such as redeemable preference shares appearing on the balance sheet at a nominal value of a minute fraction of their issue/redemption price, or convertible capital bonds represented as capital for purposes of gearing and as bonds for purposes of interest relief. As the date for mandatory adoption approached, many companies made moves towards aligning themselves with the Standard. Very seldom, however, was full adoption of the terms of the Standard seen.

Examples

Example 2.1 Wagon has in issue 7.25p (net) convertible participating preference shares of 10p each. The basis of "participation", apart from the 7.25 preference dividend, is not explained. FRS 4 states that "a brief summary of the rights of each class of shares should be given". The shares were clearly issued at a price substantially greater than 10p each. FRS 4 states that "the amount of non-equity shareholders' funds attributable to [a non-equity instrument] should be the net proceeds of the issue", and that this should be shown or referred to on the face of the balance sheet.

Example 2.1
Wagon Industrial Holdings plc *31 March 1993*
Extract from notes to the accounts:

20. SHARE CAPITAL

	Authorised		Alloted, called up and fully paid	
	Number	£000	Number	£000
Ordinary shares of 25p each				
At 1 April 1992	46,000,000	11,500	33,604,908	8,401
Authorised during year	14,000,000	3,500	—	—
Issued during year	—		10,393,285	2,598
At 31 March 1993	60,000,000	15,000	43,998,192	10,999
7.25p (net) convertible participating preference shares of 10p each				
At 1 April 1992	30,000,000	3,000	20,370,179	2,037
Converted during year	—	—	(2,533)	—
At 31 March 1993	30,000,000	3,000	20,367,646	2,037
Total share capital		**18,000**		**13,036**

The 7.25p (net) convertible participating preference shares allow conversion at the option of the shareholder into fully paid ordinary shares of 25p each during the period to 20 August 2008 on the basis of 28.5714 ordinary shares for every 100 convertible participating preference shares.

Redeemable preference shares are in issue by **Example 2.2 T Cowie**. The company is entitled to redeem these shares at a price not exceeding 120p per share at any time before 1995, failing which they will be redeemed at 31 December 1995 at par. FRS 4 states that the finance costs, which include any redemption premium, should be "recognised at a constant rate or the carrying amount of the debt". However it allows the application of commercial reality (or common sense) in assessing the finance costs. In this instance the likelihood of the company exercising its call option is pretty remote and consequently no provision is made for the premium.

Example 2.2
T Cowie plc *31 December 1993*
Extract from notes to the accounts:

	Authorised		Allotted-Fully Paid	
20 CALLED UP SHARE CAPITAL	1993	1992	1993	1992
Ordinary shares of 5p each	£9,500,000	£8,500,000	£7,154,530	£6,354,062
Number of shares	190,000,000	170,000,000	143,090,594	127,081,241
10½% Redeemable Cumulative				
Preference Shares of £1 each	£2,200,000	£2,200,000	£37,227	£37,227
Number of shares	2,200,000	2,200,000	37,227	37,227

On 14 May, 1993 Shareholders approved an increase in the authorised share capital by the creation of 20,000,000 new ordinary shares of 5p each.

The number of ordinary shares in issue during the year increased as follows:

Date	Number of Shares	Event
28 April, 1993	370,000	Exercise of share options
20 May, 1993	237,000	Scrip Dividend
27 May, 1993	13,972,956	Placement of shares for the acquisition of The Keep Trust Ltd.
2 June, 1993	410,000	Exercise of share options
4 June, 1993	900,000	Exercise of share options
26 August, 1993	30,000	Exercise of share options
29 September, 1993	30,000	Exercise of share options
15 October, 1993	59,389	Scrip Dividend
	16,009,353	

At 31 December, 1993 there were outstanding options to receive allotments of 1,688,000 ordinary shares at subscription prices ranging from 49.6p per share to 248.5p per share, exercisable at various dates up to 23 September, 2003.

In accordance with the Company's Memorandum and Articles of Association, the 10¹/₂% Redeemable Cumulative Preference Shares are redeemable at the Company's option at any time before 1995 at a price not exceeding 120p per share, failing which they will be redeemed on 31 December, 1995 at par.

An instrument which is growing in popularity is the warrant, now in issue by 6% of companies with complex financial instruments. FRS 4 states that "the net proceeds from the issue of . . . warrants for equity shares should be credited direct to shareholders' funds". **Example 2.3 Pilkington** issued warrants during the year and the proceeds are credited to other reserves.

Example 2.3
Pilkington plc *31 March 1994*
Extract from notes to the accounts:

29 Movements on Share Premium Account and Reserves For the year ended 31st March 1994	Share premium account	Revaluation reserve	Other reserves	Goodwill reserve	Profit and less account	Total
	£m	£m	£m	£m	£m	£m
Group						
At beginning of year	53.0	295.1	210.4	(345.8)	301.8	514.5
Retained profit for year	—	—	—	—	8.2	8.2
Premium on shares issued	2.3	—	—	—	—	2.3
Premium on warrants issued (note 28)	—	—	16.4	—	—	16.4
Acquisition goodwill written off (note 31)	—	—	—	(66.4)	—	(66.4)
Acquisition goodwill written back (note 6)	—	—	—	—	18.3	18.3
Revaluations in year	—	(6.9)	—	—	—	(6.9)
Unrealised exchange rate adjustments	—	24.0	1.3	(7.2)	(18.2)	(0.1)
Transfers between reserves	—	(14.9)	10.2	—	4.7	—
Other movements	—	0.9	0.3	—	(2.5)	(1.3)
At end of year	55.3	298.2	238.6	(419.4)	312.3	485.0

The redeemable convertible preference share is still the most usual of the complex capital instruments, although its popularity appears to be on the wane – down by 20% on last year. **Example 2.4 BBA**, with such shares in issue, is one of the first, and so far very few, companies to provide the "brief summary of rights" called for by FRS 4.

Example 2.4
BBA Group plc   *31 December 1993*
Extract from notes to the accounts:

13 Capital and reserves		Company		Company	
		Allotted, called up and fully paid		Authorised	
		1993 millions	1992 millions	**1993 millions**	1992 millions
Share capital	**Number of shares**				
	Ordinary 25p shares	**404.9**	313.5	**600.0**	500.0
	5% Cumulative preference £1 shares	**0.2**	0.2	**0.2**	0.2
	6.75% Cumulative redeemable convertible preference £1 shares	**89.9**	89.9	**95.0**	95.0
	Nominal value of shares	**£m**	£m	**£m**	£m
	Equity shares				
	Ordinary 25p shares	**101.1**	78.3	**150.0**	125.0
	Non-equity shares				
	5% Cumulative preference £1 shares	**0.2**	0.2	**0.2**	0.2
	6.75% Cumulative redeemable convertible preference £1 shares	**89.9**	89.9	**95.0**	95.0
		90.1	90.1	**95.2**	95.2
		191.2	168.4	**245.2**	220.2

. . . . .

Rights of non-equity interests

5% Cumulative £1 preference shares:
i. entitle holders, in priority to holders of all other classes of shares, to a fixed cumulative preferential dividend at a rate of 3.5% per annum per share payable half yearly in equal amounts on 1 February and 1 August;
ii. on a return of capital on a winding up, or otherwise, will carry the right to repayment of capital together with a premium of 12.5p per share and a sum equal to any arrears or deficiency of dividend; this right is in priority to the rights of the convertible preference and ordinary shareholders;
iii. carry the right to attend and vote at a general meeting of the Company only if, at the date of the notice convening the meeting, payment of the dividend to which they are entitled is six months or more in arrears, or if a resolution is to be considered at the meeting for winding-up the Company or reducing its share capital or sanctioning the sale of the undertaking of the Company or varying or abrogating any of the special rights attaching to them.

6.75% Cumulative redeemable convertible preference £1 shares:

i.   entitle holders (subject to the prior rights of the 5% cumulative £1 preference shares) to a fixed cumulative preferential dividend at a rate of 6.75% per annum per share, payable half yearly in equal amounts on 31 May and 30 November;

ii.   carry the right to be converted into ordinary shares at the option of the holder on 31 May in any of the years 1994 to 2005 inclusive at the rate of 54.64 ordinary shares for every £100 nominal of convertible preferences shares;

iii.   will be redeemable by the Company on 31 May 2006 at par (if not previously converted or redeemed) and any arrears of dividend will be paid;

iv.   on a return of capital on a winding up, or otherwise, will carry the right to repayment of capital and payment of accrued dividends in priority to ordinary shares but after the 5% cumulative £1 preference shares;

v.   carry the right to attend and vote at a general meeting of the Company only if, at the date of the notice convening the meeting, payment of the dividend to which they are entitled is six months or more in arrears, or if a resolution is to be considered at the meeting for winding-up the Company, or for modifying or abrogating any special rights attaching to them.

The principal reaction of companies to publication of FRED 3 (the precursor of FRS 4) was to move convertible capital bonds out of capital into debt. **Example 2.5 HIH** does this in its most recent accounts, although it continues to maintain that conversion to share capital is "highly probable". **Example 2.6 BICC** states that it intends, subject to shareholders' approval, to convert its capital bonds during 1994. Accordingly it invokes the true and fair override and includes the capital bonds in capital.

Example 2.5
HIH plc *30 September 1993*
Extract from notes to the accounts:

21. CONVERTIBLE CAPITAL BONDS

	1993 £000's	1992 £000's
Convertible Capital Bonds	33,422	28,106

On 12 August 1991, an issue of US $50,000,000 7½ per cent Convertible Capital Bonds, 2006 ("the Bonds"), was made by a subsidiary company, HIH Capital Ltd. The Bonds are guaranteed on a subordinated basis by the Company, and are convertible into Redeemable Preference Shares at HIH Capital Ltd., which in turn are immediately exchangeable for Ordinary Shares of 5 pence each in the Company. The conversion rate, which is based upon the paid-up value of the Redeemable Preference Shares and a fixed rate of exchange of £1.00 = US $1.6825, is 310 pence per Ordinary Share and is subject to adjustment in certain circumstances. At this conversion rate the number of Ordinary Shares to be issued on conversion and exchange of each unit of US $1,000 comprised in a Bond would be 191.

The terms of the issue are such that the Directors consider it highly probable that the proceeds of the Bonds will in due course become part of the Company's called up share capital and will therefore be available to the Company on a permanent basis. Accordingly, at 30 September 1992, the normal balance sheet format specified by the Companies Act 1985 was modified to include the Bonds following Capital and Reserves in the Consolidated Balance Sheet. However, at 30 September 1993 the Directors have decided, that following publication of the UK Exposure Draft "Accounting for Capital Instruments", to include the Bonds under "Creditors – amounts following due after more than one year".

Included within amounts owed to Group companies on the Company Balance Sheet is a debenture of US $50,000,000 (£33,422,000) owed to HIH Capital Ltd., given in consideration for the on-loan of the net proceeds of the Bond issue of US $47,300,000 (£31,618,000). The terms of the debenture are similar to those of the Bonds.

Example 2.6
BICC plc *31 December 1993*
Extract from notes to the accounts:

18 Convertible capital bonds

On 20 July 1990 a wholly owned subsiduary undertaking of BICC plc issued by way of rights to BICC plc ordinary shareholders £177·1m of 10·75% Convertible Capital Bonds maturing 2020. The bonds have a par value of £1 each and are convertible at the option of the holder at any date after 1 July 1992 into exchangeable redeemable preference shares of the issuer which will then be immediately exchanged for new BICC plc ordinary shares. The effective conversion price is 488p per BICC plc ordinary share subject to adjustment in certain circumstances.

Payments under the bonds are guaranteed by BICC plc on a subordinated basis. The net proceeds have been loaned to BICC plc and are included in BICC plc's loans due to subsidiary undertakings as set out in Note 9(b).

There is no put option under which bondholders can require early redemption and there are no cross default provisions or financial covenants. Also in certain circumstances the issuer may elect to suspend and accumulate coupon payments on the bonds without default. Furthermore it is the Company's intention, subject to shareholders' approval, to exercise its right to convert the bonds into cumulative convertible redeemable preference shares of BICC plc during 1994. The Companies Act 1985 would normally require that the bonds be classified as a creditor falling due after more than one year. However, for the reasons explained above, in order to give a true and fair view, the balance sheet format specified by the Companies Act has been modified to include the convertible capital bonds as permanent capital.

It is not unusual for interest rates on loan stock or bonds to be linked to LIBOR or bank base rates, and we do not include such bonds in our analysis. However **Example 2.7 Anglian Water** has in issue loans stock the value of whose capital and interest elements are linked to movements in the Retail Price Index.

Example 2.7
Anglian Water plc *31 March 1993*
Extract from notes to the accounts:

	Group		Company	
18. Loans and other borrowings falling due after more than one year	**1993 £m**	1992 £m	**1993 £m**	1992 £m
Repayable wholly after five years				
5.125% Index Linked Loan Stock 2008 (a)	117.1	112.9	117.1	112.9
12% Fixed Rate Bond 2014	100.0	100.0	100.0	100.0
European Investment Bank 1999	25.0	—	—	—
Other	0.3	0.1	—	—
Repayable by instalments, any one of which is due for repayment after five years				
European Investment Bank 1995/2007 (interest in the range 9.9–11.5%)	105.0	105.0	—	—
Finance leases (b)	100.3	41.0	—	—
Other borrowings	26.5	29.1	—	—
Repayable wholly within five years				
Other loans	22.2	1.7	21.6	1.6
Finance leases (b)	1.0	1.7	—	—
Total loans and other borrowings	497.4	391.5	138.7	214.5
Less amounts included in creditors falling due within one year	(1.8)	(1.7)	(0.4)	—
	495.6	389.8	**238.3**	214.5
Due for repayment as follows:				
Between one and two years	1.1	1.7	0.4	0.4
Between two and five years	40.1	11.2	20.8	1.2
After five years	454.4	376.9	217.1	212.9
	495.6	389.8	**238.3**	214.5

(a) The value of the capital and interest elements of the Index Linked Loan Stock are linked to movements in the Retail Price Index. The increase in the capital value during the year of £4.2m (1992 – £5.9m) has been taken to the profit and loss account as part of interest payable.

(b) Amounts due under finance leases include £0.2m (1992 – £0.7m) payable between one and five years and £100.3m (1992 – £41.0m) payable after five years.

(c) Of the unspecified loans and other borrowings £21.4m (1992 – £1.5m) are at fixed rates and the remainder are at variable rates. Loans and other borrowings include £1.4m (1992 – £1.5m) secured on the revenues of a subsidiary undertaking.

While the impact on profits of issuing deep discount loan stock, rather than loan stock at a commercial rate of interest, is not materially different, the major cash value of the finance costs does not have to be earmarked until the stock matures. The book value of 4% deep discount bonds issued by **Example 2.8 Tesco** increases year by year towards its maturity value of £125 million. By contrast, the company elects to set aside funds to provide for the excess of the net present value of the redemption value of its ⅛% deep discount bonds over its book value.

Example 2.8
Tesco plc *26 February 1994*
Extract from notes to the accounts:

Note 16	Creditors – Amounts falling due after more than one year		Group		Company	
			1994 **£m**	1993 £m	**1994** **£m**	1993 £m
		4% Unsecured deep discount loan stock 2006 (a)	**72.8**	70.8	**72.8**	70.8
		Finance leases (note 20)	**40.8**	45.1	—	—
		10³/₈% Bonds 2002 (b)	**200.0**	200.0	**200.0**	200.0
		⅛% Deep discount bond 2012 (c)	**50.0**	50.0	**63.2**	56.7
		8³/₄% Bonds 2003 (d)	**200.0**	—	**200.0**	—
		E.C.S.C. loans 1996–1998 (e)	**79.2**	73.8	**5.4**	—
		Other loans	**8.8**	—	—	—
			651.6	439.7	**541.4**	327.5
		Amounts owed to group undertakings	—	—	**200.0**	200.0
		Accruals and deferred income (note 15 (c))	**38.4**	—	—	—
			690.0	439.7	**741.4**	527.5
		Convertible capital bond (note 18)	**200.0**	200.0	—	—
			890.0	639.7	**741.4**	527.5

a) The 4% unsecured deep discount loan stock is redeemable at a par value of £125m in 2006.

b) The 10³/₈% bonds are redeemable at a par value of £200m in 2002.

c) The ⅛% deep discount bond is redeemable at a par value of £428.9m in 2012. The redemption value as at 26 February 1994 is £63.2m (1993 – £56.7m) against which a deposit balance with the same bank of £13.2m (1993 – £6.7m) has been offset under a legal right of set-off.

d) The 8³/₈% bonds are redeemable at a par value of £200m in 2003.

e) E.C.S.C. refers to the European Coal and Steel Community.

The most popular of the complex debt instruments is the convertible bond. FRS 4 increases the parameters of this classification by introducing convertible preference shares issued by subsidiaries and guaranteed by the parent. Such instruments were previously most often classified as minority interests. In its 1992 accounts **Example 2.9 Costain** switched its subsidiary's preference shares from minority interests to debt, and they remain so classified in the company's most recent accounts.

Example 2.9
Costain Group plc   *31 December 1993*
Extract from notes to the accounts

20 Redeemable preference shares
A subsidiary undertaking, Costain Finance NV, incorporated in the Netherlands Antilles
with limited liability, had in issue at 31 December 1993 24 (1992 7,521) 7½%
Guaranteed Redeemable Convertible Reference Shares 2003. The shares are
guaranteed on a subordinated basis by Costain Group PLC, and convertible, at any
time up to 17 August 2003, into ordinary shares of Costain Group PLC at £3.05 per
ordinary share. The shares can be redeemed upon the revocation, in certain
circumstances, of the subordinated guarantee at prices between the issue price and
101% thereof. Any shares outstanding on 24 August 2003 will be redeemed at their
issue price. During the year 2,464 preference shares were redeemed at a price of
£4,912.50 per share and on 24 August 1993, 5,033 preference shares were redeemed at
their issue price.

In general terms, the conversion price of convertible instruments is disclosed; the
redemption price of preference shares is usually shown while the redemption at par of
dated bonds/loan stock is taken as read. **Example 2.10 Kingfisher** discloses that its zero
coupon loan stock, book value £89 million, is £225 million.

Example 2.10
Kingfisher plc   *29 January 1994*
Extract from notes to the accounts:

18. CREDITORS

| | GROUP | | COMPANY | |
£ MILLIONS	**1994**	1993	**1994**	1993
Amounts falling due after more than one year				
8.5% Convertible Unsecured Loan Stock 2000	—	46.0	—	46.0
Zero Coupon Loan Stock 2003	**89.2**	80.7	**89.2**	80.7
Loan notes 1994	—	3.6	—	3.6
Bank loans	**294.7**	—	—	—
Medium term notes	**1.0**	2.0	**1.0**	2.0
External funding	**384.9**	132.3	**90.2**	132.3
Accruals and deferred income	**80.9**	—	—	—
	465.8	132.3	**90.2**	132.3
The external funding falls due for repayment as follows:				
Between one and two years	**62.5**	4.6	—	4.6
Between two and five years	**233.2**	1.0	**1.0**	1.0
After five years other than by instalments	**89.2**	126.7	**89.2**	126.7
	384.9	132.3	**90.2**	132.3

The company made full conversion of the 8.5% Convertible Unsecured Loan Stock 2000
at the rate of 46.119 shares per £100 of stock with effect from 30 June 1993.

The Zero Coupon Loan Stock 2003 has an implicit fixed interest rate of 10.3% which
has been swapped into a floating rate interest obligation against six month LIBOR.
Unless redeemed earlier the loan stock is repayable at its par value of £225.7m on 28
April 2003.

Both the conversion price and the redemption value of preference shares issued by **Example 2.11 Tomkins** are stated in the notes to the accounts.

Example 2.11
Tomkins plc   *1 May 1993*
Extract from notes to the accounts:

18 SHARE CAPITAL	Authorised		Allotted & fully paid	
Ordinary shares of 5p each:	Number	£million	Number	£million
At 2 May 1992	430,000,000	21.5	281,843,797	14.1
Increase	908,960,220	45.4	833,285,781	41.6
Total ordinary shares at 1 May 1993	1,338,960,220	66.9	1,115,129,668	55.7
Preference shares of £1 each:				
At 2 May 1992	95,000,000	95.0	48,834,392	48.9
Converted	—	—	(48,834,392)	(48.8)
At 1 May 1993	95,000,000	95.0	—	—
Preference shares of 20p each				
At 2 May 1992	85,000,000	17.0	82,859,474	16.6
Converted	—	—	(564,251)	(0.1)
At 1 May 1993	85,000,000	17.0	82,295,223	16.5
Total preference shares at 1 May 1993	180,000,000	112.0	82,295,223	16.5
Total share capital at 2 May 1992	610,000,000	133.5	413,537,663	79.5
Total share capital at 1 May 1993	**1,518,960,220**	**178.9**	**1,197,424,891**	**72.2**

....

The 6.25p (net) cumulative convertible redeemable preference shares of 20p each (series 2 preference shares) were issued on terms that they could be converted, at the shareholder's option, into fully paid ordinary shares of 5p each of the Company on 30 September in any of the years 1989 to 2008 on the basis of 5p nominal amount of ordinary share capital for every 54.28p nominal amount of series 2 preference share capital. When 75% or more of the series 2 preference shares have been converted, the Company then has the right to convert the remainder. Following the capitalisation issue in August 1992 the conversion terms are 10p nominal amount of ordinary share capital for every 54.28p nominal amount of series 2 preference share capital. 564,251 series 2 preference shares were converted on 30 September 1992 into 415,807 ordinary shares of 5p each. The series 2 preference shares are redeemable at 100p each on 30 September 2013.

Rather unusually, **Example 2.12 Next** states that dated convertible bonds are repayable at par, but does not disclose the conversion price.

Example 2.12
Next plc *31 January 1994*
Extract from notes to the accounts:

17 Creditors: amounts falling due after more than one year

	Group		Company	
	1994	1993	**1994**	1993
	£m	£m	**£m**	£m
5.75% Convertible bonds due 2003	**0.5**	0.5	**0.5**	0.5
Obligations under finance leases	**—**	0.5	**—**	—
Due within the periods shown below	**0.5**	1.0	**0.5**	0.5

The 5,75% convertible bonds are unsecured and are repayable at part in 2003, or earlier at the Company's option.

More usually, **Example 2.13 Allied Lyons** discloses the conversion price of dated bonds, but allows it to be assumed that redemption in 2008 would be effected at par.

Example 2.13
Allied Lyons plc *5 March 1994*
Extract from notes to the accounts

19. LOAN CAPITAL AND OTHER BORROWINGS	Redemption date	**1994 £m**	1993 £m
....			
Subsidiary undertakings			
Secured loans (5.1% to 9.7%)	—	**15**	25
Unsecured loans			
**Multiple option facility (3.3% (USS) to 5.3% (£))	1994 to 1995	**119**	54
**US $150m Guaranteed notes (6.5%)	1997	**101**	104
**US $400m Guaranteed senior notes (9.39% and 9.59%)	2001 and 2006	**268**	278
**Guaranteed convertible subordinated bonds (6³/₄%)	2008	**200**	—
Other loans (2.8% to 9.1%)	—	**388**	379
		1,076	815
Total subsidiary undertakings		**1,091**	840

....

The 6³/₄% guaranteed convertible subordinated bonds may be converted into Allied-Lyons plc ordinary shares at any time prior to redemption in 2008. The bonds may be redeemed by the issuer (Allied-Lyons Financial Services Plc) after 21 July 1998 or earlier if 85% of bond holders have elected to convert. The bonds would convert into 32m shares at the 5 March 1994 conversion price of 622p. The conversion price was adjusted to 604p with effect from 30 April 1994 as a result of the rights issue.

Example 2.14 Bodycote neither discloses the conversion price of its convertible loan stock, nor if and at what figure it will eventually be repaid.

Example 2.14
Bodycote International plc   *31 December 1993*
Extract from notes to the accounts:

14. Creditors
Amounts falling due within one year:

Bank loans	861	898	—	204
Bank overdrafts	2,886	2,717	6,709	3,995
10% convertible loan stock	100	100	100	100
10% loan notes	100	100	100	100
Trade creditors	8,120	5,198	54	27
Amounts owed to subsidiary undertakings	—	—	72	1,500
Corporation tax	903	1,353	—	—
Proposed dividends	1,878	1,794	1,878	1,794
Advance corporation tax	803	886	803	880
Other taxes and social security	1,852	1,688	21	22
Other creditors	1,751	2,113	1,239	1,174
Dividends to minority interests	184	360	—	—
Accruals and deferred income	2,828	4,031	103	194
	22,266	21,238	11,079	9,990

The income effect of dividends paid on preference shares is invariably stated in the notes to the accounts. The income effect of interest on convertible bonds/loan stock is usually not shown separately, but rolled into the overall interest figure, as in the accounts of **Example 2.15 Inchcape**. Such instruments as warrants (see **Example 2.3 Pilkington**) do not give rise to a charge against income.

Example 2.15
Inchcape plc *31 December 1993*
Extracts from notes to the accounts:

	1993	1992
6 INTEREST	**£m**	£m

Interest payable and similar charges:

	1993 £m	1992 £m
On bank loans and overdrafts and other loans:		
– repayable within 5 years not by instalments	**48.6**	40.0
– repayable within 5 years by instalments	**4.3**	2.8
	52.9	42.8
– repayable wholly or partly in more than 5 years including Subordinated Bonds	**6.1**	0.7
Other interest	**7.4**	6.8
	66.4	50.3
Interest receivable	**(39.2)**	(38.2)
	27.2	12.1

Interest includes £1.5m (1992 – £1.5m) payable in respect of finance leases.

. . . . .

	Group		Inchcape plc	
25 CREDITORS – AMOUNTS FALLING DUE AFTER MORE THAN ONE YEAR	**1993 £m**	1992 £m	**1993 £m**	1992 £m
Borrowings: – note 26				
Bank loans and secured overdrafts (secured £6.3m – 1992 £5.8m)	**8.5**	8.9	—	—
Net obligations under finance leases	**17.0**	12.6	—	—
Other borrowings (Group – secured £13.0m – 1992 £33.3m)	**13.1**	42.3	—	6.0
	38.6	63.8	—	6.0
6¼% Convertible Subordinated Bonds Due 2008 – note 26	**125.0**	—	**125.0**	—
Other:				
Trade creditors	**5.2**	13.1	—	—
Amounts owed to associates	**0.5**	—	—	—
Corporate taxation	**1.1**	1.2	—	—
Other creditors	**0.7**	1.3	—	—
Accruals and deferred income	**1.0**	—	—	—
Net disposal proceeds of Toyota (GB) – note 12	**30.0**	26.7	—	—
	38.5	42.3	—	—
Total creditors falling due after more than one year	**202.1**	106.1	**125.0**	6.0

Table 3: Contingencies

	FT-SE 100	Listed	Unlisted	Total
Number of relevant companies	85	106	29	220
Number of companies...............	100	150	50	300
	%	%	%	%

Disclosure of contingent gains and losses:
Contingency quantified in respect of:

	FT-SE 100	Listed	Unlisted	Total
Guarantees:				
to banks.........................	33	28	24	30
other..........................	7	4	10	6
unspecified	41	40	45	41
Deferred consideration	1	7	10	5
Forward foreign exchange contracts. .	16	5	7	9
Forward mercantile contracts	1	—	—	1
Warranties and indemnities..........	—	2	3	1
Discounted bills.....................	11	13	3	11
Documentary credits	2	4	3	3
Legal action:				
gains...........................	1	—	3	1
losses..........................	5	6	3	5
Other............................	17	13	14	15
Unspecified.......................	11	3	7	6
Aggregate of more than one of				
above	12	6	10	9

Contingency not quantified in respect of:

	FT-SE 100	Listed	Unlisted	Total
Guarantees:				
to banks.........................	2	—	—	1
to purchasers of former:				
subsidiaries....................	—	1	—	1
other..........................	1	1	—	1
unspecified	1	5	3	3
Deferred consideration	—	2	—	1
Forward foreign exchange contracts. .	—	2	—	1
Forward mercantile contracts	1	—	—	1
Warranties and indemnities..........	2	—	—	1
Discounted bills....................	1	1	—	1
Legal action:				
gains...........................	1	—	—	1
losses..........................	33	14	14	21
Other............................	5	5	—	4
Unspecified.......................	1	1	—	1
Aggregate of more than one of				
above	1	1	—	1

Note:
The percentages are based on the number of relevant companies, that is, those with evidence of contingent gains or losses.

Commentary

As the effective date for FRS 5 "Reporting the substance of transaction" approaches, companies will be looking closely at their contingent liabilities to establish if an asset and/or liability, as defined by the Standard, in fact exists. If so, the item will in future require to be brought on balance sheet. Meantime the majority of companies describe contingent liabilities of one sort or another in the notes to their accounts, and while most are quantified as to their potential risk, a number do not indicate the level of possible cost.

Examples

Example 3.1 Lloyds Chemists discloses that it provides bank guarantees amounting to £4 million on account of former customers, while **Example 3.2 Amber Day** discloses contingent liabilities in respect of property leases sold to third parties, without indicating the downside risk.

Example 3.1
Lloyds Chemists plc *30 June 1993*
Extract from notes to the accounts:

26. CONTINGENT LIABILITIES
Under the terms of the Pharmacy Finance Scheme, certain subsidiaries of Macarthy PLC have guaranteed liabilities of customers of its former medical wholsale business to their bankers. At 30th June 1993, the amounts outstanding for which guarantees had been given were £4,377,000 (1992: £6,188,000).

Example 3.2
Amber Day Holdings plc *31 July 1993*
Extract from notes to the accounts:

22 **Contingent Liabilities**

. . . .

There are other contingent liabilities of the Company and of the Group in respect of property leases formerly entered into by the Group in the ordinary course of business (including acting as guarantor) but which have subsequently been sold to third parties.

Other guarantees include the guarantee given by **Example 3.3 Galliford** of a minimum return to the investors in its special vehicle company. Such companies are defined by FRS 4 as quasi-subsidiaries and "the assets, liabilities, profits, losses and cash flow of a quasi-subsidiary should be included in the group financial statements . . . in the same way as if they were those of a subsidiary".

Example 3.3
Galliford plc   *30 June 1993*
Extract from notes to the accounts:

24   Contingent liability

On 23 March 1993, Galliford plc entered into a commitment to promote a Business Expansion Scheme (BES) with a maximum share subscription level of £5 million. The group's principal responsibility is to construct and provide suitable residential properties for lease to the BES company, B.EXBES I Plc. The group retains the reversionary freehold interests in the relevant properties.

The share offer was fully subscribed and guarantees investors a minimum aggregate return of £5,900,000. This amount is jointly and severally guaranteed by Galliford plc, Stamford Construction Limited and J Hodgson Limited.

The guarantees will be discharged on 5 April 1998 through the payment of £5,900,000 for either the properties or for the entire issued share capital of B.EXBES I Plc. The guarantor companies therefore have a contingent liability in respect of the potential deficiency between the ultimate realisable value of the properties and the £5,900,000 to be paid. The directors at present do not believe that there will be a liability for such a shortfall.

By 30 June 1993 advance payments totalling £4,543,000 had been received from the BES company in respect of the properties committed to the scheme, and at that date eleven properties had been completed and transferred.

The quantified contingent liabilities of **Example 3.4 Concentric** include performance bonds and forward foreign exchange contracts. **Example 3.5 Yorkshire Chemicals** quantifies the amount of bills discounted. By contrast, **Example 3.6 Lucas** refers to discounted bills and FFECs as being in the ordinary course of business, and makes no effort to quantify the risk.

Example 3.4
Concentric plc *30 September 1993*
Extract from notes to the accounts:

19. **Contingent liabilities**	**1993**	1992
	Group	*Group*
	£000	£000
(a) Customers' bills of exchange discounted	—	220
Performance bonds and guarantees	**493**	1,078
Forward exchange contracts	**4,170**	2,156
	4,663	3,454

(b) The group commitment in respect of future lease payments is not material.

Example 3.5
Yorkshire Chemicals plc *31 December 1993*
Extract from notes to the accounts:

24. **CONTINGENT LIABILITIES**	Group		Company	
	1993	1992	**1993**	1992
	£'000	£'000	**£'000**	£'000
Guarantees given in respect of bank loans	—	—	**2,011**	5,101
Bills discounted	**4,687**	4,715	**3,214**	3,343

Example 3.6
Lucas Industries plc *31 July 1993*
Extract from notes to the accounts:

Note 24: Contingent liabiities	**Group**	**Parent company**
	£million	**£million**
Bank guarantees	**4.0**	**4.0**
Guarantees of borrowings of subsidiary undertakings		**394.0**

There were contingent liabilities arising in the ordinary course of business relating principally to discounted bills, bonds outstanding, advance payments by customers and forward sales and purchase of foreign currencies. In the opinion of the directors adequate provision has been made for losses which might arise.

Deferred consideration, the amount of which is dependent on the results of the acquired business, is usually reported as a contingency. **Example 3.7 Hays** states the amount which will be payable if a specified level of earnings is achieved. **Example 3.8 Laporte** confines itself to stating that additional purchase consideration is payable, dependent on the future results of certain subsidiaries.

Example 3.7
Hays plc *30 June 1993*
Extract from notes to the accounts:

21 Contingent Liabilities

	Group		Company	
	1993	1992	**1993**	1992
	£'000	£'000	**£'000**	£'000
Bank and other guarantees	**100**	100	**20,385**	27,008
Other	**309**	502	**—**	—
	409	602	**20,385**	27,008

Performance bonds and other guarantees given in the normal course of business are not included above.

There is additional contingent purchase consideration payable in respect of the acquisition of Fril up to an estimated maximum of French Francs 75,000,000, based upon an earnings formula for the years ending 30 June 1994 and 1995.

Example 3.8
Laporte plc *2 January 1994*
Extract from notes to the accounts:

Note 25 Contingent Liabilities

	Group		Company	
	1993	1992	**1993**	1992
	£m	£m	**£m**	£m
Guarantees of loans of subsidiary undertakings...	**—**	—	**—**	5.5
Guarantees under licence agreement and other guarantees	**12.8**	11.0	**—**	—

Additional purchase consideration is payable dependent upon the future results of certain subsidiary undertakings.

Example 3.9 Raine states that its contingencies included letters of credit amounting to £3 million.

Example 3.9
Raine plc *30 June 1993*
Extract from notes to the accounts:

24. Commitments and contingent liabilities
Future capital commitments for which no provision has been made in these accounts are as follows:

....

Performance bonds amounting to £39,938,000 (1992 – £29,503,000) have been entered into by subsidiary undertakings in the normal course of business.
The Company has a contingent liability in respect of guarantees given to support borrowings and performance bonds of subsidiary undertakings amounting to £86,089,000 (1992 – £66,896,000) and a contingent liability in respect of letters of credit amounting to £3,210,000. The Company has also guaranteed the performance of certain contracts by some of its subsidiary undertakings.

The one type of contingency which does not lend itself readily to quantification is legal action. Of the small number which put a figure on the possible outcome, **Example 3.10 Westland** discloses an award in its favour which is being contested by the defendants, while **Example 3.11 GEC** quantifies the level of damages being sought against it.

Example 3.10
Westland Group plc *1 October 1993*
Extract from notes to the accounts:

30 Claims, arbitration and litigation
(i) In its Interim Award of 21 June 1991 in the arbitration proceedings in Geneva brought by Westland Helicopters Limited (WHL) in 1980 against the Arab Organisation for Industrialisation (AOI) and three of its member States (namely the State of Qatar, the Kingdom of Saudi Arabia and the United Arab Emirates) and the Arab British Helicopter Company (ABH), the Arbitral Tribunal held that AOI was liable to WHL for damages for breach of contract, that the three States were subsidiarily liable and that WHL had no responsibility for the breach. These damages were determined by the Arbitral Tribunal in its Final Award of 28 June 1993, in which it was held that the amount of damages and costs due to WHL was approximately £385 million, plus interest to the date of payment, but stated that WHL remained a debtor of ABH in respect of net advance payments of some £30 million received prior to the breach of contract. The Arbitral Tribunal ordered payment to WHL of the amount of the damages and costs, plus interest; no order was made against WHL for repayment of the net advance payments.

No appeals against the Final Award have been filed by AOI or by ABH. The three States have appealed to the Swiss Supreme Court against the Awards in so far as they affect them. WHL has filed a limited appeal in respect of that part of the Final Award relating to the net advance payments.

After the commencement of the arbitration in May 1980, various court proceedings were instituted in Egypt against WHL. In certain of these proceedings the Egyptian courts gave judgments purporting to declare the arbitration void and to hold WHL liable for specific performance and to pay damages, which may exceed £200 million;

other Egyptian court proceedings are still pending. WHL has not appeared in any of these proceedings and the Directors have been advised that no judgment in the Egyptian court proceedings would be recognised or enforced in England. The Directors continue to be satisfied that no provision need be made in respect of these proceedings.

Litigation continues to surround this matter and the ultimate financial outcome to the Group cannot be predicted with certainty. However, the Directors are hopeful that this long running dispute is approaching a satisfactory resolution.

(ii) The Company and its subsidiary undertakings are the subject of certain other claims and legal proceedings which are regarded as unlikely to succeed or to have a material effect on the consolidated financial position.

Example 3.11
The General Electric Company plc *31 March 1993*
Extract from notes to the accounts:

17   Contingent liabilities

	Group		Company	
	1993	1992	**1993**	1992
	£ million	£ million	£ million	£ million
Guarantees	**1**	1	—	—
Bills discounted	**2**	2	—	—
Other	**35**	35	—	—
	38	38	—	—

Hughes Aircraft Company has brought arbitration proceedings against the Company and certain of its subsidiaries alleging that obligations to Hughes were breached as a result of the acquisition of the Ferranti Defence Systems Group business and the subsequent award to GEC Ferranti Defence Systems Limited of the development contract for the European Fighter Aircraft's radar. Hughes also alleges that the Company conspired with the subsidiaries to misappropriate information proprietary to Hughes. Hughes is seeking damages of up to US $185 million and the payment of a royalty on sales of radars designed by the subsidiaries from the alleged misappropriation of information. The Company and the subsidiaries deny any liability to Hughes and continue to defend the proceedings. The Company and its subsidiaries have been advised that there are meritorious defences to all the claims brought by Hughes and they have counter claimed for an amount in excess of $5 million.

Among the 21% of companies which record unquantified potential losses from legal actions, **Example 3.12 British Petroleum** describes the circumstances giving rise to a number of lawsuits against it.

Example 3.12
The British Petroleum Company plc *31 December 1993*
Extract from notes to the accounts:

32 Contingent liabilities

There were contingent liabilities at 31 December 1993 in respect of guarantees and indemnities entered into as part of, and claims arising from, the ordinary course of the group's business, upon which no material losses are likely to arise.

Subsidiaries of BP America Inc. are engaged in administrative proceedings in which the State of Alaska is challenging the subsidiaries' valuation of crude oil for production tax purposes since 1979 and their determination of taxable income for income tax purposes for the years 1978–81. BP believes that its subsidiaries have complied with applicable tax legislation and the subsidiaries are disputing the State's claims. While the amounts claimed and subject to claim are substantial, it is believed that the ultimate resolution will not have a material effect on the financial position, liquidity or results of operations of the group.

Approximately 200 lawsuits are being pursued in State and Federal Courts in Alaska seeking compensatory and punitive damages arising out of the Exxon Valdez oil spill in Prince William Sound in March 1989. Most of those suits name Exxon, Alyeska Pipeline Service Company ('Alyeska'), which operates the oil terminal at Valdez, and the seven oil companies which own Alyeska. Alyeska initially responded to the spill until the response was taken over by Exxon. BP owns a 50% interest in Alyeska through a subsidiary of BP America Inc. During 1993, Alyeska and its owners settled substantially all of these lawsuits except for a small number of plaintiffs who opted out of the settlements. The accounts reflect the group's share of the estimated cost of the settlements. Although the courts approved the settlements in 1993, the approval is not final and has been appealed by Exxon on the grounds, inter alia, that the settlements may affect as yet unasserted claims between Exxon and Alyeska arising out of the oil spill. BP is unable to quantify the amounts that may be at issue. If any claims are asserted by Exxon which affect Alyeska and its owners, BP would defend the claims vigorously.

The group is subject to numerous national and local environmental laws and regulations concerning its products, operations and other activities. These laws and regulations may require the group to take future action to remediate the effects on the environment of prior disposal or release of chemical or petroleum substances by the group or other parties. Such contingencies may exist for various sites including refineries, chemical plants, oil fields, service stations, terminals and waste disposal sites. In addition, the group may have obligations relating to prior asset sales or closed facilities. The ultimate requirement for remediation and its cost is inherently difficult to estimate. However, the estimated cost of known environmental obligations has been provided in these accounts in accordance with the group's accounting policies. While the amounts of future costs could be significant and could be material to the group's results of operations in the period in which they are recognised, BP does not expect these costs to have a material effect on the group's financial position or liquidity.

The parent company has issued guarantees under which amounts outstanding at 31 December 1993 were £6,819 million (£8.126 million) including £6,781 million (£8.008 million) in respect of borrowings by its subsidiary undertakings.

Among the transactions in the ordinary course of business from which contingent liabilities are acknowledged but not quantified, **Example 3.13 Cadbury Schweppes** makes reference to forward commodity purchases while **Example 3.14 RMC** refers to discounted debt.

Example 3.13
Cadbury Schweppes plc *1 January 1994*
Extract from notes to the accounts:

<table>
<tr><td>21</td><td>**Contingent Liabilities and Financial Commitments**</td><td>(a) The Company has guaranteed overdrafts and other liabilities of certain subsidiary undertakings, the amount outstanding at 1 January 1994 being £383.9m (1992: £406.9m).
(b) Subsidiary undertakings have guarantees and indemnities outstanding amounting to £21.2m (1992: £22.2m).
(c) In the normal course of business the Group gives certain indemnities and also enters into forward commitments for the purchase of cocoa and other raw materials and for the purchase and sale of foreign currencies. Such commitments are only entered into on the basis of forecast requirements.</td></tr>
</table>

Example 3.14
RMC Group plc *31 December 1993*
Extract from notes to the accounts:

30 CONTINGENT LIABILITIES
The company has guaranteed certain loans, overdrafts and commitments of group undertakings totalling £19.7 million, and the Convertible Capital Bonds issued by RMC Capital Limited.
The group has guaranteed certain bank loans of associated undertakings totalling £55.7 million. The Directors consider that the possibility of any significant loss arising from these contingent liabilities is remote. In the normal course of business there are legal claims outstanding for the supply of goods, and bills and debts discounted, for which provision is made in the accounts for any liabilities which are expected to arise.

Another transaction which will be drawn on balance sheet by FRS 4 is the sale with repurchase options. **Example 3.14 Courts** has the right to repurchase properties which it sold and leased back, and indemnifies the lessor against loss in the event of sale to a third party.

Example 3.15
Courts (Furnishers) plc *31 March 1993*
Extract from notes to the accounts:

24 Contingent liabilities

The Parent Company has given guarantees in respect of bank borrowings of subsidiaries and trade creditors payable by bills of exchange up to a limit of £50,890,000 (1992 £65,387,000) against which £43,030,000 (1992 £50,023,000) was outstanding at 31st March 1993. Conversely, subsidiaries have guaranteed the Parent Company. The Company has also given the associate undertaking a guarantee up to a limit of £8,243,000 (1992 £3,079,000) against which £5,970,000 (1992, £3,001,000) was outstanding at 31st March 1993.

In previous years the Company entered into the following sale and 30 year leaseback arrangements, relating to store properties, realising profits of £2,895,000 in 1991 and £936,000 in 1990.

	Sale price £'000
30th March 1990	6,000
28th September 1990	3,000
24th October 1990	3,000
	12,000

The sale prices for the properties were at independent professional open market valuations. Under the terms of the leaseback agreements, certain covenants are imposed upon the Company and, in the event of a breach of these, the lessor has the right to enforce a repurchase of the properties at prices ranging from £12 million rising to £14.6 million over a five year period. At the end of the first five year period, the Company has the right to repurchase the properties for £14.6 million; and in the event that the Company has not exercised its repurchase option, the lessor has the right to dispose of the properties in the open market and any loss so incurred below £14.6 million is chargeable to the Company. In order to deal with these contingenies, the Company is, in each of the first five years, providing the increase from £12 million to 14.6 million on the same basis as the contingent liability increases (see note 15).

In respect of the remainder of the risk, the Company has arranged insurances as follows:-

(a) The first transaction – 85% of the risk.
(b) The second and third transactions – the first £1.5 million loss below £6 million.

Table 4: Consolidated financial statements

	FT-SE 100		Listed		Unlisted		Total	
Number of relevant companies ..	4	(6)	8	(5)	1	(4)	13	(15)
Number of companies...........	100	(100)	150	(150)	50	(50)	300	(300)
	%	(%)	%	(%)	%	(%)	%	(%)
Reasons given for excluding subsidiaries from consolidation:								
Lack of control	25	(33)	—	(20)	—	(—)	8	(20)
Severe long-term restrictions	—	(—)	13	(—)	100	(25)	15	(7)
Temporary control	—	(—)	13	(20)	—	(—)	8	(7)
Inclusion would be misleading...	—	(—)	—	(—)	100	(25)	8	(7)
Insignificant....................	75	(67)	38	(20)	—	(50)	46	(47)
Held for resale	—	(17)	25	(20)	—	(25)	15	(20)
Other...........................	—	(—)	13	(20)	—	(—)	8	(7)
Treatment of non-consolidated subsidiaries:								
Equity method	25	(n/a)	14	(n/a)	—	(n/a)	15	(n/a)
At cost method..................	—	(n/a)	—	(n/a)	50	(n/a)	8	(n/a)
Proportional method	—	(n/a)	—	(n/a)	50	(n/a)	8	(n/a)
Other...........................	50	(n/a)	14	(n/a)	—	(n/a)	25	(n/a)
Excluded from group accounts entirely	—	(n/a)	14	(n/a)	—	(n/a)	8	(n/a)
No disclosure of treatment of non-consolidated subsidiares ..	25	(n/a)	57	(n/a)	—	(n/a)	39	(n/a)

Note:
The above percentages are based on the number of relevant companies, that is, those with consolidated accounts.

Commentary

There has been a further modest fall in the number of companies which hold subsidiaries unconsolidated. Again, the principal reason for so doing is insignificance. This year, we have extended our table to show the various treatments accorded by companies to their unconsolidated subsidiaries.

Examples

While **Example 4.1 British Steel** holds a majority of the voting rights in a subsidiary, it is restricted in its ability to exercise its rights, and for this reason it excludes the subsidiary from consolidation on the basis of lack of control.

Example 4.1
British Steel plc   *2 April 1994*
Extract from accounting policies:

1. BASIS OF CONSOLIDATION

The accounts have been prepared under the historical cost convention and in accordance with applicable accounting standards in the U.K. They comprise a consolidation of the accounts of the Company and its subsidiary undertakings together with the Group's share of the results and net assets of its associated undertakings.

The Company holds a majority of the voting rights in UES Holdings Limited (UES), but is restricted in its ability to exercise those rights under an agreement with the other shareholder. Consequently, the investment has not been consolidated in these accounts but has been included based on the Group's share of its results and net assets.

Subsidiaries which are subject to severe long-term restrictions are neither consolidated nor included in the group accounts of **Example 4.2 Whitecroft**.

Example 4.2
Whitecroft plc   *31 March 1993*
Extract from accounting policies:

Basis of consolidation   The accounts of the parent company and its subsidiaries are made up to 31 March.

The results of subsidiaries joining or leaving the group during the year are included for the period of control. Overseas subsidiaries which are subject to severe long-term restrictions which hinder the exercise of the rights of the parent company over their assets or management are not consolidated and dividends received are included in the group accounts in the year of receipt.

Extract from notes to the accounts:

2   SUBSIDIARIES NOT CONSOLIDATED

Whitecroft owns 68% (1992 68%) of the issued share capital of Randalls Holdings (Pvt) Limited and its subsidiaries, all of which are incorporated and operate in Zimbabwe. For the reasons stated in the Accounting Policies these subsidiaries are not consolidated.

The group's share of profit before and after taxation for the year, based on unaudited management accounts (1992 audited) and translated at year-end exchange rates, of £165,000 (1992 £808,000) and £52,000 (1992 £435,000) respectively are not included in the group profit and loss account nor is any value attributed to these subsidiaries in the group accounts. The group's share of net assets at 31 march 1993, was £2,920,000 (1992 £3,172,000). Group profit before and after taxation includes dividends received during the year of £81,000 (1992 £276,000) and £42,000 (1992 £132,000) respectively.

175

Temporary control is not a reason for non-consolidation cited by either the Companies Act 1985 or FRS 2 "Accounting for subsidiary undertakings". However, **Example 4.3 News International** gives this as its justification for exclusion.

Example 4.3
News International plc   *30 June 1993*
Extract from accounting policies:

> *Basis of consolidation*
> The Group accounts are made up to 30 June 1993 and consolidate the accounts of News International plc and all its subsidiary undertakings, except those held as temporary investments.
>
> The results of subsidiary undertakings acquired or disposed of in the year are included in the consolidated profit and loss account from the date of acquisition or to the date of disposal, as appropriate.

While the Companies Act permits non-consolidation if the necessary information cannot be obtained without undue delay, FRS 2 only makes this concession if the subsidiaries are individually or collectively immaterial in the context of the group. **Example 4.4 David S Smith** plays the immateriality card in excluding two subsidiaries in respect of which the necessary information was not available without undue delay.

Example 4.4
David S Smith (Holdings) plc   *1 May 1993*
Extract from notes to the accounts:

12 **Fixed asset investments**	Group under- takings £m	Associated under- takings £m	Total £m
At 3 May 1992	0.4	0.4	0.8
Exchange differences	0.1	—	0.1
At 1 May 1993	**0.5**	**0.4**	**0.9**

The unconsolidated Group undertakings are two small waste paper collection companies, Sorepa Sarl (60% owned) in France and Sorepa GmbH (56% owned) in Germany. They have not been consolidated as they are immaterial to the Group accounts and the necessary information was not available without undue delay.

Example 4.5 J Bibby accepts the invitation of the Companies Act 1985 and obeys the dictates of FRS 2 by excluding from consolidation a subsidiary which is held exclusively for resale. The investment is represented on the balance sheet at the value of the sale agreement.

Example 4.5
J Bibby & Sons plc *25 September 1993*
Extract from notes to the accounts:

		Associated companies net assets £000's	Non-consolidated subsidiaries £000's	Other invest-ments £000's	Loans £000's	Total £000's
7	Fixed asset investments:					
	Consolidated cost					
	At 26th September 1992 ..	74	2,028	138	3,576	5,816
	Additions................	—	410	—	—	410
	Disposals................	—	—	(88)	(4,590)	(4,678)
	Fair value	—	(1,055)	—	—	(1.055)
	Exchange fluctuation......	—	(215)	(12)	1.014	787
	At 25th September 1993 ..	**74**	**1,168**	**38**	—	**1,280**
	Share of post acquisition reserves					
	At 26th September 1992 ..	337				337
	Retained for period	(14)				(14)
	At 25th September 1993 ..	**323**				**323**
	Amounts written off					
	At 26th September 1992 ..				155	155
	Disposals................				(155)	(155)
	At 25th September 1993 ..				—	—
	Net book value					
	At 25th September 1993 ..	**397**	**1,168**	**38**	—	**1,603**
	At 26th September 1992 ..	411	2,028	138	3,421	5,998

All investments are unlisted. The non-consolidated subsidiary shown above is Alequinsa of Spain which is the subject of a provisional sale agreement at the year end. The investment has been written down to the proceeds value of this sale agreement which is expected to be completed before the end of December.

Example 4.6 Smiths Industries considers that court proceedings overhanging the ownership of assets justifies non-consolidation, in a situation where the right to control is clearly not fully established.

Example 4.6
Smiths Industries plc *31 July 1993*
Extract from accounting policies:

Basis of Consolidation

Goodwill arising on consolidation and representing the difference between the cost of acquisition of a subsidiary undertaking and the fair value of its net assets at the date of acquisition is written off to reserves in the year of acquisition. Results of subsidiaries acquired during the year are consolidated from the date of acquisition.

The accounts of Ceewood Housing Association Limited have not been consolidated as the ownership of its assets is subject to court proceedings.

Methods of accounting for non-consolidated subsidiaries are varied. In addition to exclusion (**Example 4.2 Whitecroft**) and sale value (**Example 4.5 J Bibby**), **Example 4.7 Stakis** accounts on an equity basis while **Example 4.8 Nuclear Electric** uses a cost basis. **Example 4.9 Photo-Me** does not disclose if or how its non-consolidated subsidiaries are included in its accounts.

Example 4.7
Stakis plc *3 October 1993*
Extract from accounting policies:

Basis of Consolidation

With the undernoted exception, the consolidated accounts incorporate the audited accounts of the Company and all its subsidiaries which are made up to 3 October 1993.

The financial services subsidiaries being run down are not material in the context of the Group and have not been consolidated. They continue to be accounted for on an equity basis.

The subsidiary undertakings acquired during the year has been consolidated using acquisition accounting.

Example 4.8
Nuclear Electric plc *31 March 1993*
Extract from notes to the accounts:

9 Fixed asset investments

....

	1993	1992
	£m	£m
Investment in subsidiary undertakings at cost	24	24
Loans to subsidiary undertakings	18	18
Total fixed asset investments	42	42

The company's share of the combined net assets of subsidiary undertakings not consolidated amounted to £142 million at 31 March 1993 (1992: £113 million).

Example 4.9
Photo-Me International plc *30 April 1993*
Extract from accounting policies:

(b) Basis of consolidation

The Group accounts consolidate the accounts of the Company and all its subsidiary undertakings (except four small undertakings which only commenced trading during the period) made up to 30 April 1993, except for Photo-Me Hubei Co. Ltd. and Photo-Me (Cyprus) Ltd. whose accounts were made up to 31 December 1992, and Photec K.K. to 31 March 1993.

Table 5: Foreign currencies

	FT-SE 100	Listed	Unlisted	Total
Number of relevant cmpanies......	96	129	140	236
Number of companies.............	100	150	50	300
	%	%	%	%
Disclosure of exposure to risk:				
Indebtedness analysed by currency:				
comprehensively................	26	7	3	14
partially	41	19	13	26
Assets analysed by currency:				
comprehensively................	4	1	—	2
partially	2	2	5	3
No disclosure of foreign currency exposure	33	74	85	61

Note:
The percentages are based on the number of relevant companies, that is, those with evidence of foreign currency exposures.

Commentary

Although some 90% of companies surveyed acknowledge a measure of currency exposure, less than half give any indication of the amount and currency of debt and very few indeed analyse assets by currency.

Examples

The financial review in the accounts of **Example 5.1 Laporte** gives particulars of the currency make-up of the company's total indebtedness.

Example 5.1
Laporte plc   *2 January 1994*
Extract from financial review:

Debt Management
Group indebtedness at 2 January 1994 was denominated in the following currencies:

	Currency(m)	£m
US Dollars	237	160
Deutschmarks	6	2
French Francs	138	16
Canadian Dollars	18	9
Australian Dollars	25	12
		199
Sterling deposits		(64)
		135

Although the total indebtedness of **Example 5.2 British Aerospace** is not fully analysed, the currencies of the principal loans are disclosed in the notes to the accounts.

Example 5.2
British Aerospace plc *31 December 1993*
Extract from notes to the accounts:

17 Loans and Overdrafts

	Group		Company	
	1993 £m	1992 £m	1993 £m	1992 £m
Due within one year				
Bank loans and overdrafts	**141**	297	**47**	113
European Investment Bank loan (secured)	**10**	5	—	—
Obligations under finance leases	**40**	40	**1**	11
	191	342	**48**	124

Bank loans and overdrafts for the Group and Company include £17 million (1992 £24 million) secured by charges on assets.

	Group		Company	
	1993 £m	1992 £m	1993 £m	1992 £m
Due after one year				
European Investment Bank loan, final instalment 2009 (secured)	**300**	340	—	—
Medium term notes	**250**	248	—	—
US$ 8% Eurobond, repayable 1997	**235**	235	—	—
Euro-Sterling 11⅞% bond, repayable 2008	**150**	150	**150**	150
Euro-Sterling 10¾% bond, repayable 2014	**100**	100	**100**	100
Private placement 10.15% loan, repayable 2000	**68**	64	—	—
Schuldschein 9.2% bond, repayable 2000	**34**	34	—	—
Other loans	**39**	67	—	51
Obligations under finance leases	**131**	148	**2**	69
	1,337	1,386	**252**	370

Example 5.3 Tate & Lyle analyses its net assets by currency after taking account of the various borrowings and currency swaps.

Example 5.3
Tate & Lyle plc *25 September 1993*
Extract from notes to the accounts:

30 Currency Analysis of Net Assets

After taking into account the various borrowings and currency swaps entered into by the Group, the percentage of net assets by currency of the Group, which totalled £807.6 million as at 25th September 1993, was:

	1993 %
Pounds Sterling	24
United States Dollars	28
Canadian Dollars	4
Australian Dollars	11
EC currencies excluding Sterling	29
Others	4
Total	**100**

Without specifying the currencies concerned, **Example 5.4 Barings** states the aggregate amounts of assets and liabilities which are denominated in currencies other than sterling.

Example 5.4
Barings plc *31 December 1993*
Extract from notes to the accounts:

32. Assets and liabilities in foreign currencies

The aggregate amounts of assets and liabilities in the balance sheet denominated in foreign currencies were as follows:

	1993 £'000	1992 £'000
Assets	3,301,069	2,227,311
Liabilities	3,311,205	2,206,720

Due to the existence of off-balance sheet items, the above should not be taken as a measure of the Group's exposure to foreign exchange risk.

But probably the most comprehensive disclosure which we have encountered is that provided by **Example 5.5 Wolseley**, the notes to whose accounts abstract, line by line, the US$ and French Franc elements of the balance sheet.

Example 5.5
Wolseley plc *31 July 1993*
Extract from notes to the accounts:

20. Foreign assets and liabilities

The group balance sheet includes the following material assets and liabilities denominated in foreign currencies:

(i) US Dollars

	1993		1992	
	US$000	US$000	US$000	US$000
Tangible fixed assets		116,766		111,325
Stock		273,086		249,350
Construction loans receivable		92,035		65,092
Construction loan borrowings		(89,000)		(64,000)
Debtors		268,286		247,575
Creditors and provisions		(244,359)		(212,686)
Taxation		207		(8,063)
		417,021		388,593
Net (borrowings)/funds				
Short term	24,877		(110,263)	
Long term	(136,915)		(11,399)	
		(112,038)		(121,662)
		304,983		266,931

(ii) French Francs

	1993		1992	
	FRF'000	FRF'000	FRF'000	FRF'000
Tangible fixed assets		169,518		168,737
Stock		561,221		608,008
Debtors		967,344		994,009
Creditors and provisions		(1,470,405)		(1,589,042)
Taxation		4,104		(12,203)
		231,782		169,509
Net borrowings:				
Short term	(176,998)		(993,888)	
Long term	(939,776)		(141,904)	
		(1,116,774)		(1,135,792)
		(884,992)		(966,283)

Goodwill amounting to FRF950m (1992 FRF1,004m) has been written off to reserves.

Table 6: Intangibles

	FT-SE 100		Listed		Unlisted		Total	
Number of relevant companies	27	(22)	27	(25)	17	(14)	69	(61)
Number of companies................	100	(100)	150	(150)	50	(50)	300	(300)
	%	(%)	%	(%)	%	(%)	%	(%)

Disclosures and classification of intangible assets:
Classified as intangible fixed assets:

	FT-SE 100		Listed		Unlisted		Total	
research and development..........	8	(9)	22	(16)	6	(14)	13	(13)
development costs other than R&D	—	(—)	4	(4)	—	(—)	1	(2)
goodwill..........................	4	(5)	11	(16)	65	(64)	22	(23)
brand names......................	21	(23)	4	(4)	6	(7)	10	(12)
patents and trade marks............	21	(14)	11	(8)	12	(7)	15	(10)
extractive industry exploration costs	21	(27)	—	(—)	—	(—)	7	(10)
licences..........................	17	(9)	—	(—)	6	(—)	7	(3)
copyright and other publishing rights............................	8	(9)	—	(—)	3	(—)	3	(3)
technical know-how	4	(5)	4	(12)	12	(14)	6	(10)
deferred charges	8	(5)	4	(4)	—	(—)	4	(3)
other	4	(5)	11	(4)	18	(21)	10	(8)
aggregate of more than one	16	(9)	11	(24)	—	(—)	10	(13)
unidentified.......................	4	(5)	—	(—)	—	(—)	1	(2)

Classified as current assets:

	FT-SE 100		Listed		Unlisted		Total	
development costs other than R&D	4	(—)	(—)	(4)	—	(—)	1	(2)
film rights	4	(5)	7	(4)	—	(—)	4	(3)
other	—	(n/a)	4	(n/a)	—	(n/a)	1	(n/a)

Classified as tangible fixed assets:

	FT-SE 100		Listed		Unlisted		Total	
licences..........................	—	(—)	7	(4)	—	(—)	3	(2)
extractive industry exploration costs	4	(9)	4	(4)	—	(—)	3	(5)
other	—	(—)	7	(4)	—	(—)	3	(2)

Measurement of carrying value of capitalised intangible assets:

	FT-SE 100		Listed		Unlisted		Total	
Purchase cost......................	40	(n/a)	19	(n/a)	6	(n/a)	23	(n/a)
Purchase cost less amortisation.......	52	(n/a)	74	(n/a)	88	(n/a)	70	(n/a)
Valuation	4	(n/a)	15	(n/a)	6	(n/a)	9	(n/a)
No disclosure of measurement basis..	17	(n/a)	—	(n/a)	—	(n/a)	6	(n/a)

Measuremeant of amortisation charge: Amortisation rates:

	FT-SE 100		Listed		Unlisted		Total	
2–5%.............................	18	(n/a)	10	(n/a)	14	(n/a)	14	(n/a)
6–10%............................	—	(n/a)	10	(n/a)	50	(n/a)	17	(n/a)
11–20%...........................	12	(n/a)	14	(n/a)	14	(n/a)	14	(n/a)
21–33%...........................	—	(n/a)	14	(n/a)	—	(n/a)	6	(n/a)
Greater than 33%....................	—	(n/a)	14	(n/a)	—	(n/a)	6	(n/a)

Range of rates wider than specified above, spanning:

	FT-SE 100		Listed		Unlisted		Total	
not more than three bands	12	(n/a)	—	(n/a)	7	(n/a)	6	(n/a)
more than three bands	6	(n/a)	—	(n/a)	—	(n/a)	2	(n/a)
No disclosures	65	(n/a)	38	(n/a)	36	(n/a)	46	(n/a)

Note:
The percentages are based on the number of relevant companies, that is, those with evidence of intangible assets.

Commentary

The ASB has thrown a ball in the air by publishing its discussion paper "Goodwill and intangible assets", and the financial world waits to see where it will fall. Learned and erudite arguments are advanced both in favour of and against the various treatments suggested in the paper. Meantime, approximately one company in five represents intangibles of one type or another in its balance sheet. The majority of these are amortised over an appropriate period, but one in four are not prepared to accept that their intangibles have finite lives and carry them unamortised in defiance of SSAP 12 "Accounting for depreciation" and of Sch 4 para 18 of the Companies Act 1985. The following are some of the many and varied types of intangible assets carried on companies' balance sheets.

Examples

Example 6.1 Photo-Me capitalises both development costs and chemical systems. The development costs are amortised over a three-year period while the chemical systems are not subjected to amortisation.

Example 6.1
Photo-Me International plc *30 April 1993*
Extract from notes to the accounts:

11 Intangible fixed assets

	Development costs £	Chemical system £	Total £
....			
Group			
Cost:			
At 1 May 1992	800,000	167,131	967,131
Exchange adjustment	—	32,869	32,869
Additions	700,000	—	700,000
At 30 April 1993	£1,500,000	£200,000	£1,700,000
Amortisation:			
At 1 May 1992	399,999	—	399,999
Provided during year	266,667	—	266,667
At 30 April 1993	£666,666	—	£666,666
Net book value:			
At 30 April 1993	£833,334	£200,000	£1,033,334
At 1 May 1992	£400,001	£167,131	£567,132

Development costs in prior years related to software and hardware development. Costs in the current year are in respect of the development of new photographic studios.

The argument that certain intangible assets are evergreen is advanced most strongly in respect of brands and titles. **Example 6.2 Cadbury Schweppes** carries substantial brands on its balance sheet which are not subject to amortisation unless "permanent diminution" is detected at their annual review.

Example 6.2
Cadbury Schweppes plc *1 January 1994*
Extract from accounting policies:

n) Intangibles Intangibles represent significant owned brands acquired since 1985 valued at historical cost. No amortisation is charged as the annual results reflect significant expenditure in support of these brands and the values are reviewed annually with a view to write down if a permanent diminution arises.

Extract from notes to the accounts:

9 Intangible Assets

	1993 £m	1992 £m
Cost at beginning of year	385.1	308.0
Exchange rate adjustments	(0.1)	51.1
Additions (see Note 9)	160.8	26.0
	545.8	385.1

The assets of **Example 6.3 Burmah Castrol** include patents and trade marks and also oil and gas exploration expenditure. The former are amortised over an unspecified period "for which they are expected to provide a valuable benefit"; the latter is written down by the unit of production method.

Example 6.3
Burmah Castrol plc *31 December 1993*
Extract from notes to the accounts:

10. **Intangible fixed assets**	Patents, trade marks, etc	Oil and gas exploration expenditure	Total
	£ million	£ million	£ million
Cost			
At 1 January 1993	6.8	14.6	21.4
Exchange adjustments	(0.1)	(1.3)	(1.4)
Acquisitions	0.1		0.1
Capital expenditure	0.5	1.1	1.6
Disposals and other adjustments	(0.2)		(0.2)
At 31 December 1993	7.1	14.4	21.5
Amortisation			
At 1 January 1993	2.9	6.0	8.9
Exchange adjustments		(0.8)	(0.8)
Charge for year	0.6		0.6
Disposals and other adjustments	(0.3)		(0.3)
At 31 December 1993	3.2	5.2	8.4
Net per group balance sheet			
At 31 December 1993	3.9	9.2	13.1
At 31 December 1992	3.9	8.6	12.5

Example 6.4 Thomas Cook carries as an intangible asset a country-specific licence giving the right to use its trade mark. This is being amortised at a rate of 10% per annum.

Example 6.4
The Thomas Cook Group plc *31 December 1993*
Extract from notes to the accounts:

7. Fixed assets Group	Land Buildings £000	Furniture, Fixtures & Equipment £000	Total Tangible Assets £000	Total Intangible Assets £000
Cost or valuation				
At 1 January 1993	46,586	109,898	156,484	4,106
Exchange and other adjustments	168	730	898	—
Additions at cost	2,144	23,713	25,857	—
Assets of subsidiary undertakings acquired	1,027	1,820	2,847	—
Reclassification (partly to current assets)	(464)	(11)	(475)	—
Disposals at cost or valuation	(1,963)	(7,880)	(9,843)	
At 31 December 1993	47,498	128,270	175,768	4.106
Depreciation				
At 1 January 1993	10,720	57,510	68,230	1,541
Exchange and other adjustments	36	723	759	—
Assets of subsidiary undertakings acquired	—	315	315	—
Reclassification (partly to current assets)	79	6	85	—
Disposals	(1,388)	(6,690)	(8,078)	—
Change for the year	2,216	15,236	17,452	410
At 31 December 1993	11,663	67,100	78,763	1,951
Net book value				
At 31 December 1993	35,835	61,170	97,005	2,155
At 31 December 1992	35,866	52,388	88,254	2,565
Comparable amounts determined according to the historical cost convention:				
Cost	35,445	128,270	163,715	4,106
Accumulated depreciation	11,663	67,100	78,763	1,951
Net book value				
At 31 December 1993	23,782	61,170	84,952	2,155
At 31 December 1992	23,812	52,388	76,200	2,565

Intangible fixed assets relate to a country-specific licence which gives a third party the right to use the Thomas Cook trade mark.

Some 15% of the fixed assets of **Example 6.5 Carlton Communications** comprise intangibles, being pre-transmission revenue expenditure and publishing rights.

Example 6.5
Carlton Communications plc *30 September 1993*
Extract from notes to the accounts:

9 Intangible assets	Pre-transmission revenue expenditure £'000	Publishing rights and other £'000	Total £'000
The Group			
Cost			
At 1 October 1992	16,045	6,699	22,744
Exchange rate movements	—	(185)	(185)
Expenditure	14,212	4,163	18,375
Retirements	—	(2,361)	(2,361)
At 30 September 1993	**30,257**	**8,316**	**38,573**
Amortisation			
At 1 October 1992	—	3,172	3,172
Exchange rate movements	—	(120)	(120)
Charge for the year	2,140	1,514	3,654
Retirements	—	(1,766)	(1,766)
At 30 September 1993	**2,140**	**2,800**	**4,940**
Net book value of assets at 30 September 1993	**28,117**	**5,516**	**33,633**
Net book value of assets at 30 September 1992	16,045	3,527	19,572

Technical know-how, or intellectual properties, first made its appearance a few years ago. This category of intangible is on the wane, and now appears in the accounts of only 5% of companies which account for intangible assets, including **Example 6.6 Westland.**

Example 6.6
Westland Group plc   *1 October 1993*
Extract from notes to the accounts:

12 Intangible assets	Consolidated £m
Know-how Agreement – Black Hawk	
Cost	
Balance at beginning of year	5.0
Balance at end of year	5.0
Amortisation	
Balance at beginning of year	2.3
Provided during year	0.4
Balance at end of year	2.7
Net book value at 1.10.93	**2.3**
Net book value at 2.10.92	**2.7**

Example 6.7 Medeva rolls brands, licences, trademarks and patents together and present them as an aggregate figure. Exploration expenditure, goodwill and other (unspecified) intangibles are recorded by **Example 6.8 British Petroleum**.

Example 6.7
Medeva plc   *31 December 1993*
Extract from notes to the accounts:

10 INTANGIBLE FIXED ASSETS	Group	Company
BRAND NAMES, LICENCES, TRADEMARKS AND PATENTS	£'000	£'000
Cost at 1st January 1993	48,578	—
Purchases and acquisitions	8.114	2,432
Disposals	—	—
Exchange differences	(1,512)	—
Cost at 31st December 1993	**55,180**	**2,432**
AMORTISATION		
At 1st January 1993	3,239	—
Charge for the year	3,189	—
Exchange differences	(138)	—
At 31st December 1993	**6,290**	—
NET BOOK VALUE		
At 31st December 1993	**48,890**	**2,432**
At 31st December 1992	45,339	—

The intangible assets above include £7.5 million (1992: £4 million) of assets which have yet to generate commercial sales of the product to which they relate and upon which no amortisation has been charged. As described in note 22, legal costs totalling £695,000 have been included in the above costs of intangible assets.

Example 6.8
The British Petroleum Company plc *31 December 1993*
Extract from notes to the accounts:

18 Intangible assets

£ million

	Exploration expenditure	Goodwill	Other intangibles	Total
Cost				
At 1 January 1993	1,243	248	277	1,768
Exchange adjustments	5	(4)	(5)	(4)
Additions	390	—	6	396
Transfers	(314)	—	—	(314)
Deletions	(474)	(82)	(122)	(678)
At 31 December 1993	**850**	**162**	**156**	**1,168**
Depreciation				
At 1 January 1993	206	152	125	483
Exchange adjustments	3	(3)	1	1
Charge for the year	450	10	16	476
Transfers	(10)	—	—	(10)
Deletions	(470)	(39)	(50)	(559)
At 31 December 1993	**179**	**120**	**92**	**391**
Net book amount				
At 31 December 1993	**671**	**42**	**64**	**777**
At 31 December 1992	1,037	96	152	1,285

The foregoing companies all classified intangible assets as such on the face of their balance sheet. A small number of companies introduce them under different headings. **Example 6.9 British Aerospace** includes unamortised launch costs in its stocks figure.

Example 6.9
British Aerospace plc *31 December 1993*
Extract from notes to the accounts:

14 Stocks

	Group		Company	
	1993 £m	1992 £m	1993 £m	1992 £m
Raw materials and consumables	**155**	180	—	128
Work in progress	**3,305**	4,105	—	3,564
Finished goods and goods for resale	**575**	754	—	168
Development properties	**662**	582	**318**	280
Progress payments	**(1,350)**	(2,173)	—	(2,075)
	3,348	3,448	**318**	2,065

Included within work in progress for the Group are unamortised launch costs relating to programmes supported by launch aid of £486 million (1992 £500 million for the Group and Company) and net costs less foreseeable losses on long term contracts of £242 million for the Group (1992 £549 million for the Group and £250 million for the Company). The payments on account applicable to these contracts and included within progress payments are £242 million for the Group (1992 £486 million for the Group and £220 million for the Company).

Development properties for the Group include capitalised interest of £39 million (1992 £39 million) and rationalisation costs of £343 million for the Group (1992 £303 million) and £293 million for the Company (1992 £280 million).

Example 6.10 STV also uses the stock section to accommodate film rights, while **Example 6.11 Gleeson** includes ground rents under this heading.

Example 6.10
Scottish Television plc *31 December 1993*
Extract from notes to the accounts:

16 Stocks, Film Rights and Recorded Programmes	Group		Company	
	1993	1992	**1993**	1992
	£'000	£'000	**£'000**	£'000
Stocks	**163**	32	**163**	32
Film rights	**8,927**	7,662	**8,927**	7.662
Recorded programmes and films	**11,672**	15,313	**2,352**	14,992
	20,762	23,007	**11,442**	22,686

Future instalments amounting to £2,095,000 (1992: £2,728,360) payable for film rights are incorporated where transmission rights are in existence at the balance sheet date. Contracts for £461,000 (1992: £465,000) where transmission rights commence after this date are included. The valuation of recorded programmes stock includes £4,513,000 (1992: £5,916,000) of attributable staff costs and overheads on programmes produced for the ITV network and Comataidh Telebhisein Gaidhlig.

Example 6.11
MJ Gleeson Group plc *30 June 1993*
Extract from notes to the accounts:

	Group 1993	Group 1992	Company 1993	Company 1992
	£000	**£000**	**£000**	**£000**
10. Stock and work in progress				
Residential, commercial and industrial developments	37,764	42,601	37,467	42,601
Properties held by BES companies (see note 20)	3,954	—	3,954	—
Raw materials and consumables	372	381	—	—
Ground rents	694	679	413	398
Long term contract balances:				
Net cost less foreseeable losses	—	4,937	—	—
Applicable payments on account	—	(4,937)	—	—
	42,784	43,661	41,834	42,999

Example 6.12 Sema does not raise a separate heading for intangibles in its balance sheet, but includes software licences in tangible fixed assets, into which classification **Example 6.13 Costain** slots mining pre-production expenditure and coal contracts.

Example 6.12
Sema plc *31 December 1993*
Extract from notes to the accounts:

10. TANGIBLE ASSETS

	Land and buildings £000	Prepaid software licences £000	Computer equipment £000	Office furniture cars and equipment £000	Total £000
COST					
At 1 January 1993	38,152	5,597	46,798	29,913	120,460
On acquisition of DAFA Norr Group	—	—	15,263	13,527	28,790
Additions	4,179	—	11.016	7.421	22,616
Disposals	(1,006)	—	(9,025)	(6,781)	(16,812)
Foreign exchange adjustment	(2,683)	(232)	(1,545)	(1,150)	(5,610)
AT 31 DECEMBER 1993	**38,642**	**5,365**	**62,507**	**42,930**	**149,444**
DEPRECIATION					
At 1 January 1993	3,512	4,476	32,446	11,665	52,099
On acquisition of DAFA Norr Group	—	—	9,126	9,929	19,055
Charge for year	1,338	1,096	9,757	6,901	19,092
On disposals	(520)	—	(9,110)	(6,232)	(15,862)
Foreign exchange adjustment	(177)	(207)	(1,221)	(658)	(2,263)
AT 31 DECEMBER 1993	**4,153**	**5,365**	**40,998**	**21,605**	**72,121**
NET BOOK AMOUNT – 31 DECEMBER 1993	**34,489**	**—**	**21,509**	**21,325**	**77,323**
Net book amount – 31 December 1992	34,640	1,121	14,352	18,248	68,361

Example 6.13
Costain Group plc *31 December 1993*
Extract from notes to the accounts:

14 Tangible assets

....

Analyses of the movements of operating assets and investment properties during the year are set out below.

Operating assets	Land and buildings			Mining assets	Plant and equipment		Total
	Freehold	Leasehold over 50 years	Leasehold 50 years and under		Owned	Leased	
	£m	£m	£m	£m	£m	£m	£m
Cost or valuation							
At 1 January 1993	29.8	2.1	20.5	184.9	400.8	25.5	663.6
Currency realignment	—	—	0.5	4.3	6.6	0.7	12.1
Additions	0.8	—	—	6.9	27.5	—	35.2
Disposals	(0.9)	—	—	(2.8)	(17.9)	—	(21.6)
Disposal of subsidiary undertakings	(1.7)	—	(16.0)	(25.8)	(101.9)	(26.2)	(171.6)
At 31 December 1993	**28.0**	**2.1**	**5.0**	**167.5**	**315.1**	**—**	**517.7**
Depreciation							
At 1 January 1993	5.8	1.3	10.4	69.5	216.0	7.9	310.9
Currency realignment	—	—	0.2	1.6	2.7	0.2	4.7
Provided in year	1.2	—	0.4	11.7	29.1	0.7	43.1
Disposals	—	—	—	(2.3)	(10.2)	—	(12.5)
Disposal of subsidiary undertakings	(0.2)	—	(6.2)	(4.1)	(57.7)	(8.8)	(77.0)
At 31 December 1993	**6.8**	**1.3**	**4.8**	**76.4**	**179.9**	**—**	**269.2**
Net book value							
At 31 December 1993	**21.2**	**0.8**	**0.2**	**91.1**	**135.2**	**—**	**248.5**
At 31 December 1992	24.0	0.8	10.1	115.4	184.8	17.6	352.7

Mining assets comprise mineral rights and mining pre-production expenditure of £72.2m (1992 £94.0m) and coal contracts purchased of £18.9m (1992 £21.4m).

Example 6.14 IMI includes in tangible fixed assets computer software incorporated in products sold by its computing group.

Example 6.14
IMI plc *31 December 1993*
Extract from notes to the accounts:

13 Tangible fixed assets

	Land and Buildings			Plant and machinery			Assets in course of construction	Total
	Gross book value	Depre-ciation	Net book value	Gross book value	Depre-ciation	Net book value	Net book value	Net book value
	£m	£m	£m	£m	£m	£m	£m	£m
At 31 December 1992	143.1	44.0	99.1	400.1	251.2	148.9	19.4	267.4
Exchange adjustments	(1.2)	(0.2)	(1.0)	(2.3)	(1.2)	(1.1)	0.2	(1.9)
Acquisitions	0.1	—	0.1	1.8	0.2	1.6	—	1.7
Additions	0.7	—	0.7	29.4	—	29.4	17.6	47.7
Revaluation	4.3	·	4.3	—	—	—	—	4.3
Disposals	—	—	—	(13.5)	(11.5)	(2.0)	—	(2.0)
Transfers	0.5	—	0.5	24.1	—	24.1	(24.6)	—
Depreciation for year	—	3.9	(3.9)	—	35.7	(35.7)	—	(39.6)
At 31 December 1993	**147.5**	**47.7**	**99.8**	**439.6**	**274.4**	**165.2**	**12.6**	**277.6**

(i) The net book value of land and buildings comprises:

	1993 £m	1992 £m
Freehold: land	10.8	10.5
buildings	53.8	56.7
Long leasehold	7.4	7.6
Short leasehold	5.2	5.3
Investment properties	22.6	19.0
At 31 December	99.8	99.1

The value of intangibles (usually acquired) reflected in the accounts of the foregoing companies is dwarfed by the value of intangible assets, homegrown or otherwise, owned by virtually all companies, which are not incorporated in the balance sheet. **Example 6.15 Bass** is only one of a number of companies which can point to substantial assets which are not represented in their financial statements.

Example 6.15
Bass plc *30 September 1993*
Extract from Operating and financial review:

....

Commitment to brands continued through a planned programme of revenue investment including research and development, marketing and advertising to support existing brands and to extend ranges. The very significant value of acquired and internally generated brands and other intangible assets (including trademarks, hotel franchises and management contracts) is not incorporated in the balance sheet, associated costs being charged to the profit and loss account as incurred.

Extract from accounting policies:

FIXED ASSETS AND DEPRECIATION
i) Intangible assets
No value is attributed to trademarks, concessions, patents and similar rights and assets, including hotel franchises and management contracts. Costs incurred on trademarks, concessions, patents and similar rights, whether purchased or created by the Group, are charged to the profit and loss account in the period in which they are incurred.

Example 6.16 Guinness carries brands at cost, while **Example 6.17 SmithKline Beecham** amortises the purchase price of intangibles over 20 years.

Example 6.16
Guinness plc *31 December 1993*
Extract from accounting policies:

BRANDS
The fair value of businesses acquired and of interests taken in associated undertakings includes brands, which are recognised where the brand has a value which is substantial and long term. Acquired brands are only recognised where title is clear, brand earnings are separately identifiable, the brand could be sold separately from the rest of the business and where the brand achieves earnings in excess of those achieved by unbranded products.
Amortisation is not provided except where the end of the useful economic life of the acquired brand can be foreseen. The useful economic lives of brands and their carrying value are subject to annual review and any amortisation or provision for permanent impairment would be charged against the profit for the period in which they arose.

Example 6.17
SmithKline Beecham plc *31 December 1993*
Extract from accounting policies:

Intangible assets
From 1 January 1993, the Company has adopted a new accounting policy for intangible fixed assets in recognition of the increase in the amount expended on acquiring them as it forges strategic alliances across all business sectors. The costs of separately identifiable intangible assets such as patents, licences and marketing rights to develop compounds for future commercial production, have been capitalised separately from goodwill and will be amortised over.

Example 6.18 News International carries publishing rights and titles at directors' estimate of current cost, which is considerably greater than historical cost.

Example 6.18
News International plc   *30 June 1993*
Extract from notes to the accounts:

12. Intangible fixed assets

....

	Group	
The movement in the year was as follows:	Pubishing rights and titles £000's	Goodwill on consolidation £000's
Cost or valuation		
Beginning of year	1,074,332	3,994
Addition	—	27,577
Exchange movement	1,831	—
End of year	1,076,163	31,571
Amortisation		
Beginning of year	—	409
Amortisation in year	—	1,553
End of year	—	1,962
Net book value		
Beginning of year	1,074,332	3,585
End of year	1,076,163	29,609

All of the Group's United Kingdom newspaper titles unaccompanied by the assets and other rights and interests which go to make up the associated businesses taken as a whole have been incorporated in the consolidated balance sheet at the Directors' estimate of current cost of £1,068,000,000 (1992 – £1,068,000,000), The Directors have reviewed the current cost of these newspaper titles, taking into account the principles of the valuation placed on them by Hambros Securities Limited at 30 June 1990 and have concluded, based on this review, that there has been no significant change in current cost in the year to 30 June 1993. Corporation tax that could arise (maximum – £332,912,000) in the event of disposal at the revalued amount has not been provided in these accounts since it is not the Directors' intention to dispose of these titles.

The original cost of publishing rights and titles is £67,339,000 (1992 – £67,339,000).

Introducing intangibles to its balance sheet for the first time, **Example 6.19 Smith & Nephew** does not disclose the basis of amortisation.

Example 6.19
Smith & Nephew plc   *31 December 1993*
Extract from notes to the accounts:

12 Intangible fixed assets

During the year £5.4m of patents, licences and distribution rights were acquired and £0.5m of amortisation provided.

Table 7: Goodwill

	FT-SE 100		Listed		Unlisted		Total	
Number of relevant companies	93	(88)	136	(136)	28	(28)	257	(252)
Number of companies................	100	(100)	150	(150)	50	(50)	300	(300)
	%	(%)	%	(%)	%	(%)	%	(%)
Disclosure and classification of goodwill:								
Capitalised goodwill:								
intangible assets	1	(1)	2	(3)	36	(29)	5	(5)
fixed asset investments.............	—	(n/a)	1	(n/a)	—	(n/a)	—	(n/a)
No capitalised goodwill..............	99	(99)	97	(97)	64	(71)	94	(95)
Disclosure of income effect of goodwill:								
Disclosed:								
in income.........................	—	(1)	5	(4)	32	(30)	5	(6)
in reserves........................	98	(97)	99	(100)	65	(71)	95	(94)
No disclosure	2	(2)	—	(—)	7	(15)	3	(1)

Note:
The percentages are based on the number of relevant companies, that is, those with evidence of goodwill.

Commentary

As they await the outcome of the ASB review, initiated by the discussion paper "Goodwill and intangible assets", UK companies continue in the main to write off goodwill through reserves as it arises, as permitted by UK accounting standards and contrary to international practice. Of those which show evidence of having purchased goodwill, only 3% of companies carry this asset on their balance sheet. an increasing number of chairmen and finance directors, however, are given to referring to the hidden value of this asset in their respective reports.

Examples

Example 7.1 News International capitalises acquisition goodwill, which it writes off over 20 years.

Example 7.1
News International plc *30 June 1993*
Extract from notes to the accounts:

12. Intangible fixed assets

....

The movement in the year was as follows:	Group	
	Publishing rights and titles £000's	Goodwill on consolidation £000's
Cost or valuation		
Beginning of year	1,074,332	3,994
Addition	—	27,577
Exchange movement	1,831	—
End of year	1,076,163	31,571
Amortisation		
Beginning of year	—	409
Amortisation in year	—	1,553
End of year	—	1,962
Net book value		
Beginning of year	1,074,332	3,585
End of year	1,076,163	29,609

Goodwill is also carried on the balance sheet of **Example 7.2 Attwoods**. In this instance it relates to an investment in an associated company, and appears under fixed asset investments. On this occasions the goodwill is being written off over 40 years.

Example 7.2
Attwoods plc *31 July 1993*
Extract from notes to the accounts:

8 FIXED ASSET INVESTMENTS

Group	Associated undertakings £'000	Loans to associated undertakings £'000	Trade investments £'000	Total £'000
At 1 August 1990	14,823	13,655	2	28,480
Additions	—	244	142	386
Dividends received/disposals	(89)	(640)	(2)	(731)
Currency adjustments	58	373	—	431
Premium amortisation	(285)	—	—	(285)
Retained profit for the period	112	—	—	112
At 31 July 1991	14,619	13,632	142	28,393
Additions	34	1,666	41	1,741
Dividends received/disposals	(25)	—	(101)	(126)
Currency adjustments	(44)	(550)	2	(592)
Premium amortisation	(287)	—	—	(287)
Retained loss for the period	(537)	—	—	(537)
At 31 July 1992	13,760	14,748	84	28,592
Additions	195	3,599	16	3,810
Dividends received/disposals	(19)	—	—	(19)
Currency adjustments	(59)	1,451	11	1,403
Premium amortisation	(293)	—	—	(293)
Retained loss for the period	(1,550)	—	—	(1,550)
Provided in period	—	—	(40)	(40)
At 31 July 1993	12.034	19,798	71	31,903

The Group has the following interestes in associated undertakings:

(a) A 40% interest in the ordinary share capital of Vesta Technology Ltd, a company engaged in providing the service and sales of mobile incinerators for the disposal of hazardous waste, operating and incorporated in the USA.
(b) A 49% interest in the ordinary share capital of A&J Bull (Holdings) Limited, a company engaged in mineral extraction and waste management services, operating, registered and incorporated in England.
(c) A 50% interest in the ordinary share capital of Green Land Reclamation Ltd, a company engaged in the provision of environmental and power generation consultancy services, operating, registered and incorporated in England.
(d) A 50% interest in the ordinary share capital of Cranford Realty Ltd, a company engaged in the rental of property operating, registed and incorporated in England.

The associated undertaking investments comprise:

	31 July 1993 £'000	31 July 1992 £'000	31 July 1991 £'000
Share of net assets	943	2,911	3,483
Premium on acquisition	11,956	11,421	11,421
Premium amortisation	(865)	(572)	(285)
	12,034	13,760	14,619
Long-term loans	19,798	14,748	13,632
	31,832	28,508	28,251

Example 7.3 Bass follows the popular line by writing off goodwill through reserves. The written off value of goodwill expressed in foreign currencies is, however, maintained at its current sterling level by exchange adjustments, against the day that it may require to be resurrected.

Example 7.3
Bass plc *30 September 1993*
Extract from accounting policies:

BASIS OF CONSOLIDATION

iii) ....

Any difference between the purchase consideration and the fair value attributed to the tangible assets and liabilities represents discount or goodwill. Any discount is taken to capital reserves; goodwill is eliminated against reserves. To the extent that goodwill in foreign currencies (arising on acquisitions of overseas subsidiary undertakings) continues to have value, the amount is adjusted at each balance sheet date. On disposal of a business, any goodwill previously eliminated on acquisition is included in determining the surplus or loss on disposal. Where the disposal materially effects the nature and focus of the Group's operations the business sold is treated as discontinued. In such circumstances prior year results are restated to show the results of the discontinued business. The results of those businesses acquired or disposed of during the year are included for the period during which they were within the Group's control.

Extract from notes to the accounts:

19 RESERVES	Share premium account £m	Revalu- ation reserve £m	Capital reserve £m	Profit and loss account £m	Total £m
GROUP					
At 30 September 1992	499	1,107	—	1,521	3,127
Premium on allotment of Ordinary shares	18	—	—	—	18
Retained earnings for the year	—	—	—	142	142
Goodwill (see below)	—	—	—	(205)	(205)
Realised revaluation surplus transfer	—	(42)	—	42	—
Revaluation element in depreciation charge	—	(2)	—	2	—
Exchange adjustments on:					
assets	—	(12)	—	293	281
borrowings	—	—	—	(167)	(167)
AT 30 SEPTEMBER 1993	517	1,051	—	1,628	3,196

....

	Group		
GOODWILL	Cost of goodwill eliminated £m	Exchange adjustment £m	Total £m
Eliminated to 30 September 1992	1,391	(50)	1,341
Acquisitions	1	—	1
Disposals	(9)	—	(9)
Exchange adjustments	—	213	213
ELIMINATED TO 30 SEPTEMBER 1993	**1,383**	**163**	**1,546**

The annual amortisation of goodwill capitalised by **Example 7.4 Ford** is seen as a charge to profit and loss account.

Example 7.4
Ford Motor Company Ltd   *31 December 1993*
Extract from notes to the accounts:

4   Operating loss

	1993			1992		
	Continuing operations £m	Discontinued operations £m	**Total** **£m**	Continuing operations £m	Discontinued operations £m	Total £m
....						
Financial services segment						
Financial services operating profit comprises:						
Finance income						
Conditional sale	**10**	**107**	**117**	14	229	243
Operating lease	**—**	**77**	**77**	—	140	140
Finance lease	**20**	**9**	**29**	26	25	51
Loans secured on property	**16**	**—**	**16**	19	—	19
Other interest and insurance income	**29**	**2**	**31**	36	1	37
Inter-segment income (see note below)	**—**	**18**	**18**	—	77	77
	75	**213**	**288**	95	472	567
Interest expense						
Group undertakings	**(15)**	**—**	**(15)**	(20)	(6)	(26)
Bank loans, overdrafts and other loans repayable within five years	**(14)**	**(89)**	**(103)**	(23)	(246)	(269)
Finance leases	**(1)**	**—**	**(1)**	(1)	—	(1)
	(30)	**(89)**	**(119)**	(44)	(252)	(296)
Goodwill amortisation	**(8)**	**—**	**(8)**	(12)	—	(12)
Provision for bad and doubtful debts	**(14)**	**—**	**(14)**	(29)	5	(24)
Other operating expenses	**(19)**	**(89)**	**(108)**	(26)	(173)	(199)
Financial services operating profit	**4**	**35**	**39**	(16)	52	36

The potential for confusion in UK accounts of calling both the revenue account and the profit and loss reserve "profit and loss account" is highlighted in the accounts of **Example 7.5 Polypipe**. The goodwill write off through profit and loss account is of course a charge against reserves.

Example 7.5
Polypipe plc *30 June 1993*
Extract from consolidated profit and loss account and statement of movements in profit and loss account:

Consolidated profit and loss account

For the year ended 30th June, 1993

	Notes	1993 £'000	1992 £'000
Turnover			
Continuing operations	2	**120,459**	108,257
Operation profit			
Continuing operations	3	**17,369**	15,433
Interest payable less receivable	5	**(266)**	(54)
Profit on ordinary activities before taxation		**17,103**	15,379
Tax on profit on ordinary activities	7	**(5,611)**	(5,040)
Profit on ordinary activities after taxation		**11,492**	10,339
Dividends	8	**(3,278)**	(3,045)
Retained profit for the year		**8,214**	7,294
Retained as follows:			
Polypipe plc		**3,636**	4,679
Subsidiary companies		**4,578**	2,615
		8,214	7,294
Earnings per share	9	**7.40p**	6.69p

The Group has no recognised gains or losses other than those included in the profits above, and therefore, no separate statement of total recognised gains and losses has been presented.

There is no difference between the result stated above, and the result on an unmodified historical cost basis.

Statement of movements in profit and loss account

		1993 £'000	1992 £'000
Retained profits at 1st July 1992		**32,018**	25,916
Goodwill written off	19	**(2,518)**	(1,192)
Retained profits for the year		**8.214**	7,294
Retained profits at 30th June 1993		**37,714**	32,018

Table 8: Inventories

	FT-SE 100		Listed		Unlisted		Total	
Number of relevant companies	83	(84)	144	(143)	47	(47)	274	(274)
Number of companies................	100	(100)	150	(150)	50	(50)	300	(300)
	%	(%)	%	(%)	%	(%)	%	(%)
Disclosure and classification of inventories:								
Development land & properties	14	(11)	17	(19)	10	(13)	15	(15)
Minerals and other extractive industry mined product....................	1	(1)	—	(—)	—	(—)	—	(—)
Livestock..........................	—	(—)	1	(1)	—	(—)	1	(1)
Raw materials.......................	76	(74)	71	(71)	68	(72)	72	(72)
Work in progress:								
long-term contracts	10	(7)	14	(13)	9	(9)	12	(11)
other	71	(69)	66	(68)	53	(64)	65	(68)
Finished goods......................	73	(70)	63	(66)	55	(60)	64	(66)
Consumables	14	(14)	14	(12)	19	(11)	15	(12)
Goods held for resale	16	(14)	19	(15)	23	(23)	18	(16)
Goods held for hire	—	(—)	—	(—)	—	(2)	—	(1)
Payments on account.................	15	(14)	21	(21)	13	(9)	18	(17)
Capitalised interest..................	9	(8)	3	(7)	2	(2)	4	(7)
Intangibles.........................	4	(4)	3	(1)	2	(—)	3	(2)
Various other single items...........	6	(10)	(13)	(12)	15	(17)	11	(12)
Inventories analysed by line of businesses	—	(n/a)	1	(n/a)	—	(n/a)	1	(n/a)
All in: no categories................	12	(10)	3	(4)	9	(2)	7	(5)

Note:
The above percentages are based on the number of relevant companies, that is, those with evidence of inventories.

Measurement of carrying value on long-term contracts:								
Lower of cost and net realisable value	6	(n/a)	—	(n/a)	—	(n/a)	1	(n/a)
Cost plus attributative profit	—	(n/a)	—	(n/a)	8	(n/a)	1	(n/a)
Cost plus attributable profit less provisions for losses:								
without distinguishing between debtors & inventory	33	(n/a)	31	(n/a)	50	(n/a)	35	(n/a)
explicitly restricted to LTC carried in debtors	22	(n/a)	49	(n/a)	33	(n/a)	39	(n/a)
Cost less provisions for losses	6	(n/a)	5	(n/a)	—	(n/a)	4	(n/a)
Other methods......................	22	(n/a)	13	(n/a)	8	(n/a)	15	(n/a)
No disclosure	12	(n/a)	3	(n/a)	—	(n/a)	4	(n/a)

Note:
The above percentages are based on the number of relevant companies, that is, those with evidence of long-term contracts.

Commentary

There are no surprises in this year's table. By and large the same classes of inventory appear in approximately the same proportion. As one would expect, the most popular items are raw materials, work in progress and finished goods, which appear in the majority of the accounts reviewed. We have expanded our table this year to show the various treatments of long-term work in progress.

Examples

The stock in trade of development companies is development land and properties. **Example 8.1 Trafalgar House** carries principally commercial and residential property, but also provides examples of raw materials, work in progress (both long-term and other), finished goods and consumables.

Example 8.1
Trafalgar House plc *30 September 1993*
Extract from notes to the accounts:

19 Current asset developments

	Group	
	1993	1992
		restated
	£m	£m
Commercial Property:		
United Kingdom	**73.2**	124.6
United States	**24.4**	22.4
	97.6	147.0
Residential Property:		
United Kingdom	**148.3**	189.1
United States	**109.1**	97.2
Continental Europe	**9.5**	24.3
	266.9	310.6
	364.5	457.6

Certain properties have a programme of development extending over a period of years. Commercial and residential development properties have been valued by directors at the lower of cost and net realisable value, as explained in notes 2(f) and 2(g).

1992 comparatives have been restated for the change in accounting policy for financing charges on developments (see Note 1).

20 **Stocks**

	1993	1992
	£m	£m
Work in progress	20.6	20.4
Long term contract balances	22.4	12.1
Raw materials and consumables	34.0	36.5
Finished goods and goods for resale	6.0	8.9
Shipping, aircraft and hotel stores	7.5	8.6
	90.5	86.5

Not surprisingly, the principal item of stock in the accounts of **Example 8.2 British Petroleum** is extractive industry mined products. **British Petroleum** is one of the few companies to disclose a replacement cost of stocks which differs from the book value.

Example 8.2
The British Petroleum Company plc *31 December 1993*
Extract from notes to the accounts:

21 **Stocks**	£ million	
	1993	1992
Petroleum	1,951	2,322
Chemicals	250	330
Nutrition	122	287
Other	43	87
	2,366	3,026
Stores	302	353
	2,668	3,379
Replacement cost	2,725	3,463

Livestock is an unusual stock classification, but it features in the accounts of grain merchants and pig producers, **Example 8.3 Usborne**.

Example 8.3
Usborne plc *30 June 1993*
Extract from notes to the accounts:

11. **Stocks**	30 June 1993	31 December 1991
	£000's	£000's
Grain, raw materials and stores	887	7,606
Development work-in-progress	2,963	4,787
Livestock valuations	7,385	3,778
Finished goods	697	591
	11,932	16,762

In addition to the standard analysis of stock, **Example 8.4 Whessoe** analyses it by line of business.

208

Example 8.4
Whessoe plc   *30 September 1993*
Extract from notes to the accounts:

13   Stocks

	Group	
Stocks are classified as follows:	**1993**	1992
	£000	£000
Fire Security	**4,628**	1,954
Marine Instrumentation	**2,412**	—
Liquid Measurement and Control	**4,717**	3,949
Piping Systems	**303**	277
Project Engineering	**10**	10
	12,070	6,190
Finished goods	**2,785**	1,638
Work in progress	**1,985**	890
Raw materials and consumables	**7,300**	3,662
	12,070	6,190

Items purchased for resale are separately identified in the notes to the accounts of
Example 8.5 Arjo Wiggins Appleton.

Example 8.5
Arjo Wiggins Appleton plc   *31 December 1993*
Extract from notes to the accounts:

12.   Stocks

	Group	
	1993	1992
	£m	£m
Raw materials	**93.5**	102.3
Consumable stores	**42.2**	41.4
Work-in-progress	**31.0**	36.2
Finished goods	**147.6**	169.5
Goods purchased for resale	**50.3**	59.8
	364.6	409.2

Payments on account are sometimes itemised in the stocks schedule; other times they are quantified in a note showing their effect on the stock concerned, as in the accounts of **Example 8.6 GKN**.

Example 8.6
GKN plc *31 December 1993*
Extract from notes to the accounts:

13 STOCKS	1993	1992
	£m	£m
Raw materials and consumables	**70.2**	82.6
Work-in-progress	**60.7**	73.6
Long-term work in progress	**4.9**	6.0
Finished goods and goods for resale	**128.8**	144.7
	264.6	306.9

Long-term work in progress consists of costs of £67.8 million (1992 – £6.6 million) less payments on account of £62.9 million (1992 – £0.6 million). Payments received from customers are deducted from stock and work in progress to the extent of the cost of the work carried out and any excess is shown as customer advances. Sales and attributable profit on long-term contracts are recognised on the delivery of units under the contracts.

Stocks are valued at the lower of cost and estimated net realisable value, due allowance being made for obsolete or slow-moving items. Cost includes the relevant proportion of works overheads assuming normal levels of activity. The replacement cost of stocks is not materially different from the historical cost value.

5% of companies accrue capitalised interest in their stocks figure, as in the accounts of **Example 8.7 Dixons**.

Example 8.7
Dixons Group plc *1 May 1993*
Extract from notes to the accounts:

	1993	1992
	Group	Group
	£million	£million
17 Stocks		
Finished goods and goods for resale	**332.9**	295.8
Properties held for development or resale	**147.2**	158.0
	480.1	453.8
Properties held for development include interest of	**14.3**	9.7

Intangible assets classed as stocks are not as rare as one might expect, appearing as they do in the accounts of 3% of companies. In the case of **Example 8.8 Gleeson**, these take the form of ground rents, based on a valuation of 7.5 years' purchase.

Example 8.8
MJ Gleeson Group plc *30 June 1993*
Extract from notes to the accounts:

		Group 1993	Group 1992	Company 1993	Company 1992
		£000	£000	£000	£000
10.	**Stock and work in progress**				
	Residential, commercial and industrial developments	37,764	42,601	37,467	42,601
	Properties held by BES companies (see note 20)	3,954	—	3,954	—
	Raw materials and consumables	372	381	—	—
	Ground rents	694	679	413	398
	Long term contract balances:				
	Net cost less foreseeable losses	—	4,937	—	—
	Applicable payments on account	—	(4,937)	—	—
		42,784	43,661	41,834	42,999

Extract from accounting policies:

Stock and work in progress
i) Stock is valued at the lower of cost and net realisable value.
ii) Contract work in progress is accounted for in turnover and in accordance with the provisions of SSAP9 (revised). The excess of book value over payments receivable is included in debtors as "Amounts recoverable on contracts".
iii) Land held for industrial, commercial and residential estate developments and related work in progress is stated at the lower of cost and net realisable value as estimated by the directors.
iv) Ground rents are included in stock on a consistent basis at a valuation of 7.5 years' purchase.

Among the sundry items, not separately classified in our table and appearing in the accounts of 11% of companies, is metals, minerals and securities which comprise the bulk of the stocks of metal dealers **Example 8.9 Wogen**.

Example 8.9
Wogen Group Ltd   *30 September 1993*
Extract from notes to the accounts:

17. **Stocks** (see note 1e)	The Group	
	1993	1992
	£'000	£'000
Raw materials and consumables	**419**	131
Work in progress	**331**	224
Metals and minerals	**5,952**	4,864
Securities	**70**	46
	6,772	5,265

In 5% of accounts stock is not analysed, but is represented as a single figure only. The policies notes in the accounts of **Example 8.10 BBA** describe the nature of the items rolled into the stock figure.

Example 8.10
BBA Group plc   *31 December 1993*
Extract from accounting policies:

Stocks   Stocks are valued at the lower of cost and net realisable value. Cost comprises the actual cost of raw materials and an appropriate proportion of labour and overheads in the case of work in progress and finished goods.

The accounting treatment accorded to long-term work in progress is dependent on the point at which it is considered appropriate to introduce the profit element. In **Example 8.6 GKN** work in progress comprises cost less payments on account. **Example 8.11 VSEL** makes allowance for expected losses and carries the proportion on which profit has been taken as receivables – amounts recoverable on contracts.

Example 8.11
VSEL Consortium plc *31 March 1993*
Extract from accounting policies:

7 Work in progress

a Cost

Work in progress is valued at cost of materials, direct labour and relevant overhead expenses (other than interest) allocated on an estimated normal level of activity.

b Provisions for losses

Provision is made for all losses expected to arise to completion of contracts in progress, or entered into up to the balance sheet date, whether or not work has commenced. Loss provisions are calculated after making detailed assumptions about future labour, material and overhead costs. The proportion of total loses applicable to progress to date is deducted from the cost of work in progress. The remainder is stated without deduction of anticipated future profits on other contracts and is shown as 'provision for future losses' within provisions for liabilities and charges.

c Profit

Credit is taken for attributable profits to date on long-term contracts where the outcome of these contracts can be assessed with reasonable certainty. Any such profits are added to the cost of work in progress.

Extracts from notes to the accounts:

11 Stocks and work in progress	1993 £000	1993 £000	1992 £000	1992 £000
Group:				
Raw materials and consumables		2,755		3,528
Work in progress at cost	1,823,826		1,520,042	
Plus attributable profit	169,419		125,924	
Less provisions for losses on work carried out to date	(6,718)		(12,778)	
	1,986,527		1,633,188	
Less instalments received and receivable	(1,986,527)		(1,633,168)	
		0		0
Finished goods and stock items		937		951
		3,692		4,479

In the case of most shipbuilding contracts, title to materiels and other components which are the subject of the contract vests in the customer from the date of allocation to the contract. Nevertheless, such materiels and other components have, in accordance with recognised accounting practice, been included, net of instalments and provisions for losses, as work in progress.

		Group		Company	
		1993	1992	**1993**	1992
12	**Debtors**	**£000**	£000	**£000**	£000
	Due within one year:				
	Amounts recoverable on contracts	**75,034**	50,782	—	—
	Trade debtors	**18,042**	10.436	—	—
	Amounts owed by subsidiary undertakings	—	—	**84,000**	59,548
	Other debtors	**2,031**	1,675	—	—
	Loans	**145**	120	**145**	118
	Prepayments and accrued income	**21,540**	27,729	**2,216**	1,713
		116,792	90,742	**86,361**	61,379
	Due after one year:				
	Corporation tax recoverable	**2,161**	2,104	**2,161**	2,104
	Deferred tax asset	**18,470**	22,031	—	—
		137,423	114,877	**88,522**	63,483

The deferred tax asset arises from short-term timing differences relating to provisions and work in progress contract profit recognition.

Example 8.12 Sema does not account for stocks of any description in its balance sheet, and long-term work in progress appears in receivables, inclusive of "a prudent proportion of profit" and net of losses incurred or foreseen.

Example 8.12
Sema Group plc *31 December 1993*
Extract from accounting policies:

AMOUNTS RECOVERABLE ON CONTRACTS

Work is undertaken for customers either on the basis that time and materials are billed as incurred or according to the terms of fixed or limited-price contracts (which are substantially long term).

With respect to the former, turnover and profit are recognised according to time worked.

With respect to fixed or limited-price contracts, turnover is recognised according to the percentage of the estimated total contract value completed or the achievement of contractual milestones and a prudent proportion of profit is also recognised as the contract progresses. All losses are recognised as soon as incurred or foreseen.

Extract from notes to the accounts:

13. Debtors

	Group 1993	1992	Company 1993	1992
	£000	£000	£000	£000
Trade debtors	88,493	92,192	—	—
Amounts recoverable on contracts	62,698	50,207	—	—
Amounts owed by Group undertakings	—	—	209	211
Amounts owed by associated undertakings	366	684	—	—
Advance corporation tax recoverable	1,934	2,147	1,601	1,558
Other debtors	9,657	10,705	17	—
Prepayments and accrued income	10,327	5,031	—	—
	173,475	160,966	1,827	1,769

Of the amount shown in other debtors above, £1,060,000 (1992: £797,000) falls due after more than one year.

There is no indication that **Example 8.13 British Telecommunications** accounts for profit during the run of contract, long-term work in progress being accounted for at cost less provision for losses.

Example 8.13
British Telecommunications plc *31 March 1994*
Extract from accounting policies:

X Stocks
Stocks mainly comprise items of equipment held for sale or rental and consumable items. They are stated at the lower of cost, including appropriate overheads, and estimated net realisable value, after provisions for obsolescence.

Stocks also include work in progress on long-term contracts which is stated at cost, after deducting payments on account, less provisions for any foreseeable losses.

Example 8.14 Crest Nicholson explains in its policies notes that the point at which profit is accounted for depends on the nature of the contract.

Example 8.14
Crest Nicholson plc *31 October 1993*
Extract from accounting policies:

(d) Income recognition
Profit is recognised on houses when contracts are exchanged and building is substantially complete. Profit is recognised on commercial property developments or units of development which, at the year end, are substantially complete and subject to binding, and unconditional contracts of sale and where legal completion has occurred shortly thereafter. Where the sale price is conditional upon letting, profit is restricted by reference to the space unlet at the year end.
  Profit in respect of construction is recognised when the contract is complete.
  In the case of contracts that are regarded as long term, profit is recognised during execution provided a binding contract for sale exists and the outcome can be foreseen with reasonable certainty.

Table 9: Operating fixed assets

	FT-SE 100	Listed	Unlisted	Total
Number of relevant companies......	98	150	50	298
Number of companies..............	100	150	50	300
	%	%	%	%
Measurement of carrying value:				
Purchase or construction cost.......	27	22	46	28
Purchase or construction cost plus capitalised interest	13	5	6	7
Cost modified by periodic valuation	34	62	46	51
Cost modified by perodic valuation plus interest......................	21	11	2	13
No disclosure	5	—	—	2

Note:

The above percentages are based on the number of relevant companies, that is, those with evidence of operating fixed assets.

Most recent valuation of operating properties recognised in accounts:

	FT-SE 100	Listed	Unlisted	Total
Current year........................	38	28	17	30
Previous year	21	10	8	13
2 years ago	2	6	17	6
3 years ago	4	6	4	5
4 years ago	7	17	4	13
5 years ago	5	2	13	4
Within past 5 years.................	—	10	4	6
Within past 6–10 years..............	7	6	8	6
More than 10 years ago.............	2	10	8	8
No disclosure	7	4	17	7

Proportion of operating properties carried at historical cost:

	FT-SE 100	Listed	Unlisted	Total
81–100%...........................	20	17	13	17
61–80%............................	5	8	8	7
41–60%............................	13	19	17	17
21–40%............................	15	15	8	14
1–20%	22	19	29	21
0%............................	3	5	4	4
No disclosure	17	19	21	19
No revaluations recognised in accounts...........................	5	—	—	2
	100	100	100	100

Notes:

1 The above percentages are based on the number of relevant companies; that is, those with revaluations recognised in the accounts.

2 The percentage carried at historical cost is calculated by dividing the amount carried at historical cost by the amount shown as "cost or valuation" for properties before depreciation.

3 Investment properties are not included within the scope of this table.

Commentary

As long ago as March 1993 the ASB published its Discussion Paper "The role of valuation in financial reporting". Until this matures into a Standard, accounting for properties will remain the most undisciplined of all accounting issues. Our tables show that 65% of companies carry some property assets at valuation, that the latest valuations range from current year to over ten years ago, and that the proportion of properties valued ranges from under 20% to over 80%. In addition, a few companies value their properties but do not introduce the valuation into their accounts.

Examples

Example 9.1 AF Blakemore is one of the 25% of companies which account for their property assets at cost, while **Example 9.2 Wm Low** refines this figure with the introduction of capitalised interest.

Example 9.1
AF Blakemore & Son Ltd *30 April 1993*
Extract from accounting policies:

....

b) Tangible fixed assets
Tangible fixed assets are shown at original cost less accumulated depreciation.

Example 9.2
Wm Low & Company plc *4 September 1993*
Extract from notes to the accounts:

11 Tangible Fixed Assets	Land and Buildings			Fixtures Fittings &	Assets in course of Con-	
Group	Freehold	Long Leasehold	Short Leasehold	Equipment	struction	Total
Cost	£000	£000	£000	£000	£000	£000
5 September 1992	138,786	19,487	11,157	48,000	22,575	240,005
Additions	8,968	560	1,555	7,119	23,518	41,720
Transfers	12,001	(2,167)	2,678	1,037	(13,549)	—
Disposals	(595)	—	(216)	(4,126)	—	(4,937)
4 September 1993	159,160	17,880	15,174	52,030	32,544	276,788
Depreciation						
5 September 1992	8,752	1,099	2,840	22,141	—	34,832
Provided during period	2,341	252	570	6,161	—	9,324
Disposals	(65)	—	(106)	(1,787)	—	(1,958)
4 September 1993	11,028	1,351	3,304	26,515	—	42,198
Net Book Amounts						
4 September 1993	148,132	16,529	11,870	25,515	32,544	234,590
5 September 1992	130,034	18,388	8,317	25,859	22,575	205,173

Included in group freehold land and buildings is £33,053,000 (1992–£28,516.00) for land not depreciated.

Included in group land and buildings at cost is £13,766,000 (1992–£11,456,000) for interest capitalised.

Among the majority of companies, **Example 9.3 Wolseley** reveals valuations over a number of years, while **Example 9.4 Asda** both values assets and incorporates capitalised interest.

Example 9.3
Wolseley plc *31 July 1993*
Extract from notes to the accounts:

11. **Tangible fixed assets**

a Movements	Total £000	Freehold land and buildings £000	Long term leasehold land and buildings £000	Short term leasehold land and buildings £000	Plant, equipment, land and fixtures and fittings £000	Motor vehicles £000
Cost or valuations						
1 August 1992	333,644	95,833	7,316	30,789	148,889	50,817
Exchange rate adjustment	30,225	11,502	492	5,037	7,980	5,214
New businesses	31,796	6,791	—	179	22,668	2,158
Additions	36,815	5,632	614	3,645	13,733	13,191
Disposals at cost or valuation	(25,921)	(405)	(9)	(486)	(15,240)	(9,781)
Reclassification	(1,245)	(223)	—	(7)	(746)	(269)
Own manufacture	143	—	—	—	143	—
Real property awaiting disposal	(2,263)	(1,013)	(1,250)	—	—	—
Cost or valuations 31 July 1993	**403,194**	**118,117**	**7,163**	**39,157**	**177,427**	**61,330**
Being balance remaining of valuation – 1979	889	889	—	—	—	—
– 1982	4,427	4,427	—	—	—	—
– 1986	10,973	9,818	1,155	—	—	—
– 1987	69	69	—	—	—	—
– 1991	10,424	9,752	672	—	—	—
– 1993	422	422	—	—	—	—
Cost	375,990	92,740	5,336	39,157	177,427	61,330
Balance at 31 July 1993	**403,194**	**118,117**	**7,163**	**39,157**	**177,427**	**61,330**

The above valuations are on either an existing use or open market basis and, in the main, were provided by external professional valuers. They were principally undertaken for the purpose of ascribing fair value to land and buildings on the acquisition of new subsidiary undertakings.

The freehold properties acquired with the acquisition of Wipac Group Ltd and Form Fittings Ltd were professionally valued in February 1993 and June 1993 respectively. The valuations, undertaken by Grimley JR Eve, were on an Open Market Existing Use basis.

Example 9.4
Asda Group plc *1 May 1993*
Extract from notes to the accounts:

10. TANGIBLE FIXED ASSETS

	FREEHOLD PROPERTIES £M	LEASEHOLD PROPERTIES £M	PLANT MACHINERY EQUIPMENT & VEHICLES £M	TOTAL £M
COST OR VALUATION				
At beginning of year	988.7	739.4	565.8	2,293.9
Reclassification	(6.3)	6.3	—	—
Additions	7.0	27.7	53.0	87.7
Disposals	(71.8)	(2.0)	(99.7)	(173.5)
At end of year	917.6	771.4	519.1	2,208.1
COST OR VALUATION AT END OF YEAR IS REPRESENTED BY:				
Valuation at 2 May 1992	566.2	416.3	—	982.5
Cost	351.4	355.1	519.1	1,225.6
	917.6	771.4	519.1	2,208.1
DEPRECIATION				
At beginning of year	6.2	28.5	270.3	305.0
Reclassification	(1.1)	1.1	—	—
Charge for the year	1.5	8.7	82.2	92.4
Disposals	(2.2)	(0.2)	(69.6)	(72.0)
At end of year	4.4	38.1	282.9	325.4
Net book amounts at 1 May 1993	913.2	733.3	236.2	1,882.7
Assets under construction (1992: £14.7 million)				49.8
Net book amounts at 1 May 1993				1,932.5
Net book amounts at 2 May 1992				2,003.6

Food retailing properties were revalued at 2 May 1992 by the Group's own surveyors. This was carried out on the basis of open market valuation for existing use, with the exception of certain properties which, in the opinion of the Directors, had a limited future life in existing use. In respect of these properties, a Directors' valuation was undertaken on the basis of their lower, alternative use value.

The historical cost of food retailing properties included at valuation is as follows:

	1993 £M	1992 £M
Freehold properties	705.4	714.3
Leasehold properties	474.6	474.6
	1,180.0	1,188.9

An amount of £0.7 million (1992: £3.9 million) has been included in additions in respect of interest capitalised during the year, after deducting tax relief of £0.3 million (1992: £1.9 million).

219

Example 9.5 Owners Abroad valued the greatest part of its tangible fixed assets in the current year, whereas **Example 9.6 Acatos & Hutcheson** last valued in 1987.

Example 9.5
Owners Abroad Group plc *31 October 1993*
Extract from notes to the accounts:

12 Tangible fixed assets	Land and buildings Freehold	Short leasehold	Aircraft under finance lease	Aircraft equipment and spares	Other fixed assets	Total
Group cost or valuation	£'000	£'000	£'000	£'000	£'000	£'000
At 1st November, 1992	9,881	2,205	22,954	38,728	13.640	87,408
Additions	581	60	—	3,321	3,066	7,028
Exchange adjustments	(333)	—	—	—	(179)	(512)
Valuation adjustment						
– profit and loss account	(4,497)	—	—	—	—	(4,497)
– revaluation reserve	171	—	1,898	—	—	2,069
Transfer from current assets	350	—	—	—	—	350
Disposals	(285)	—	—	(1,064)	(1,528)	(2,877)
At 31st October, 1993	**5,868**	**2,265**	**24,852**	**40,985**	**14,999**	**88,969**
Group depreciation						
At 1st November, 1992	819	1,451	—	8,892	7,380	18,542
Provided during the year	163	551	174	4,015	5,150	10,053
Exchange adjustments	(51)	—	—	—	(60)	(111)
Valuation adjustment						
– profit and loss account	(708)	—	—	—	—	(708)
– revaulation reserve	(29)	—	(174)	—	—	(203)
Disposals	(69)	—	—	(346)	(808)	(1,223)
At 31st October, 1993	**125**	**2,002**	**—**	**12,561**	**11,662**	**26,350**
Net book value						
At 31st October, 1993	**5,743**	**263**	**24,852**	**28,424**	**3,337**	**62,619**
Net book value						
At 31st October, 1992	9,062	754	22,954	29,836	6,260	68,866
Cost or valuation						
At 31st October, 1993						
is represented by:						
Cost	995	2,265	—	40,985	14,999	59,244
Valuation in 1993	4,873	—	24,852	—	—	29,725
	5,868	**2,265**	**24,852**	**40,985**	**14,999**	**88,969**

Revalued assets

The Boeing 757-200 aircraft, held under a finance lease, the terms of which give the Group the right to participate in the final sale proceeds, was revalued at US$36,930,000 (Sterling equivalent £24,852,000) by Airclaims Ltd., aircraft consultants and valuers, on the basis of an open market valuation in October 1993.

The Group's UK freehold property was revalued at £1,600,000 by Dunlop Heywood, consultant surveyors, on the basis of an open market valuation as at 31st October, 1993.

The resultant net valuation adjustment of £1,516,000 after provision for deferred taxation, has been dealt with through the revaluation reserve.

Example 9.6
Acatos & Hutcheson plc *3 October 1993*
Extract from notes to the accounts:

12 Tangible assets

| | Land and buildings | | | Plant, Vehicles and | |
Consolidated	Freehold £000	Long Leasehold £000	Short Leasehold £000	Equipment £000	Total £000
Cost or valuation:					
At 27th September 1992	11,175	1,083	110	52,831	65,199
Additions	314	1,017	15	3,969	5,315
Disposals	—	(173)	—	(948)	(1,121)
At 3rd October 1993	**11,489**	**1,927**	**125**	**55,852**	**69,393**
Accumulated depreciation:					
At 27th September 1992	1,959	370	33	31,575	33,937
Provision for period	212	58	7	3,703	3,980
Additional provision (note 3)	185	—	—	851	1,036
Disposals	—	—	—	(740)	(740)
At 3rd October 1993	**2,356**	**428**	**40**	**35,389**	**38,213**
Net book value:					
At 3rd October 1993	**9,133**	**1,499**	**85**	**20,463**	**31,180**
At 27th September 1992	9,216	713	77	21,256	31,262

The net book value of tangible assets held under finance leases included as plant, vehicles and equipment above is £259,000 (1992: £424,000).

Cost or valuation at 3rd October 1993 comprises:					
At cost	2,326	975	125	55,852	59,278
At 1987 valuation	9,163	952	—	—	10,115
at 3rd October 1993	**11,489**	**1,927**	**125**	**55,852**	**69,393**

Freehold and long leasehold land and buildings were revalued in the 1987 financial statements on the basis of open market value or, where considered appropriate, depreciated replacement cost.

Historical costs at 3rd October 1993 for land and buildings incuded at valuation:

	Freehold £000	Long Leasehold £000
Cost	6,349	1,908
Accumulated depreciation	1,174	1,188
Net book amounts	5,175	720

A small proportion of companies, like **Example 9.7 Wogen**, disclose that their tangible fixed assets have been revalued, without disclosing which, how much or when.

Example 9.7
Wogen Group Ltd   *30 September 1993*
Extract from notes to the accounts:

13.   Tangible fixed assets – Group

	Properties (including improvements)		Plant and Machinery	Furniture, Fittings and Office Equipment	Motor Vehicles	Total
	Freehold	Short Leasehold				
	£'000	£'000	£'000	£'000	£'000	£'000
Cost or valuation:						
At 1st October 1992	335	53	328	954	306	1,976
Additions	—	24	10	56	52	142
Disposals	—	—	—	(43)	(51)	(94)
Exchange variations	—	7	—	12	8	27
At 30th September 1993	335	84	338	979	315	2,051
Decpreciation:						
At 1st October 1992	4	30	147	779	196	1,156
Charge for the year	4	18	51	75	58	206
Eliminated on disposal	—	—	—	(15)	(36)	(51)
Exchange variations	—	3	—	7	5	15
At 30th September 1993	8	51	198	846	223	1,326
Net book value at 30th September 1993	327	33	140	133	92	725
Net book value at 30th September 1992	331	23	181	175	110	820

Valuations can be disclosed without being accounted for. **Example 9.8 PowerGen** valued its properties in 1990 but elected to continue to account for them at cost.

Example 9.8
PowerGen plc   *3 April 1994*
Extract from Directors' report

Fixed Assets
Changes in fixed assets during the year are shown in note 10 on page 30 of the accounts. Edward Erdman (now Erdman Lewis), property consultants, updated the valuation of the Company's properties, excluding the specialised parts of its power stations' sites and certain minor properties, on the basis of the properties' open market value within their existing use in the Company's occupation, as at 31 December 1990.

That valuation of £135m is approximately £115m in excess of the net book value of the properties as at 3 April 1994. The directors consider that there has been no significant reduction in value since the date of the valuation.

The Company's properties are subject to the property clawback debenture arrangements entered into shortly before flotation which entitle HM Government to a proportion of any property gains (above certain thresholds) accruing to the Company. Further details of these arrangements are set out in note 27e on page 42 of the accounts.

Extract from accounting policies:

Tangible fixed assets
Tangible fixed assets, including plant spares, are stated at original cost less accumulated depreciation. In the case of assets constructed by the Company, related works, administrative overheads and commissioning costs are included in cost. Assets in the course of construction are included in tangible fixed assets on the basis of expenditure incurred at the balance sheet date. Where assets in the course of construction involve material accelerated payments, interest payable not exceeding the actual amount incurred during the relevant period of construction is capitalised as part of the cost of the asset.

The proportion of properties carried at cost varies widely. **Example 9.9 Williams** carries 90% of its properties at cost while **Example 9.10 British Vita** carries a like proportion at valuation.

Example 9.9
Williams Holdings plc *31 December 1993*
Extract from notes to the accounts:

12 Fixed assets – tangible

	Land and buildings		Plant, equipment	Total
	Freehold	Leasehold	and vehicles	
	£m	£m	£m	£m
Group				
Cost and valuation:				
At 1st January 1993	156.8	24.7	374.9	**556.6**
Currency adjustment	(2.0)	0.1	(0.8)	**(2.7)**
Subsidiaries acquired	4.8	2.4	39.9	**47.1**
Additions	1.7	1.8	30.2	**33.7**
Reclassification and transfer	(0.8)	0.2	—	**(0.6)**
Disposals	(7.2)	(4.5)	(44.6)	**(56.3)**
At 31st December 1993	153.3	24.7	399.6	**577.6**
Valuation in 1988	18.1	0.3	—	**18.4**
Valuation in 1989	0.8	—	—	**0.8**
Cost to group	134.4	24.4	399.6	**558.4**
	153.3	24.7	399.6	**577.6**

Example 9.10
British Vita plc *31 December 1993*
Extract from notes to the accounts:

£000

11 Tangible fixed assets		Group		Company
	Land & buildings	Plant & vehicles	Total	Plant & vehicles
Cost of valuation				
Balance 31 December 1992	115,604	266,944	382,548	311
Exchange rate adjustments	(4,960)	(11,352)	(16,312)	—
Additions	11,717	23,413	35,130	1
New subsidiary undertakings	3,182	11,814	14,996	—
Disposal of subsidiary undertakings	(14,306)	(23,618)	(37,924)	(34)
Disposals	(450)	(5,256)	(5,706)	—
Balance 31 December 1993*	110,787	261,945	372,732	278
Accumulated depreciation				
Balance 31 December 1992	—	164,526	164,526	215
Exchange rate adjustments	—	(7,792)	(7,792)	—
New subsidiary undertakings	1,474	7,536	9,010	—
Disposal of subsidiary undertakings	(198)	(15,877)	(16.075)	(33)
Disposals	(238)	(4,523)	(4,761)	44
Charge for year	3,203	24,673	27,876	—
Balance 31 December 1993	4,241	168,543	172,784	226
Net book value				
31 December 1993	106,546	93,402	199,948	52
31 December 1992	115,604	102,418	218,022	96
*Cost and valuation analysis:				
Valuation 1993	96,024	—	96,024	—
Cost	14,763	261,945	276,708	278
	110,787	261,945	372,732	278
Land and buildings comprise:				
Freehold	102,013			
Long leasehold buildings	5,024			
Buildings subject to finance leases	3,750			
	110,787			

If land and buildings had not been revalued they would have been included at cost of
£97,518,000 (£106,674,000) less accumulated depreciation of £20,504,000 (£24,034,000).
Land at a valuation of £18,564,000 is not depreciated.

Example 9.11 BTR does not divulge how much of its property assets are carried at cost and how much at valuation.

Example 9.11
BTR plc *31 December 1993*
Extract from notes to the accounts:

12   TANGIBLE ASSETS

	Land and buildings	Plant and machinery	Total
Cost or valuation			
Beginning of year	1.616	4,546	6,162
Currency fluctuations	(10)	(15)	(25)
Acquisitions less divestments	42	106	148
Additions	57	454	511
Disposals	(26)	(110)	(136)
Revaluation	2		2
End of year	1,681	4,981	6,662
Accumulated depreciation			
Beginning of year	195	1,952	2,147
Currency fluctuations	(2)	(5)	(7)
Acquisitions less divestments	6	4	10
Charge for the year	32	328	360
Disposals	(11)	(89)	(100)
End of year	220	2,190	2,410
Net book value at beginning of year	1,421	2,594	4,015
Net book value at end of year	1,461	2,791	4,252

The most recent professional revaluations were carried out in 1989 in BTR Nylex and BTR Dunlop Limited on an open market existing use basis. These revaluations give rise to an increase of £227 million in the net book value at the end of the year.

The net book value of tangible fixed assets includes capitalised finance leases of £59 million (£56 million) and interest capitalised gross amounting to £51 million (£39 million).

The net book value of land and buildings comprises freehold £1,175 million (£1,148 million), long leasehold £58 million (£49 million), short leasehold £94 million (93 million) and quarries and mineral rights £134 million (£131 million).

Included in the net book value of plant and machinery is £142 million (£137 million) in respect of railway rolling stock leased to North American railroad operators by CGTX Inc., the 55% subsidiary of Hawker Siddeley Canada Inc. Rental income from these operations, included in sales, amounted to £37 million (£31 million).

The historic cost of tangible assets is as follows:

	Land and buildings	Plant and machinery	Total
Cost	1,509	5,054	6,563
Accumulated depreciation	216	2,332	2,548
Net book value at beginning of year	1,246	2,524	3,770
Net book value at end of year	1,293	2,722	4,015

Table 10: Pensions: Defined benefit schemes

	FT-SE 100		Listed		Unlisted		Total	
Number of relevant companies	98	(100)	133	(140)	43	(45)	274	(285)
Number of companies...................	100	(100)	150	(150)	50	(50)	300	(300)
	%	(%)	%	(%)	%	(%)	%	(%)
Disclosure and classification of surplus or deficit on valuation of funded schemes:								
Amount disclosed:								
amortised over remaining service lives	2	(2)	2	(2)	—	(—)	2	(2)
taken to reserves immediately	1	(1)	1	(—)	—	(—)	1	(—)
not accounted for:								
contributions adjusted...............	3	(2)	5	(2)	5	(7)	5	(3)
both benefits and contributions								
adjusted........................	—	(—)	—	(2)	—	(—)	—	(1)
treatment unknown	3	(3)	2	(—)	2	(2)	2	(2)
Amount not disclosed:								
not accounted for:								
benefits adjusted...................	—	(n/a)	1	(n/a)	2	(n/a)	1	(n/a)
contributions adjusted...............	67	(66)	64	(72)	79	(73)	69	(70)
both benefits and contributions								
adjusted..........................	7	(6)	5	(11)	—	(—)	5	(7)
treatment unknown	16	(19)	18	(10)	12	(17)	16	(14)
	100	(100)	100	(100)	100	(100)	100	(100)
Disclosure and classification of provisions for unfunded schemes:								
Disclosed:								
amount of full provision..............	8	(n/a)	28	(n/a)	20	(n/a)	16	(n/a)
amount of provision and amount of								
any unprovided commitment.......	8	(9)	—	(—)	—	(—)	4	(4)
amount of provision only.............	58	(59)	56	(67)	60	(100)	57	(66)
No disclosure..........................	27	(32)	17	(33)	20	(—)	22	(30)
	100	(100)	100	(100)	100	(100)	100	(100)
Disclosure of incidental information relating to most recent valuations:								
Market value of assets..................	99	(97)	96	(94)	87	(91)	96	(95)
Date of most recent valuation...........	65	(66)	78	(75)	78	(82)	73	(73)
Range of dates of most recent valuation..	26	(28)	18	(19)	7	(9)	19	(21)
Ratio of asset valuation to accrued								
benefits:								
at least 100%	88	(91)	87	(91)	88	(87)	86	(90)
less than 100%.......................	17	(14)	19	(11)	17	(20)	18	(14)
Frequency of valuation:								
less than 3 years......................	1	(2)	2	(2)	4	(2)	2	(2)
every 3 years	41	(29)	39	(42)	41	(40)	40	(37)
greater than 3 years..................	—	(n/a)	1	(n/a)	—	(n/a)	—	(n/a)
not disclosed	52	(64)	55	(50)	46	(49)	53	(55)

Actuarial assumptions:								
rate of return on investments..........	58	(58)	47	(47)	61	(78)	54	(56)
rate of increase of future salaries	58	(57)	45	(45)	59	(76)	52	(54)
rate of increase of future pensions	52	(51)	40	(38)	41	(44)	44	(44)
rates expressed as a percentage of one								
another	40	(40)	50	(49)	30	(16)	43	(41)
not disclosed	—	(2)	—	(1)	—	(7)	—	(3)
Actuarial assumptions:								
rate of change of new entrants.........	—	(n/a)	1	(n/a)	—	(n/a)	—	(n/a)
not disclosed	1	(n/a)	1	(n/a)	9	(n/a)	2	(n/a)
No disclosure of any information relating								
to most recent valuation	1	(1)	1	(3)	2	(—)	1	(2)

Note:
The above percentages are based on the number of relevant companies, that is, those with evidence of defined benefit pension schemes.

Commentary

More than 90% of companies continue to operate defined benefits pension schemes, although our database shows that the number which operate defined contribution schemes also or only has increased from 38% to 40%. Generally speaking, the level of disclosure called for by SSAP 24 "Accounting for pension costs" is being provided.

Examples

A majority of companies with overfunded schemes apply the surplus to reduce their contribution, without quantifying the amounts involved. A small number of companies go down different tracks. **Example 10.1 Alfred McAlpine** recognises the overfunding as a current asset.

Example 10.1
Alfred McAlpine plc *31 October 1993*
Extracts from notes to the accounts:

18. Debtors	**Group** **1993** **£000**	Group 1992 £000	**Company** **1993** **£000**	Company 1992 £000
Amounts falling due within one year:				
Trade debtors	**28,402**	25,619	—	—
Amounts owed by subsidiary undertakings	—	—	**55,120**	75,504
Amounts owed by related undertakings	**24**	45	**1,448**	1,415
Prepayments and accrued income	**2,587**	2,224	**447**	155
Amounts recoverable on contracts	**57,989**	52,695	—	—
Other debtors	**13,474**	15,550	**3,249**	1,526
	102,476	96,133	**60,264**	79,600
Amounts falling due after more than one year:				
Pension prepayments (note 27)	**35,011**	34,111	**35,011**	34,111
Advance corporation tax	**491**	2,235	**491**	651
Other debtors	**14,310**	12,112	**11,343**	12,230
	49,812	48,458	**46,845**	46,992

....

27. Pension Costs

The Group operates a defined benefit pension scheme in the United Kingdom. The Alfred McAlpine Retirement Benefits Plan (1973) provides benefits based on final pensionable salary for eligible employees. The assets of the Scheme are held separately from the Group and are managed on the Trustees' behalf by investment managers. The Plan is funded by contributions from the employer and employees, and investment returns. The contributions are determined by a qualified actuary using the projected unit method.

The most recent valuation was at 1st November, 1991 and incorporated the assumption that investment returns wil be 2.5% per annum greater than the rate of future salary increases to normal retirement date or earlier death or withdrawal from the scheme and 5% greater than the rate of increase in present and future pensions.

The actuary reported that the market value of the Fund's assets at 1st November, 1991 was approximately £105 million which was sufficient to cover 135% of the benefits that had accrued to members allowing for future salary projections.

This overfunding is recognised as a prepayment in the accounts. With effect from 1st November, 1992 the Group recommenced company contributions to the pension scheme at a rate of 4% per annum. Contributions made to the Scheme in the year to 31st October, 1993 totalled £1.2 million. The actuarially calculated pension charge under SSAP 24 was £0.3 million – this amount was charged in the profit and loss account with £0.9 million being added to the pension prepayment (note 18). The regular cost of £3.6 million (1992 – £3.5 million) has been largely offset by interest on the prepayment of £3.3 million (1992 – £3.5 million). In the United States of America a non-qualified defined contribution retirement plan is operated for selected senior management, and qualified savings and security plans cover substantially all employees. The total charged against profits was £0.2 million (1992 – £0.2 million).

Example 10.2 Wilson Bowden removed the surplus by arranging a refund.

Example 10.2
Wilson Bowden plc *31 December 1993*
Extract from notes to the accounts:

31 Pensions
The Group operates a number of defined contribution pension schemes for certain employees, under which the Group has no obligation other than to make regular contributions to independent investment managers at a pre-determined proportion of each participating employee's salary. The Group's contributions to these defined contribution pension schemes amounted to £502,000 (1992 £452,000) and are charged against the profits of the year in which the contributions are made.

Another scheme, the Wilson Executive Pension Scheme established in 1978, of which the Chairman is a member at the accounting date, is a scheme which aims to provide certain target level of pension based on final salary and the length of service within the Group. The amount of pension is limited, however, to that which can be funded by the member's accumulated fund at normal retirement age and hence the Group's obligation to the scheme is not open ended.

The refund of £5.5m from this scheme to the Group, together with other measures, removed the pension scheme surplus at 31st December 1992. The most significant of the actuarial assumptions used in calculating the surplus relate to the difference between the investment return and the rate of salary increase (assumed to be 1.5% per annum), and the rate of increase in pensions in payment (6.5% per annum) and dividend income (3.5% per annum). On these assumptions no further pension charge arose in the period. Company contributions to this scheme remain suspended.

Example 10.3 John Menzies quantifies the prepayment, notional interest on which is deducted from the company's annual charge to income.

Example 10.3
John Menzies plc *1 May 1993*
Extract from notes to the accounts:

5 Employees	**1993**	1992
	£m	£m
Wages and salaries	**101.3**	100.5
Social security costs	**8.8**	9.0
Other pension costs	**0.6**	0.4
	110.7	109.9

The average number of employees during the year was **12.327** (1992: 12,831).
The charge to income for pensions in the year of **£0.6m** (1992: £0.4m) was assessed in accordance with independent actuarial advice using the projected unit method and after crediting notional interest of **£2.5m** (1992: £2.5m) on the pension prepayment of £25.9m as at 2nd May 1992. Principal assumptions used in calculating the charge for the year were:

Gap between investment growth and:	%
– earnings increases	0.5 to 2.5
– pension increases	4.5
– dividend growth	4.5

At 1st April 1992, the date of the latest actuarial valuation, the market value of scheme assets was £85.7m. The actuarial value of the assets represented 146% of the value of the benefits accrued to members, after allowing for expected future increases in earnings and pensions.

Example 10.4 Attwoods identifies a modest surplus but does not comment on its application.

Example 10.4
Attwoods plc   *31 July 1993*
Extract from notes to the accounts:

2 PROFIT ON ORDINARY ACTIVITIES BEFORE TAXATION

....

(c) Particulars of employees

....

The Company maintains a pension plan for Directors and senior management in the UK. The plan is administered by Godwins Limited and takes the form of a defined benefit plan. The pension plan is funded, on the basis of recommendations by an actuary, partly by contribution from members and partly by the Company.

	31 July 1993 £'000	31 July 1992 £'000	31 July 1991 £'000
The pension expense in respect of this plan was:	293	319	217

The following are the accumulated plan benefits and plan net assets in the latest actuarial valuation which was carried out in August 1992.

	£'000
Actuarial present value of accumulated plan benefits (projected unit method)	2,054
Net assets available for benefits	2,091

The assumed rate of return used in determining the actuarial present value of accumulated plan benefits is 9.0%. The balance of other pension costs relates to payments to defined contribution personal pension plans.

While most companies apply funding surpluses for their own benefit, **Example 10.5 Henry Boot** utilises a substantial part of the surplus to provide improved benefits.

Example 10.5
Henry Boot & Sons plc   *31 December 1993*
Extract from notes to the accounts:

4. Directors and Staff Costs

....

Pensions:
The Henry Boot Staff Pension and Life Assurance Scheme is a final salary scheme for eligible staff which is funded to provide for future pension liabilities, including anticipated increases in earning and pensions. The assets of the scheme are held in a fund independently administered by trustees. Contributions are determined by a qualified actuary on the basis of triennial valuations using the projected unit method.

Although independent actuarial reviews are carried out at each year end for the purposes of SSAP 24, the most recent triennial valuation was at 1st January 1992. The assumptions which have the most significant effect on the results of that valuation were that the investment returns would be 9% per annum, that salary increases would average 7% per annum and that present and future pensions would increase at the rate of 5% per annum. That latest actuarial valuation showed that the market value of the assets of the scheme was £28,549,000 and that the actuarial value of those assets represented 111% of the benefits accrued to the members, after allowing for anticipated future increases in earnings.

A substantial part of the surplus has been utilised in providing improved benefits.

Example 10.6 Unilever is among the 67% of companies which do not specifically quantify the overfunding, but state that it is applied to reduce the company's contribution.

Example 10.6
Unilever plc   *31 December 1993*
Extract from notes to the accounts:

28 Pension schemes
In the majority of countries in which the Group operates, employees' retirement arrangements are provided defined benefit schemes. These are either externally funded, with the assets of the scheme held separately from those of the Group in independently administered funds, or are unfunded but with provisions maintained in the Group balance sheet. All are subject to regular actuarial review. Actuarial advice is provided by both external consultants and actuaries employed by the Unilever Group.

Valuations are usually carried out using prospective benefit methods, the aims of which are to ensure that current and future charges remain a stable percentage of pensionable payroll. The principal actuarial assumptions adopted usually assume that, over the long term, the annual rate of return on investments will be higher than the annual increase in pensionable renumeration or in present and future pensions in payment.

The market value of the assets of externally funded defined benefit schemes at 31 December 1993 was £7,474 million (1992: £6,220 million). The level of funding of all defined benefit schemes at the dates of the valuations, in aggregate, was 118% (1992:

125%). The levels of funding represent the actuarial value of fund assets and the provisions held in the consolidated accounts at the dates of the most recent valuations expressed as a percentage of the aggregate benefits that had accrued to members at those dates, after allowing for future increases expected thereafter in pensionable remuneration and pensions in the course of payment.

Pension costs and company contributions to defined benefit schemes have been reduced in recent years by the amortisation of surpluses in some funds. This situation is expected to continue for a number of years, although there will be a gradual increase in costs and contributions as the level of surpluses declines.

The Group also operates a number of defined contribution schemes throughout the world. The assets of all the Group's defined contribution schemes are held in independently administered funds. The pension costs charged to the profit and loss account represents contributions payable by the Group to the funds.

Both the company and its employees share in the pension scheme surplus of **Example 10.7 Asda**, although in what ratio it is not stated.

Example 10.7
Asda Group plc   *1 May 1993*
Extract from notes to the accounts:

26. PENSIONS
The Group operates defined benefit schemes for full time employees, the assets of which are held in a separate trustee administered common investment fund. The trustees of the schemes have been specifically selected from a wide range of existing employee members in different functions throughout the Group. In addition a pensioner trustee has recently been appointed as well as an independent trustee, a pensions lawyer who has no connection with the Group.

The pension cost relating to the schemes is assessed in accordance with the advice of an independent qualified actuary using the projected unit method. The latest actuarial assessment of the schemes relevant for the period of these accounts was at 1 March and 6 April 1992. The most significant influence on the results of the valuation is the relationship between the long term rate of investment return and the rates of increase in salaries and pensions. In this respect, it was assumed that the long term rate of investment return would exceed the rates of increase in salaries by 1 to 2% per annum and exceed the rates of increase in pensions by 6% per annum.

At the year end the market value of the schemes' assets was £121.3 million and the actuarial value of these assets represented 143% of the benefits that had accrued to members, after allowing for expected future increases in salaries. The schemes' trustees, after consulting with the Company, decided to utilise the surplus in part by improving benefits with effect from 1 July 1992 and in part by reducing employer contributions, spread over the average service life of scheme members, with effect from 3 May 1992.

The schemes comply with the ruling of the European Court in May 1990 ("the Barber decision") concerning equality for men and women, both in respect of retirement ages and commutation factors.

The total pension cost to the Group was £3.3 million 1992: £6.8 million).

The Group also operates a defined contribution pension scheme for certain employees.

As year by year the levels of surplus are whittled down, so the number of companies which do not state how their small surpluses are applied increases. **Example 10.8 P&O** is among the 16% of companies which do not indicate how the surplus is treated.

Example 10.8
The Peninsular & Oriental Steam Navigation Company plc *31 December 1993*
Extract from notes to the accounts:

23 Pensions

The Group operates a number of pension schemes throughout the world. For UK employees, the Group opeates a defined benefit pension scheme (The P&O Pension Scheme) and makes contributions to the industrywide merchant navy pension schemes; each of these schemes has assets managed on behalf of the trustee by independent fund managers. Outside the UK, the Group operates a number of small defined benefit schemes and defined contribution schemes and makes contributions to various industry schemes. These generally have assets held in separate trustee administered funds; where this is not the case, the unfunded liabilities are included in provisions. At 31 December 1993 these amounted to £17.8m (1992 £19.7m).

The pension charge for the year was:	1993	1992
	£m	£m
The P&O Pension Scheme	6.4	6.6
Merchant navy pension schemes	4.9	5.1
Other UK pension schemes	1.3	1.8
Overseas schemes	14.6	9.7
	27.2	23.2

Formal actuarial valuations of The P&O Pension Scheme ("the Scheme") are carried out triennially by R Watson & Sons, consulting actuaries, using the projected unit method, the latest being as at 1 April 1991. The principal assumptions adopted in the valuation were that, over the long term, the annual rate of return on investments would be 2.5 percentage points higher than the annual increase in total pensionable remuneration and 5 percentage points higher than the annual increase in present and future pension payments. The market value of the Scheme's assets at 1 April 1991 was £655m and the actuarial value of those assets represented 116 per cent. of the value of the benefits accrued to members allowing for future increases in earnings. The next formal valuation is due to take place on 1 April 1994. In the meanwhile, the charge for the year has been assessed in consultation with the Scheme's actuaries, having regard to changes since the last valuation relating principally to investment conditions, UK taxation legislation and the sale of subsidiaries. Differences between the amounts charged and payments made by the Group are included in creditors and amounted to £19.6m (1992 £16.3m).

The merchant navy pension schemes are defined benefit schemes. The schemes' actuaries have advised that the actuarial value of the schemes' assets represents approximately 105 per cent. of the value of the benefits accured to members allowing for future increases in earnings.

Contributions to overseas schemes are assessed in accordance with the advice of independent actuaries.

The number of companies disclosing the existence of unfunded defined benefits schemes has increased from 14% last year to 19% this year. Disclosures vary with regard to the level of provisions made. **Example 10.9 HP Bulmer** states the amount of the full provision made.

Example 10.9
HP Bulmer Holdings plc *30 April 1993*
Extract from notes to the accounts:

29. PENSION SCHEMES

....

The group makes certain unfunded ex-gratia payments, including some to former directors, and provision has been made for the expected future cost of these payments as follows:

	1993	1992
	£000	£000
At beginning of the year	**4,940**	4,937
Amount provided	**420**	420
Payments during year	**(456)**	(417)
At end of year	**4,904**	4,940

Example 10.10 British Petroleum states the total unfunded obligation and also the amount which has been provided.

Example 10.10
The British Petroleum Company plc *31 December 1993*
Extract from notes to the accounts:

36 Pensions

....

At 31 December 1993 the obligation for accrued benefits in respect of the principal unfunded schemes was £888 million (£864 million). Of this amount, £726 million (£717 million) has been provided in these accounts.

Example 10.11 API discloses the total provision made in respect of unfunded schemes.

Example 10.11
API Group plc   *2 October 1993*
Extract from notes to the accounts:

18   Provision for liabilities and charges

....

Pension scheme provision

....

The Group still pays pensions under three unfunded, non-contributory pension schemes, membership of which is now closed. A provision of £368,000 stood at 2 October 1993 (1992: £403,000) for the present value of future payments under these schemes and the charge to the accounts in the year ended 2 October 1993 was £40,000 (1992: £44,000). The amount amortised from the provision for the year was £35,000 (1992: £35,000).

Provision is made by **Example 10.12 Howden** for unfunded commitments, but the amount is not separately disclosed.

Example 10.12
Howden Group plc   *3 May 1993*
Extract from accounting policies:

Pensions
Pensions are arranged through the pension schemes whose assets are completely separate from the Group's assets, except in Germany where the practice is to retain pension fund assets within the company. Commitments are funded on the advice of external actuaries.

The costs of the Group's defined benefit plans are charged to the profit and loss account over the anticipated working lives of the pension plan members currently in service.

Extract from notes to the accounts:

21.   CREDITORS

	Due within one year		Due after one year	
	1993	1992	**1993**	1992
	£'000	£'000	**£'000**	£'000
The Group				
Progress Payments	**12,018**	11,173	—	—
Trade Creditors	**49,951**	40,022	—	6
Other Creditors	**14,298**	9,656	**999**	800
Buffalo Forge consideration payable	**21,815**	—	—	—
Contract Loss Provisions	**1,792**	3,598	**205**	—
Taxation	**7,909**	7,289	—	—
Pension and Medical Benefits	**987**	900	**10,876**	7,311
Social Security and Other Taxes	**5,105**	3,999	—	—
Obligations under Finance Leases	**353**	276	**558**	752
Accruals and Deferred Income	**24,778**	16,826	—	182
Dividends	**4,071**	4,376	—	—
	143,077	98,124	**12,638**	9,051

Holding Company

Other Creditors	**3,667**	2,160	—	—
Subsidiaries	**15,857**	5,185	—	—
Taxation	**1,932**	1,716	—	—
Dividends	**4,061**	4,356	—	—
	25,517	13,417	—	—

Pension and Medical Benefits, represent the pension commitments of German subsidiaries and unfunded pension and medical benefits in U.S. subsidiaries.

The level of disclosure with regard to its funded defined benefit scheme made by **Example 10.13 Dalgety** is fairly typical of most companies, showing the date and amount of the most recent valuation, its ration to accrued benefits, and the actuarial assumptions used. **Dalgety** is among the 39% of companies which state that valuations are carried out every three years, and among the increasing number of companies which state comparative, rather than absolute, assumed increases in rates.

Example 10.13
Dalgety plc *30 June 1993*
Extract from notes to the accounts:

25 PENSIONS
The Group operates a number of pension schemes throughout its businesses, of both the defined contribution and defined benefit type.

a) The pension cost for defined contribution schemes, which represents contributions payable by the Group, amounted to £4.7m (£3.9m). Included in creditors is £2.3m (£1.6m) in respect of contributions to the schemes.

b) The pension cost for defined benefit schemes amounted to £0.7m (£0.4m), and is assessed in accordance with the advice of qualified independent actuaries on triennial bases. Included in debtors is £3.9m (£1.9m) in respect of prepayment to the schemes.

The most significant scheme is the Dalgety Pension Fund, a defined benefit type scheme for employers in the UK, the assets of which are held separately from the assets of the Group and are administered by trustees and managed professionally.
  The latest valuation of the Dalgety Pension Fund was made as at 5 April 1991 by R Watson & Sons, consulting actuaries, using the entry age method. The principal assumptions adopted in the valuation were that the investment return would be 2% per annum higher than the annual increase in pensionable salaries, 4% per annum higher than the annual increase in future pensions in payment and 4½% per annum higher than the rate of annual growth in dividends from existing equity holdings. The investment assumptions were stated to include a margin of prudence. For the purposes of the Group's accounts calculations used to assess the pension cost are based on the above assumptions but allowing for an extra ½% per annum on investment returns. At April 1991 the market value of the assets of the Fund was £411m and this was sufficient to cover 140% of the benefits that had accrued to members, after allowing for benefit improvements effected from April 1992 and for expected future increases in earnings. As a result of amortising the surplus, the company's regular pension cost for current employees is reduced to zero over the average remaining service lives of current employees, of some 10 years.

Example 10.14 Siebe is among the 20% of companies which, having more than one scheme, disclose a range of valuation dates.

Example 10.14
Siebe plc   *3 April 1993*
Extract from notes to the accounts:

27 Pensions
The Group operates pension schemes for the majority of employees. The larger schemes, in the UK and USA, are of the defined benefit type, and costs are assessed with the advised of independent qualified actuaries using either the projected unit method or the attained age method. These schemes cover 48% of Group employees. The assets of these schemes are held in separate trustee administered funds.

The dates of the latest actuarial valuations fall between 6 April 1991 and 31 March 1993 and the market value of the assets of the principal schemes was £312.7 million.

For the purposes of assessing funding levels and contributions under SSAP24 and FAS87, the principal actuarial assumptions used were investment returns of 8% to 9% per annum and pay growth of 5% to 7% per annum. Actuarial asset values were determined for the UK Schemes using discounted future investment income methods assuming dividend growth rates of 4% per annum. For the remainder, market or smoothed market value methods were adopted. The aggregate actuarial value of assets was sufficient to cover 98.7% of the aggregate actuarial value of accrued liabilities (after allowing for future increases in pensionable earnings). There is no deficiency on a current funding level basis.

Debtors falling due within one year, creditors falling due within one year and creditors falling due after more than one year include £29.0 million, £6.1 million and £11.3 million respectively for pension prepayments and accruals (1992 £28.3 million, £12.0 million and £8.0 million respectively).

The great majority of defined benefit schemes are fully funded. Among those which are not, however, **Example 10.15 Imperial Chemical Industries** discloses a modest 2% underfunding, which is being provided for by an increase in contributions.

Example 10.15
Imperial Chemical Industries plc   *31 December 1993*
Extract from notes to the accounts:

36 PENSION COSTS
The Company and most of its subsidiaries operate retirement plans which cover the majority of employees (including directors) in the Group. These plans are generally of the defined benefit type under which benefits are based on employees' years of service and average final remuneration and are funded through separate trustee-administered funds.

The total pension cost for the Group for 1993 was £175m (1992 £208m). Formal actuarial valuations of the Group's main plans are undertaken triennially. Actuarial valuations of these funds have been undertaken on varying dates. The actuarial assumptions used to calculate the projected benefit obligation of the Group's pension plans vary according to the economic conditions of the country in which they are situated. The weighted average discount rate used in determining the actuarial present values of the benefit obligations was 9.6 per cent. The weighted average expected long-term rate of return on investments was 9.7 per cent. The weighted average rate of increase of future earnings was 6.7 per cent. The actuarial value of the fund assets of these plans was sufficient to cover 98 per cent of the benefits that had accrued to members after allowing for expected future increases in earnings. The contribution rate paid by the Company to the major plan, which is in deficit, has been increased in line with actuarial advice.

The market value of the assets of the major plans in the Group at the date of the latest actuarial valuations was £4,910m. Accrued pension costs amounted to £29m (1992 £43m) and are included in other creditors (note 19); provisions for the benefit obligation of a small number of unfunded plans amounted to £119m (£220m) and are included in provisions for employee benefits (note 21). Prepaid pension costs amounting to £48m (£78m) are included indebtors (note 16).

Example 10.16 TSB is one of the few companies which value their pension schemes more frequently than triennially – in this instance every year.

Example 10.16
TSB Group plc   *31 October 1993*
Extract from notes to the accounts:

Note 27   The TSB Group Pension Scheme, which covers approximately 92% of the
Pensions   Group's employees, is of the defined benefit, final salary type. It is self-administered and funded to cover future pension liabilities, based on accrued service to date, including expected future earnings and pension increases.

Formal actuarial valuations are carried out by qualified actuaries annually, the latest being at 1 November 1992. This valuation showed that the market value of the assets of the scheme was £1,968m. The actuarial value of the assets represented 174% of the actuarial value of the benefits accrued to members, calculated on the basis of pensionable earnings projected to retirement or earlier exit, and service as at the date of the valuation. The nil rate of contribution to the scheme, reflected in the current year charge, has been established so as to eliminate the surplus over a period not less than the average remaining service life of current employees.

The valuation of the scheme was carried out using the projected unit method. The principal actuarial assumptions used in the valuation of the scheme were that the annual rate of price inflation would be 5.5%, the annual rate of return on investments would be 9.5%, annual dividend increases would be 5.5% and annual increases in earnings would be 7.5%. The scheme allows for annual pension increases between 4.5% and 5.5%.

The actuaries to the scheme are employed by Noble Lowndes & Partners Limited, until 30 September 1993 a Group company. The assumptions used in the valuation have been reviewed by independent actuaries.

Companies like **Example 10.17 TI**, which provide specific rather than comparative rates for their actuarial assumptions, are still in the majority, but only just.

Example 10.17
TI Group plc *31 December 1993*
Extract from notes to the accounts:

27   PENSIONS AND OTHER POST-RETIREMENT BENEFITS

The Group operates a number of pension schemes, the majority being defined benefit arrangements the assets of which are held independently of the Group's finances. Gross pension costs of £24.4m (1992 £18.6m) included £11.4m (1992 £9.4m) for overseas schemes. These costs were offset by a credit of £11.0m (1992 £11.0m) in respect of actuarial surpluses in the TI Group Pension Scheme. At 31st December 1993 there was a prepayment in respect of pensions of £38.5m (1992 £37.9m) and a provision for post-retirement healthcare benefits of £79.5m (1992 £74.0m) was included in provisions for liabilities and charges.

UK Pension Schemes

The Group's UK pension schemes are valued by independent actuaries at not more than three-yearly intervals. The valuation methods used and assumptions made by the actuaries take into account the differing membership profiles and benefit promises of the schemes.

The main UK schemes are the TI Group Pension Scheme and the Dowty Group Pension Scheme. The assets of these schemes are held in separate trustee-administered funds. The latest actuarial valuations were carried out as at 31st December 1991 and 1st April 1992 respectively using the projected unit method.

The principal actuarial assumptions used for accounting purposes were:

Long-term annual rate of return on investments	9.0% to 9.5%
Annual dividend increases	4.5% to 5.0%
Average annual increase in pensionable salaries (inclusive of promotion and merit increases)	7.5%
Average annual increase in pensions in payment	4.5% to 5.0%

The actuarial value of the assets of the schemes on this basis was sufficient to cover 114% of the benefits that had accrued to members after allowing for expected future increases in pensionable pay.

For funding purposes the actuaries in their report to the Trustees and members of the Schemes used alternative assumptions in calculating the cost of providing pension benefits. For this purpose the actuaries calculated the pension cost using the method set out above but with annual dividend increases of 4.0% to 5.0% and average annual increases in pensions in payment of 3.0% to 4.5%. The remaining assumptions were unaltered. At the date of the valuations, actuarial surpluses amounted to £99.3m and the market value of the assets was £711.4m.

There still remains the occasional company, like **Example 10.8 Guardian & Manchester Evening News**, which does not disclose the actuarial assumptions used.

Example 10.18
The Guardian & Manchester Evening News plc   *3 April 1993*
Extract from notes to the accounts:

30. Pensions

The majority of the group's employees are members of defined contribution pension schemes operated by the parent company. The group also contributes to a number of pension schemes which are of the defined benefit type. Pension scheme assets are held in separate trustee administered funds. The total pension charge for the group is shown in note 3(a).

The most recent triennial actuarial valuations of the defined benefit pension schemes stated that the assets of the schemes were sufficient to cover the liabilities as at the date of valuation. The actuaries' recommendations on the level of funding are being followed.

While **Example 10.19 Reuters**, with numerous defined benefit schemes throughout the world, which are individually of a relatively minor nature, gives no information concerning the most recent valuations save to say that they accord with local accepted practice and standards.

Example 10.19
Reuters Holdings plc   *31 December 1993*
Extract from notes to the accounts:

24. Pensions and similar obligations

Reuters has established various pension arrangements covering the majority of its employees.

Defined contribution plans Reuters operate 27 defined contribution plans covering approximately 56% of its employees, of which the largest plan, the Reuters Pension Fund, covers approximately 23% of employees. Members of this plan contribute 6% of basic salaries and Reuters is required to make an annual contribution of 9.525% of members' basic salaries regardless of the funding status of the plan. Reuters does not have the ability to recover assets held by the plan, nor can it be required to make additional payments to the plan over and above the annual contributions referred to above. Benefits in respect of these contributions are initially calculated by reference to a formula related to salary near to retirement and to length of service. Normal retiring age is the same for men and women. Benefits may be increased at the discretion of the managing committee which administers the plan, subject to actuarial approval. However, all benefits are subject to the plan being adequately funded. Independent actuarial valuations are performed every three years. The most recent actuarial valuation, undertaken at 31 December 1992 using the aggregate funding method, showed the plan to be in surplus. The principal actuarial assumptions were that over the long term the investments yield would be 9% per annum, salary increases would average 7% per annum plus modest increases for promotion; and pensions would increase by 4% per annum; the assets are valued assuming growth in equity income of about 4% per annum. Custodial responsibility for the assets of the plan rests with two substantial and independent UK investment managers.

Defined benefit plans Reuters also operates 32 defined benefit plans covering approximately 23% of employees. Individually, these plans are of a relatively minor nature. They are subject to regular valuations based on the accepted actuarial practice and standards within the country in which each plan is established. The largest plans are directly invested, others are invested in insurance contracts and by remainder are internally funded in accordance with local practice with provisions in the subsidiary undertakings to recognise the pension obligations.

Where necessary, additional provisions have been established for the group's plans in accordance with UK Statement of Standard Accounting Practice number 24 based on independent actuarial advice.

In all plans, except those which are internally funded, the assets are held separately from those of the company and are independently administered. Reuters policy is that no funded pension plan should have any direct investment in shares of, or property occupied by, Reuters Holdings PLC or its subsidiary undertakings.

Table 11: Post balance sheet events

	FT-SE 100		Listed		Unlisted		Total	
Number of relevant companies	21	(35)	51	(46)	11	(17)	82	(98)
Number of companies	100	(100)	150	(150)	50	(50)	300	(300)
	%	(%)	%	(%)	%	(%)	%	(%)
Disclosure and classification of post balance sheet events:								
Classified as post balance sheet events:								
acquisition, merger or sale of subsidiary, trading division or major investment.....	71	(66)	45	(61)	46	(24)	54	(56)
share issues made or announced	10	(9)	11	(13)	–	(18)	10	(12)
loan stock or other loans arranged or redeemed	10	(9)	8	(9)	9	(6)	8	(8)
sale and leaseback of fixed assets..........	–	(–)	–	(–)	–	(6)	–	(1)
redundancy programme announced........	5	(–)	–	(–)	–	(–)	1	(–)
other....................................	9	(3)	8	(7)	18	(47)	10	(12)
Unclassified:								
acquisition, merger or sale of subsidiary, trading division or major investment.....	–	(n/a)	8	(n/a)	–	(n/a)	5	(n/a)
acquisition by, or merger with, another company..............................	–	(–)	–	(–)	–	(6)	–	(1)
share issue made or announced	5	(n/a)	2	(n/a)	–	(n/a)	2	(n/a)
significant debtor or creditor in liquidation	–	(n/a)	2	(n/a)	–	(n/a)	1	(n/a)
trading division or major investment	–	(3)	–	(7)	–	(6)	–	(5)
resignation of directors....................	18	(20)	38	(20)	27	(18)	33	(19)
redundancy programme announced........	–	(–)	2	(–)	–	(–)	1	(–)
other....................................	–	(3)	4	(7)	–	(12)	2	(6)
loan stock or other loans arranged or redeemed	–	(3)	2	(–)	–	(–)	1	(1)

Note:

The percentages are based on the number of relevant companies, that is, those with evidence of post balance sheet events.

Commentary

As in previous years, approximately one company in three makes mention of post balance sheet events in their annual reports. These vary widely in nature and significance, and while the majority are clearly flagged as post balance sheet events, others are slipped into the notes to the accounts or the annual report under some other description.

Examples

The most common post balance sheet event mentioned is the acquisition or sale of an asset or investment. **Example 11.1 Redrow** announces an acquisition of a subsidiary as a post balance sheet event in the notes to its accounts, while the directors of **Example 11.2 Unitech** include news of a disposal in their report without mentioning that its date falls after the company's year end.

Example 11.1
Redrow Group plc *30 June 1993*
Extract from notes to the accounts:

Note 21.	POST-BALANCE SHEET EVENT

On 16 July 1993, Redrow Homes Limited acquired Costain Homes Limited. Further details are provided in the Chairman's Statement.

Example 11.2
Unitech plc *31 May 1993*
Extract from report of the directors:

Disposals and acquisitions
The Group made two acquisitions during the year:
In June 1992 the Switchmaster business was acquired for £0.6 million.
On 12 March 1993 the Group acquired Drayton Controls (Engineering) Ltd and Oreg Drayton Energietchnik GmbH for £5.5 million.

In July 1993 the 51% shareholding in Erie Controls Iberica SA was sold for a nominal amount.

SURVEY TABLES AND EXAMPLES

Example 11.3 Try publishes a "pro forma post rights balance sheet" to illustrate the effect of a post balance sheet rights issue and reduction of share premium account, while the chairman of **Example 11.4 YJ Lovell** discusses a proposed placing of ordinary shares in his statement.

Example 11.3
Try Group plc *31 December 1993*
Extract from pro forma post rights balance sheet:

The following pro forma balance sheet is provided for illustrative purposes only and cannot by its nature give a complete picture of the financial position of the Group. It is derived from the consolidated balance sheet of Try Group PLC as at 31 December 1993. Adjustments have been made to reflect the Rights Issue and the reduction of share premium account. No adjustment has been made for trading since 31 December 1993.

	31 December 1993 £000	Reduction of share premium account £000	Rights issue £000	Pro forma as at 31 December 1993 £000
FIXED ASSETS	11,479			11,479
CURRENT ASSETS				
Stocks	214			214
Developments	7,461			7,461
Debtors — due within one year	16,940			16,940
— due after one year	1,538			1,538
Cash at bank and in hand	8,680		5,583	14,263
CREDITORS: AMOUNTS FALLING DUE WITHIN ONE YEAR				
Bank loans and overdrafts	(3,132)			(3,132)
Obligations under finance leases	(550)			(550)
Trade creditors	(22,369)			(22,369)
Other taxation and social security	(676)			(676)
Other creditors	(1,835)			(1,835)
Accruals and deferred income	(1,461)			(1,461)
	16,289		5,583	21,872
CREDITORS: AMOUNTS FALLING DUE AFTER MORE THAN ONE YEAR				
Obligations under financial leases	(584)			(584)
Bank loans	(5,591)			(5,591)
Provisions	(621)			(621)
	9,493		5,583	**15,076**
CAPITAL AND RESERVES				
Called up ordinary share capital	4,325		2,595	6,920
Share premium account	11,652	(11,652)	2,988	2,988
Revaluation reserve	1,760			1,760
Profit and loss account	(8,244)	7,260		(984)
Other reserve	–	4,392		4,392
	9,493		5,583	**15,076**

The Rights Issue adjustments reflects the issue of 25,951,200 new Ordinary shares of 10p each at 23p per share to raise £5,583,000 net of the expenses of £386,000 relating to the Rights Issue.

Example 11.4
YJ Lovell (Holdings) plc *30 September 1993*
Extract from chairman's statement:

CHAIRMAN'S STATEMENT

Placing and open offer, capital restructuring and revised banking arrangements
Lovell will announce proposals to strengthen Group's balance sheet by means of a conversion of debt to equity together with a placing and open offer. In conjunction with these proposals, Lovell intends to complete a capital reorganisation to enable the Company to issue the New Ordinary Shares. The key features of the proposals are:

- conversion of a total of approximately £45.8 million of debt, and other liabilities into Convertible Preference Shares;
- placing of 316,136,314 New Ordinary Shares to raise approximately £31.6 million gross, available for clawback by existing shareholders under the Open Offer;
- committed banking arrangements with the Group's principal UK banks;
- reorganisation of the share capital involving the sub-division and conversion of the existing Ordinary Shares; and
- reduction of capital to eliminate the accumulated deficit on the Company's profit and loss account to remove restrictions on the Company's ability to pay dividends.

The financial impact of the proposals will be to increase the pro forma net assets of the Group as at 30 September 1993 to £60.6 million and to reduce pro forma on balance sheet gearing as at the same date to 29.5 per cent. The Board believes that this significant strengthening of the Group balance sheet should enable the trading prospects for the Group operating companies to be enchanced and allow the Group to share in the improving industry trend.

A P Hichens
Chairman

21 December 1993

A post balance sheet bonds issue by **Example 11.5 London Electricity** is clearly labelled as such, while the repayment of a mezzanine loan from the proceeds of a syndicated facility is mentioned in the notes to the accounts of **Example 11.6 Compass**.

Example 11.5
London Electricity plc *31 March 1993*
Extract from notes to the accounts:

36 Post balance sheet events
Bond issue On 28 April 1993 London Electricity issued unsecured 8% bonds due 2003, with a par value of £100.0m. Net proceeds after commission and other issue expenses were £98.2 million.

The proceeds were used for general corporate purposes, including the refinancing of borrowings made in connection with the acquisition of certain electricity distribution systems from BAA plc (see note 30).

Example 11.6
Compass Group plc   *26 September 1993*
Extract from notes to the accounts:

14.   Creditors

....

		Group		Company	
	26 Sept **1993** **£M**	27 Sept 1992 £M	**26 Sept** **1993** **£M**	27 Sept 1992 £M
Bank loans:				
Repayable otherwise than by instalments within 5 years	**47.9**	17.5	**43.5**	17.5
Repayable by instalments within 5 years	**6.0**	19.0	**6.0**	19.0
Repayable by instalments after 5 years	**4.5**	6.0	**4.5**	6.0
	58.4	42.5	**54.0**	42.5
Less amounts falling due after more than one year	**1.5**	7.2	**1.5**	7.2
Amounts falling due after more than one year	**56.9**	35.3	**52.5**	35.3

The mezzanine loan is secured by fixed and floating charges on assets of the Company and certain subsidiaries.

During the 52 week period ended 26 September 1993, the Group replaced its existing loan arrangements with a £122.5M facility with a syndicate of banks which is repayable in 1998. This facility was used to repay the mezzanine loan in October 1993.

The restructuring programme initiated by Xerox Corporation impacts on Rank Xerox, a joint venture with **Example 11.7 Rank Organisation**. The number of redundancies, and the proportion of the restructuring costs applicable to the Rank Xerox group, are quantified in a post balance sheet events note.

Example 11.7
The Rank Organisation plc   *31 October 1993*
Extract from notes to the accounts:

31   POST BALANCE SHEET EVENTS

On 29th October 1993, the Group announced the exchange of contracts for the sale of the Royal Lancaster Hotel, London to The Lancaster Landmark Hotel Co. Ltd. The consideration is £60.75m which approximates to revalued net book amount with completion due in February 1994.

On 8th December 1993, Xerox Corporation announced a worldwide restructuring programme. This programme is expected to result in a reduction of more than 10,000 employees worldwide. The proportion of the restructuring cost applicable to the Rank Xerox Group is expected to be approximately £125m after tax. This will be included in the 1994 results.

The substantial payments earned by PJ Wood, chief executive of Direct Line Insurance, a subsidiary of **Example 11.8 Royal Bank of Scotland**, was the subject of much publicity at the time. The steps taken by the company's board to degear the renumeration agreement are detailed in a post balance sheet events note.

Example 11.8
The Royal Bank of Scotland Group plc *30 September 1993*
Extract from notes to the accounts:

31 Post balance sheet events

....

(b) Variation of the existing service agreement with Mr P. J. Wood.
The existing service agreement, dated 3rd August 1990, between Direct Line Insurance plc and its chief executive, Mr P. J. Wood, provides for Mr Wood to be remunerated by way of a basic salary and a bonus linked to the underlying growth in the value of Direct Line. The exceptional growth of Direct Line Insurance plc since then has resulted in correspondingly large bonus payments being earned by Mr Wood. In the year to 30th September 1993, Mr Wood's emoluments incuded a bonus payment of £18.2 million (see note 29) calculated under the terms of the existing service agreement.
During the year, the directors concluded that it would be desirable to vary the existing service agreement. The terms of the transaction have been confirmed as fair and reasonable, so far as the shareholders of the company are concerned, by Goldman Sachs International Limited as advisers to the company. The terms of the existing service agreement are to be varied (subject to the approval of shareholders) as follows:–
- The bonus element of Mr Wood's remuneration will cease and he will receive a payment of £13 million in place of all future bonuses.
- Mr Wood will be paid a bonus of £4 million representing the accrued bonus for the period from 1st October 1993 to 13th January 1994.
- Mr Wood will receive an index-linked annual salary of £350,000 and Direct Line Insurance plc will make a payment of £7 million into his pension scheme.

In addition, Mr Wood has agreed that he will hold for at least five years £10 million worth of the company's shares. The company has also announced that it is to create a new joint venture insurance company with Mr Wood which will cater for non-standard risks in the motor and household insurance markets.
Full details of the proposals are contained in the letter to shareholders regarding additional business to be transacted at the annual general meeting to be held on 13th January 1994.

The great majority of post balance sheet events, which are not specifically identified as such in the annual reports, comprise the resignation of directors. The report by the directors of **Example 11.9 Diploma** records the termination of the short engagement of BM Walker.

Example 11.9
Diploma plc   *30 September 1993*
Extract from report of the directors:

Directors

The present Directors are shown on page 2. Directors' shareholdings are shown on page 21, note 3.

Mr. B. M. Walker was appointed as a director on 8th January 1993 and resigned on 28th October 1993.

Lord Stewartby retires by rotation and being eligible offers himself for re-election. Lord Stewartby is chairman of an investment trust and a director of several other public companies including a bank; he has had several Ministerial appointments, including Economic Secretary.

No Director was materially interested in any contract subsisting during or at the end of the financial year and which was significant in relation to the Group's business.

Table 12: Research and development

	FT-SE 100		Listed		Unlisted		Total	
Number of relevant companies	64	(65)	69	(65)	22	(18)	155	(148)
Number of companies....................	100	(100)	150	(150)	50	(50)	300	(300)
	%	(%)	%	(%)	%	(%)	%	(%)
Disclosure and classification of capitalised R&D:								
Intangible assets:								
amortised	3	(2)	6	(8)	5	(11)	5	(5)
No disclosure of amounts capitalised.......	9	(3)	19	(3)	9	(6)	14	(3)
No capitalised research and development ..	88	(95)	74	(89)	86	(83)	81	(92)
	100	(100)	100	(100)	100	(100)	100	(100)
Disclosure of income effect:								
Disclosed and:								
charged to income	88	(86)	74	(69)	68	(56)	79	(75)
No disclosure of income effect in financial statements:								
disclosed elsewhere..................	5 } 14		1 } 31		5 } 144		3 } (25)	
not disclosed anywhere	8		25		27		18	
	100	(100)	100	(100)	100	(100)	100	(100)

Note:

The above percentages are based on the number of relevant companies, that is, those with evidence of research and development.

Commentary

Although most companies presumably expect to benefit from their R&D activities for some years after it is undertaken, the vast majority write off the expenditure in the year in which it is incurred, with only 4% carrying any forward as a depreciating asset. A further 16% of companies state that a proportion of their expenditure is carried forward where it is recoverable under contract, or recoverability is likely, or it relates to fixed assets, or for some other similar reason. Very seldom is the amount so capitalised quantified. A number of companies state that R&D expenditure is incurred, without specifying the outlay; and a very small number of such companies state that it is impracticable to make an acurate distinction between R&D and other expenditure.

Examples

Example 12.1 Amstrad is one of the small minority of companies which capitalises and amortises its development expenditure, while **Example 12.2 Control Techniques** states that expenditure of a capital nature is capitalised, without quantifying the amount involved.

Example 12.1
Amstrad plc *30 June 1993*
Extract from notes to the accounts:

11. Intangible fixed assets

CONSOLIDATED AND COMPANY

	£000
Development costs:	
Cost at 1 July 1992	569
Additions	993
Amount fully written down	(444)
Cost at 30 June 1993	1,118
Amortisation at 1 July 1992	110
Charged in year	802
Amount fully written down	(444)
Amortisation at 30 June 1993	468
Net book value	
At 30 June 1993	650
Net book value	
At 30 June 1992	459

Example 12.2
Control Techniques plc *30 September 1993*
Extract from accounting policies:

RESEARCH AND DEVELOPMENT
Expenditure on research and development is charged to the profit and loss account as incurred for certain development expenditure and expenditure of a capital nature which is included in fixed assets and depreciated as described above.

The not insubstantial R&D costs written off by **Example 12.3 Wellcome** is disclosed in the notes to its accounts. The capital expenditure referred to in its policies notes is not so identified.

Example 12.3
Wellcome plc *31 August 1993*
Extract from accounting policies:

(D) RESEARCH AND DEVELOPMENT EXPENDITURE
Revenue expenditure on research and development is charged to the profit and loss account in the year in which it is incurred. Capital expenditure on laboratories and equipment is included in tangible fixed assets and depreciation thereon is included in the annual charge for research and development.

Extract from notes to the accounts:

3   OTHER OPERATING COSTS

	1993 £m	1992 £m
Distribution	(40.0)	(34.8)
Selling, general and administrative	(703.5)	(600.4)
Research and development	(325.5)	(254.6)
Miscellaneous trading income	16.4	7.0
Income from interests in associated undertakings	0.4	1.0
	(1,052.2)	(881.8)

While the majority of companies disclose their R&D spend in the notes to their accounts, a few such as **Example 12.4 Logica** provide this information only in the directors' report, and so constitute a technical breach of the requirements of SSAP 13 "Accounting for research and development".

Example 12.4
Logica plc *30 June 1993*
Extract from report of the directors:

RESEARCH AND DEVELOPMENT
During the year Logica invested £4.6 million in research and development (1992 – £4.8 million). These figures are net of funding by European research institutions and other clients. No development costs have been capitalised.

Example 12.5 Adwest is among the silent minority of companies which refer to R&D expenditure without disclosing how much, a practice which is misleading and should be stopped.

Example 12.5
Adwest Group plc *30 June 1993*
Extract from report of the directors:

Research and development
During the year the Group continued its programmes of research and development expenditure, the majority of which is contracted for by third parties.

Extract from acounting policies:

(k) Research and development expenditure incurred by the Group on its own account is written off during the year in which it is incurred.

Table 13: Segmental disclosure: Items disclosed by type of segment

	FT-SE 100		Listed		Unlisted		Total	
Number of relevant companies	96	(95)	133	(136)	35	(36)	264	(267)
Number of companies..............	100	(100)	150	(150)	50	(50)	300	(300)
	%	(%)	%	(%)	%	(%)	%	(%)
By line of business:								
turnover.........................	83	(82)	81	(79)	57	(58)	79	(77)
turnover between segments	9	(12)	15	(15)	3	(3)	11	(12)
operating profit	78	(75)	72	(72)	37	(42)	70	(69)
profit before tax..................	8	(12)	9	(10)	9	(14)	8	(11)
assets	84	(81)	78	(76)	34	(36)	75	(72)
investment	5	(4)	2	(2)	–	(–)	3	(2)
number of employees	38	(38)	45	(43)	11	(17)	38	(38)
Geographically:								
turnover by origin.................	80	(71)	67	(60)	31	(25)	68	(59)
turnover by destination............	48	(56)	52	(66)	66	(78)	52	(64)
turnover between segments	8	(7)	12	(10)	–	(3)	9	(8)
operating profit	84	(78)	59	(67)	14	(28)	63	(66)
profit before tax..................	5	(11)	6	(4)	11	(6)	7	(6)
assets	86	(80)	66	(71)	23	(28)	68	(68)
investment	3	(6)	1	(2)	–	(–)	1	(3)
number of employees	50	(45	29	(27)	14	(19)	35	(33)
Share of associated companies:								
turnover.........................	3	(5)	3	(3)	3	(–)	3	(3)
turnover by destination...........	–	(3)	–	(2)	–	(–)	–	(2)
operating profit	5	(7)	3	(5)	3	(3)	4	(6)
profit before tax..................	1	(3)	1	(2)	3	(–)	2	(2)
assets	5	(8)	2	(5)	3	(3)	3	(6)
number of employees	7	(2)	2	(2)	–	(–)	1	(2)

Note:
The above percentage are based on the number of relevant companies, that is, those with evidence of segmented operations.

253

Commentary

The level of disclosure in terms of SSAP 25 "Segmental reporting" remains high. Our database shows that 4% of companies included in this survey restrict their disclosures to some extent on the basis that additional disclosure would be prejudicial to their interests, while 2% maintain that it is not practicable to provide meaningful information in certain areas.

Examples

Example 13.1 Tiphook provides comprehensive segmental disclosure by line of business. Most companies analyse operating profit with a small minority analysing profit before tax – **Tiphook** does both! It is also one of the very small number of companies which analyses capital expenditure or investment by line of business, an area of disclosure which is not called for by SSAP 25.

Example 13.1
Tiphook plc *30 April 1993*
Extract from notes to the accounts:

1 Analysis of turnover, profit and capital employed
The turnover, operating profit, (loss)/profit before tax and capital employed attributable to the different classes of the Group's business are:

1993	Containers £m	Trailers £m	Rail £m	Total £m
Turnover				
– Continuing operations	177.2	131.9	14.9	324.0
– Revaluation of forward US dollar contracts	(30.6)	–	–	(30.6)
– Total turnover from continuing operations	146.6	131.9	14.9	293.4
Operating profit				
– Continuing operations	61.8	35.5	2.9	100.2
– Revaluation of forward US dollar contracts	(30.6)	–	–	(30.6)
– Total	31.2	35.5	2.9	69.6
(Loss)/profit before tax				
– Continuing operations	13.6	(2.4)	(2.4)	8.8
– Revaluation of forward US dollar contracts	(30.6)	–	–	(30.6)
– Total	(17.0)	(2.4)	(2.4)	(21.8)
Gross capital employed	628.8	544.4	76.1	1,249.3
Capital expenditure				
– Operating assets	58.0	28.5	1.1	87.6
– Advance payments	–	107.8	–	107.8
– Other assets	9.9	10.8	1.0	21.7
Depreciation				
– Operating assets	38.4	26.5	0.9	65.8
– Other assets	1.5	2.6	0.1	4.2

Analysis of inter-segmental activity is provided by one company in ten. **Example 13.2 Thames Water** analyses both inter and intra segmental movements by line of business and geographical segment. This company is also one of the very few which define each line of business as a preamble to the segmental analysis tables.

Example 13.2
Thames Water plc *31 March 1993*
Extract from notes to the accounts:

2 **Segmental analysis**
The selected segments by class of business are:
Water supply: the provision, treatment, and distribution of potable water supply to customers served by Thames Water Utilities Limited.
Sewerage services: the conveyance, treatment, and disposal of sewage from customers served by Thames Water Utilities Limited.
PWT: the design and management of the construction of water and waste-water treatment plant and the supply of industrial, commercial, and defence water treatment systems as well as pipeline products and membrane systems.
Other trading activities: the remaining trading activities comprising contracting, environmental services, international training and consultancy, insurance, and property development.
Other activities: those carried out by the Company in managing its investments.

Turnover	1993			1992		
	Intra-segment	Inter-segment	Third parties	Intra-segment	Inter-segment	Third parties
By class of business	£m	£m	£m	£m	£m	£m
Water supply	–	–	333.4	–	0.2	322.0
Sewerage services	–	–	469.5	–	0.4	424.6
PWT	1.4	25.5	150.8	1.8	13.2	131.6
Other trading activities	0.2	13.6	89.1	0.2	10.5	21.1
Total	1.6	39.1	1,042.8	2.0	24.3	899.3

	1993			1992		
Geographical segment by origin	Intra-segment £m	Inter-segment £m	Third parties £m	Intra-segment £m	Inter-segment £m	Third parties £m
UK	39.9	0.3	911.5	25.9	0.1	823.8
Continental Europe	–	–	69.5	–	–	6.7
Americas	–	–	29.8	–	–	25.0
Africa	–	–	4.5	–	–	4.0
Australasia	0.5	–	21.4	0.1	0.1	35.5
Asia	–	–	6.1	0.1	–	4.3
Total	40.4	0.3	1,042.8	26.1	0.2	899.3

Turnover is derived from the following sources:
- third parties: transactions between Group companies and external customers.
- inter-segment: transactions between Group companies trading in different segments.
- intra-segment: transactions between Group companies trading in the same segment.

Turnover by destination does not materially differ from turnover by origin.

Another area of disclosure which is not mandatory but which is provided by the majority of companies is the analysis of employees. Most companies provide an analysis either by line of business or geographical location. **Example 13.3 BOC** provides both.

Example 13.3
The BOC Group plc *30 September 1993*
Extract from notes to the accounts:

		1993		1992[4]	
6. EMPLOYEES	**a) Number of employees by business**	**Year end**	**Average**	Year end	Average
	Gases & related products	**27 615**	**26 037**	24 667	25 060
	Health care	**6 228**	**6 459**	6 671	6 694
	Vacuum technology & distribution services	**6 193**	**5 723**	5 570	5 515
	Corporate	**230**	**215**	196	193
	Continuing operations	**40 266**	**38 434**	37 104	37 462
	Discontinued operations	**–**	**–**	–	1 240
		40 266	**38 434**	37 104	38 702
	b) Number of employees by region				
	Europe	**13 506**	**12 746**	12 606	12 661
	Africa	**7 602**	**7 493**	7 706	7 862
	Americas	**9 691**	**9 760**	9 557	9 744
	Asia/Pacific	**9 467**	**8 435**	7 235	7 195
	Continuing operations	**40 266**	**38 434**	37 104	37 462
	Discontinued operations	**–**	**–**	–	1 240
		40 266	**38 434**	37 104	38 702

Rather more companies have multiple lines of business than have multiple countries of operation. **Example 13.4 Imperial Chemical Industries** has both. In its geographical analysis the company provides separate details of turnover by origin and by destination. Our database shows that, like **Example 13.2 Thames Water**, 17% of companies state only that there is no material difference between these figures.

Example 13.4
Imperial Chemical Industries plc *31 December 1993*
Extract from notes to the accounts:

9 SEGMENT INFORMATION
....

Geographic areas
The information opposite is re-analysed in the table below by geographic area. The figures for each geographic area show the turnover and profit made by, and the net operating assets owned by, companies located in that area; export sales and related profits are included in the areas from which those sales were made.

	Turnover		Trading profit before exceptional items		Profit before interest and taxation after exceptional items	
	1993 £m	1992 £m	**1993 £m**	1992 £m	**1993 £m**	1992 £m
Continuing operations						
United Kingdom						
Sales in the UK	**1,927**	1,939				
Sales overseas	**1,566**	1,501				
	3,493	3,440	**39**	(63)	**47**	(364)
Continental Europe	**1,486**	1,573	**21**	46	**32**	(51)
The Americas	**2,409**	2,007	**127**	87	**(2)**	(67)
Asia Pacific	**1,871**	1,576	**107**	72	**108**	49
Other countries	**374**	335	**40**	30	**55**	29
	9,633	8,931	**334**	172	**240**	(404)
Sales to discontinued operations	**(132)**	(284)				
Inter-area eliminations	**(1,071)**	(1,090)	**1**	1	**1**	1
Share of profits less losses of associated undertakings					**45**	22
	8,430	7,557	**335**	173	**286**	(381)
Discontinued operations	**2,256**	4,614	**298**	562	**239**	208
Sales to continuing operations	**(54)**	(110)				
Share of profits less losses of associated undertakings					**2**	5
	2,202	4,504	**298**	562	**241**	213
	10,632	12,061	**633**	735	**527**	(168)

Inter-area turnover shown above includes sales of £682m (1992 £912m) from the United Kingdom to overseas subsidiaries.

	Net operating assets	
	1993 £m	1992 £m
Continuing operations		
United Kingdom	**1,531**	1,727
Continental Europe	**575**	520
The Americas	**1,362**	966
Asia Pacific	**1,424**	1,220
Other countries	**114**	135
	5,006	4,568
Discontinued operations	**–**	2,530
	5,006	7,098

Geographic markets	Turnover	
	1993 £m	1992 £m
Turnover in each geographic market in which customers are located		
Continuing operations		
United Kingdom	**1,876**	1,810
Continental Europe	**1,678**	1,570
The Americas	**2,383**	2,028
Asia Pacific	**1,957**	1,686
Other countries	**536**	463
	8,430	7,557
Discontinued operations	**2,202**	4,504
	10,632	12,061

The number of companies which provide separate segmental information in respect of their associated undertakings are fewer this year than last. Among those which do so is **Example 13.5 Powell Duffryn**.

Example 13.5
Powell Duffryn plc *31 March 1993*
Extract from notes to the accounts:

1 OPERATING RESULTS

....

	TURNOVER		OPERATING PROFITS		OPERATING ASSETS	
	1993 **£m**	1992 £m	**1993** **£m**	1992 £m	**1993** **£m**	1992 £m

Turnover and operating results for the year ended 31 March and operating assets at 31 March are analysed over the following activities:

	TURNOVER		OPERATING PROFITS		OPERATING ASSETS	
Group						
Fuel Distribution	**362.0**	369.4	**5.4**	9.5	**35.5**	34.7
Port Services and Shipping	**64.7**	49.8	**7.3**	3.4	**21.3**	17.4
Storage	**38.1**	35.1	**7.2**	4.0	**62.2**	57.0
Engineering						
– Marine and Industrial Products	**90.8**	98.1	**8.4**	7.8	**66.0**	69.9
– Transport Equipment	**29.0**	28.2	**0.5**	0.9	**15.2**	14.3
– Environmental Systems and Services	**112.9**	103.5	**7.4**	6.6	**17.5**	16.7
Continuing activities	**697.5**	684.1	**36.2**	32.2	**217.7**	210.0
Discontinued activities	**7.6**	65.2	**(2.4)**	0.7	**2.5**	35.6
	705.1	749.3	**33.8**	32.9	**220.2**	245.6
Share of associated undertakings						
Fuel Distribution	**9.2**	–	**1.1**	–	**2.8**	–
Port Services and Shipping	**56.5**	41.4	**7.0**	3.1	**26.2**	22.9
Storage	**4.4**	4.2	**0.7**	0.7	**2.6**	2.3
Engineering						
– Marine and Industrial Products	**3.3**	15.4	**0.1**	2.4	**0.2**	1.1
– Environmental Systems and Services	**14.3**	13.4	**0.9**	0.8	**0.2**	0.1
Continuing activities	**87.7**	74.4	**9.8**	7.0	**32.0**	26.4
Discontinued activities	**2.3**	15.5	**0.2**	2.1	–	1.3
	90.0	89.9	**10.0**	9.1	**32.0**	27.7

Table 14: Separately disclosed items: Incidence of differing classifications

	EXCEP-TIONAL		EXTRA-ORDINARY		RESERVE MOVEMENT	
Number of relevant companies	285	(298)	9	(78)	268	(272)
Number of companies	300	(300)	300	(300)	300	(300)
	%	(%)	%	(%)	%	(%)
Foreign currency differences	11	(12)	–	(–)	81	(84)
Goodwill	8	(6)	–	(14)	76	(77)
Intangibles:						
immediate write-off	–	(–)	–	(1)	–	(–)
amortisation	5	(6)	–	(–)	–	(–)
Profits & losses on sales of fixed assets, investments, businesses or subsidiaries	63	(55)	56	(54)	2	(2)
Revaluations of tangible fixed assets	9	(11)	–	(13)	34	(38)
Issues/redemption of loan stocks and preference share	–	(–)	–	(–)	3	(2)
Discontinuance, reorganisation and redundancy	36	(37)	22	(32)	–	(–)
Provisions:						
for losses on non-tangible fixed assets and long term contracts and debtors	23	(21)	11	(17)	–	(–)
Purchase of own shares	–	(–)	–	(–)	1	(–)
Employee incentive schemes	11	(10)	–	(–)	–	(–)
Government grants	12	(11)	–	(–)	–	(–)
Insurance & legal claims	1	(–)	–	(1)	–	(–)
Taxation	1	(–)	–	(6)	–	(1)
Share premium credited to reserves under merger relief	–	(n/a)	–	(n/a)	7	(n/a)
Share premium credited to reserves under merger relief or court order					2	(12)
Cancellation of share capital	–	(–)	–	(–)	2	(1)
Taxation	1	(n/a)	–	(n/a)	–	(n/a)
Merger or acquisition bid or defence costs	2	(–)	11	(1)	–	(–)
Royalties or licencing	3	(3)	–	(–)	4	(–)
Prior year items:						
changes of accounting policy	–	(–)	–	(–)	17	(11)
other	–	(–)	–	(–)	1	(2)
Other	13	(18)	–	(12)	8	(11)
Unspecified	1	(1)	–	(3)	4	(3)

Notes:

1 The above percentages are based on the number of relevant companies; that is, the number of companies with either exceptional items, extraordinary items or reserve movements as appropriate.

2 Exceptional items include items disclosed separately even though not necessarily classified by the company as exceptional.

3 Reserve movements do not include movements solely between reserves.

Commentary

The coming of age in June 1993 of FRS 3 "Reporting financial performance" has had a dramatic effect on the incidence of extraordinary items. During the period under review ony 3% of companies recorded extraordinaries, compared with 26% in the previous 12 month period and 51% in the year before that. Otherwise the number of companies disclosing exceptional items and reserve movements have decreased modestly.

Examples

Example 14.1 Attwoods refers to goodwill amortisation as "amortisation of associated undertakings' premium". Among the other exceptionals featuring in these accounts are exchange gains, insurance claims surpluses and provisions for settlement of legal actions.

Example 14.1
Attwoods plc *31 July 1993*
Extract from notes to the accounts:

2   PROFIT ON ORDINARY ACTIVITIES BEFORE TAXATION

	31 July 1993 £'000	31 July 1992 £'000	31 July 1991 £'000
(a) Stated after charging/(crediting):			
Depreciation:			
Owned assets	**30,297**	23,148	18,286
Leased assets	**1,968**	1,901	608
Amortisation of associated undertakings' premium	**293**	287	285
Auditors' remuneration	**534**	472	255
Operating lease rentals:			
Hire of plant and machinery	**3,004**	2,598	2,862
Other	**3,134**	2,372	2,330
Income from listed investments	**–**	–	(113)
Net property income	**(147)**	(283)	(151)
Repairs and maintenance expenses	**6,682**	9,514	9,824

....

(d) Other income

	31 July 1993 £'000	31 July 1992 (As restated*) £'000	31 July 1991 (As restated*) £'000
Exchange gains	**5,417**	78	256
Surpluses on insurance claims	**3,672**	–	–
Rental income	**243**	283	151
Commodity hedging loss	**(1,290)**	–	–
Miscellaneous income	**318**	202	2,183
	8,360	563	2,590

(e) Exceptional items

	31 July 1993 £'000	31 July 1992 (As restated*) £'000	31 July 1991 (As restated*) £'000
Provision for settlement of legal actions	**2,011**	–	–
Investigative costs and related customer settlements on prior years' billing irregularities	**–**	5,300	–
Settlement of Marion County, Florida, legal claim	**–**	–	233
	2,011	5,300	233

*Comparative figures have been restated for the effects of FRS 3 and/or FRED 3 (see Statement of Accounting Policies page 47).

Among the 5% of companies which amortise intangibles other than goodwill, **Example 14.2 Racal** writes down the value of know how (otherwise known as intellectual property).

Example 14.2
Racal Electronics plc *31 March 1993*
Extract from notes to the accounts:

3 OPERATING PROFIT

....

c) **Operating profit has been arrived at after:**	**1993** Adjusted £000	1992 Adjusted £000	**1993** Statutory £000	1992 Statutory £000
Directors' emoluments (Note 6)	**2,732**	2,889	**2,732**	3,045
Auditors' remuneration	**1,425**	1,477	**1,920**	2,444
Payments made to auditors in respect of non-audit work — UK only	**1,107**	3,361	**1,110**	3,419
Depreciation of tangible fixed assets:				
Own assets	**50,199**	48,109	**62,398**	91,920
Finance leased assets	**2,189**	1,782	**2,660**	2,862
Amortisation of know how	**993**	764	**993**	796
Research and development	**69,191**	67,011	**72,997**	79,514
Payments under operating leases:				
Land and buildings	**18,711**	18,415	**22,404**	28,591
Other assets	**9,962**	10,436	**13,442**	36,684
Receipts under operating leases	**31,329**	30,915	**45,445**	51,400

Profits and losses on sales were popular extraordinary items pre-FRS 3, but are now invariably classified as exceptional. With its year end before the effective date of the Standard, **Example 14.3 Sheffield Forgemasters** treated the loss on disposal of River Don Stampings as an extraordinary charge, while **Example 14.4 Unilever**, whose year ended subsequently to the effective date, treats profits on disposals as exceptional.

Example 14.3
Sheffield Forgemasters Ltd *31 March 1993*
Extract from notes to the accounts:

8. **Extraordinary item**	**1993** **£'000**	1992 £'000
Disposal of River Don Stampings Limited	**1,383**	–
Related taxation	—	–
Extraordinary loss	**1,383**	–

Example 14.4
Unilever plc *31 December 1993*
Extract from notes to the accounts:

3 Exceptional items

....

	£ million	
	1993	1992
Non-operating exceptional items		
Profit in continuing operations on disposal of:		
Properties	**34**	–
Fixed investments	**54**	–
Loss on disposal of discontinued operations	–	(76)
less: provision in the prior year	–	76
	88	–

Once the revaluation reserve has been absorbed, further reductions in the value of fixed assets are charged to profit and loss account, as in the case of **Example 14.5 Ladbroke**.

Example 14.5
Ladbroke Group plc *31 December 1993*
Extract from notes to the accounts:

	3 Exceptional items	
	1993 **£m**	1992 £m
Investment property revaluation reserve net deficit	**39.4**	118.8
Write down of dealing properties	**–**	27.9
Additional stock provisions and other reorganisation costs at Texas Homecare	**20.6**	–
Special dividend from Satellite Information Services (Holdings) Limited	**(9.8)**	–
Loss/(profit) on sale of fixed assets	**5.2**	(3.3)
	55.4	143.4
Tax thereon	**(1.7)**	(23.6)
	53.7	119.8

Another area of charges which found favour as extraordinary pre-FRS 3 were discontinuance, reorganisation and redundancy. **Example 14.6 Racal** treats demerger costs as extraordinary, whereas **Example 14.7 Fenner** classes redundancy, rationalisation and aborted merger costs as exceptional.

Example 14.6
Racal Electronics plc *31 March 1993*
Extract from notes to the accounts:

9 EXTRAORDINARY ITEMS

	1993 £000	1992 £000
a) Adjusted		
Cost of demerger of Chubb Security	**(3,719)**	–
Cost of demerger of Vodafone Group	–	(7,744)
Bid defence costs	–	(14,712)
(Loss)/profit on the disposal and closures of business	**(51)**	1,852
Provisions for disposals and closures of loss making overseas businesses (£12,500,000) and acquisition goodwill written off in prior years (£5,651,000)	–	(18,151)
	(3,770)	(38,755)
Taxation on the above	**207**	(1,220)
	(3,563)	(39,975)
b) Statutory		
Cost of demerger of Chubb Security	**(3,719)**	–
Cost of demerger of Vodafone Group	–	(8,118)
Bid defence costs	–	(14,736)
Loss on the disposals and closures of businesses	**(1,994)**	(1,149)
Provisions for disposals and closures of loss making overseas businesses (£18,000,000) and acquisition goodwill written off in prior years (£12,167,000).........	–	(30,167)
	(5,713)	(54,170)
Taxation on the above	**258**	(33)
	(5,455)	(54,203)
Attributable to minority interests	–	75
	5,455	(54,128)

Example 14.7
Fenner plc *31 August 1993*
Extract from notes to the accounts:

4 Exceptional items

Redundancy and rationalisation costs	**6,765**	2,268
Aborted merger costs	**1,155**	—
	7,920	2,268

Unlike **Example 14.1 Attwoods, Example 14.8 Asda** classifies a provision as extraordinary.

Example 14.8
Asda Group plc   *1 May 1993*
Extract from notes to the accounts:

7. EXTRAORDINARY ITEMS	1993 £M	1992 £M
Profit on disposal of investment in MFI Furniture Group Plc	71.9	–
Taxation thereon	(2.8)	–
	69.1	–
Provision for cessation of food manufacturing activities	(26.6)	–
Tax relief thereon	7.5	–
	(19.1)	–
	50.0	–

The incidence of employee incentive payments continues at approximately the same level as previously and appear in 11% of accounts as exceptional items, as in **Example 14.9 Scottish & Newcastle.**

Example 14.9
Scottish & Newcastle plc   *2 May 1993*
Extract from notes to the accounts:

6 STAFF COSTS, EMPLOYEES AND DIRECTORS' REMUNERATION	1993 £m	1992 £m
(i) Staff costs		
Wages and salaries	227.1	222.6
Social security costs	29.8	27.5
Other pension costs	9.9	9.9
Employee profit sharing scheme	3.7	8.3
	270.5	268.3

Example 14.10 Sulzer is one of the 12% of companies whose profit and loss account is credited with government grant payments.

Example 14.10
Sulzer (UK) Holdings Ltd   *31 December 1993*
Extract from notes to the accounts:

4 OPERATING PROFIT

	£000	£000
Is after charging/(crediting):–		
Profit on sale of tangible fixed assets	(62)	(50)
Operating lease rentals:–		
hire of plant and machinery	673	671
other operating leases	505	430
Auditors' remuneration:–		
audit fees	94	103
other services	20	54
Directors' remuneration (see note 3)	376	378
Government Grant Credits	(225)	(50)

Specific taxation credits are rarely seen in exceptional items, but **Example 14.11 RTZ** introduces reductions in ACT and deferred tax under this heading.

Example 14.11
The RTZ Corporation plc *31 December 1993*
Extract from notes to the accounts:

3 EXCEPTIONAL ITEMS			**1993**			**1992**
	Gross	**Tax**	**Net**	Gross	Tax	Net
	£m	**£m**	**£m**	£m	£m	£m
Provisions for losses on businesses to be discontinued	–	–	–	(86)	19	(67)
Provisions for losses on disposal of fixed assets	(10)	–	(10)	(7)	5	(2)
Losses on sale or termination of discontinued businesses	(207)	42	(165)	–	(30)	(30)
Reduction in Advance Corporation Tax payable as a result of enhanced scrip dividends	–	68	68	–	–	–
Reduction in deferred tax following a change in Australian tax rates	–	21	21	–	–	–
Net exceptional items	(217)	131	(86)	(93)	(6)	(99)
RTZ and subsidiaries	(207)	110	(97)	(89)	(6)	(95)
Share of associates	(10)	21	11	(4)	–	(4)
Net exceptional items	(217)	131	(86)	(93)	(6)	(99)

Among items not separately classified, **Example 14.12 European Motor** charges legal costs as an exceptional item.

Example 14.12
European Motor Holdings plc *31 March 1993*
Extract from notes to the accounts:

4. Loss on disposal/termination of discontinued operations

	1993 £'000	1992 £'000
Profit on disposal of businesses	89	—
Legal costs connected with disposal	(105)	—
Net liabilities disposed of in liquidated business	—	3,260
Provision against amounts due to the Group	—	(3,106)
Post cessation provisions	—	(239)
Residual costs of operations disposed of in previous years	(48)	(18)
	(64)	(103)
Attributable goodwill originally written off against reserves	(663)	—
	(727)	(103)
Settlement of claims against KPMG Peat Marwick	439	—
	(288)	(103)

The great majority of companies write off acquisition goodwill through reserves. In the accounts of **Example 14.13 British Telecommunications** goodwill is written off through profit and loss account on acquisition of a subsidiary, while other goodwill, previously written off, is recredited as it is charged to profit and loss account on disposal of a subsidiary, in terms of FRS2 "Accounting for subsidiary undertakings". This example also shows the effect of currency movements arising on consolidation of overseas businesses after taking account of related currency borrowings.

Example 14.13
British Telecommunications plc *31 March 1994*
Extract from notes to the accounts:

		Other reserves			
	Share premium account	Capital redemption reserve	Other reserves	Profit and loss account	Total
20 Reserves	£m	£m	£m	£m	£m
GROUP					
Balances at 1 April 1993	314	750	8	9,600	10,672
Premium on allotment of ordinary shares	50	–	–	–	50
Retained profit for the financial year	–	–	–	728	728
Goodwill, on acquisition of subsidiary undertakings, written off	–	–	–	(5)	(5)
Goodwill, previously written off to reserves, taken back to profit and loss account *(a)*	–	–	–	12	12
Currency movements arising on consolidation of foreign subsidiary and associated undertakings and translation of other fixed asset investments *(b)*	–	–	–	16	16
Other movements	–	–	3	(3)	–
Balances at 31 March 1994	**364**	**750**	**11**	**10,348**	**11,473**

....

(a) Aggregate goodwill in respect of acquisitions in the current and earlier years of £538m (1993–£545m) has been written off against the group's reserves.

(b) The currency movements for the group and the company included net losses, in respect of currency borrowings, of £9m and £6m, respectively.

The accounts of **Example 14.14 Royal Insurance** show the credits to reserves resulting from both realised and unrealised (revaluation) gains on investments.

Example 14.14
Royal Insurance Holdings plc *31 December 1993*
Extract from "Movements in consolidated capital & reserves including Statement of shareholder recognised gains".

Movements in Consolidated Capital & Reserves including Statement of Shareholder Recognised Gains
for the year ended 31st December 1993

	Share Capital/ Share Premium £m	Realised Investment Reserve £m	Profit & Loss Account £m	Other Reserves £m	Investment Fluctuation Account £m	Long-term Insurance Business Reserve/ Minorities £m	1993 £m	1992 £m
Capital & Reserves at 1st January	259	1,122	(321)	(547)	540	427	**1,480**	1,500
Shareholder Consolidated Recognised Gains								
Realised Investment Gains/(Losses)		143					**143**	262
Unrealised Investment Gains/(Losses)					160		**160**	(184)
Investment Gains/(Losses)		143			160		**303**	78
Exchange Gains/(Losses)		5	3	(5)	3		**6**	111
Taxation on Reserve Movements		(45)			5		**(40)**	(87)
Capital Surplus for the period		103	3	(5)	168		**269**	102
Profit & Loss Account			137				**137**	9
Shareholder Consolidated Recognised Gains		103	140	(5)	168		**406**	111
Goodwill written back				5			**5**	–
Increase in Share Capital	40						**40**	–
Increase/(Decrease) in Share Premium	361						**361**	(2)
Dividend to Shareholders			(49)				**(49)**	(24)
Decrease in Value of Long-term Insurance Business						(10)	**(10)**	(60)
Development Finance				(12)			**(12)**	(32)
Other Reserve Movements				(26)		7	**(19)**	(13)
Change in Capital & Reserves	401	103	91	(38)	168	(3)	**722**	(20)
Capital & Reserves at 31st December	660	1,225	(230)	(585)	708	424	**2,202**	1,480

The costs of a bonds issue are charged to share premium in the accounts of **Example 14.15 Inchcape.** From the effective date of FRS 4 "Capital instruments", such costs will in the first instance be deducted from the carrying value of the bonds.

Example 14.15
Inchcape plc *31 December 1993*
Extract from notes to the accounts:

33 RESERVES	Share Premium Account £m	Special Capital Reserve £m	Non dis-tributable Reserve £m	Re-valuation Reserve £m	Profit and Loss Account £m	Goodwill on Con-solidation £m
(a) Group						
Balance at 1st January 1993	58.9	–	365.4	146.7	531.6	(588.7)
Exchange adjustments	–	–	–	2.4	1.1	(6.2)
Premium on ordinary shares issued	46.0	–	–	–	–	–
Costs of vendor placing	(0.7)	–	–	–	–	–
Costs of bond issue	(3.3)	–	–	–	–	–
Goodwill on acquisition – note 34	–	–	–	–	–	(52.1)
Net surplus on revaluation of properties	–	–	–	32.7	–	–
Transfers to profit and loss account	–	–	–	–	–	4.3
Transfers on realisation of property surpluses	–	–	–	(9.0)	9.0	–
Other transfers	–	–	–	2.8	(2.8)	–
Retained profit for the year	–	–	–	–	99.5	–
Balance at 31st December 1993	100.9	–	365.4	175.6	638.4	(642.7)

During the year **Example 14.16 Reuters** repurchased share capital, resulting in the creation of a capital redemption reserve for a sum equivalent to the nominal value of the shares repurchased.

Example 14.16
Reuters Holdings plc *31 December 1993*
Extract from notes to the accounts:

26. Capital and reserves	Called-up share capital £m	Capital redemption reserve £m	Share premium account £m	Profit and loss account reserve £m	Goodwill elimination reserve £m	Other reserves £m	Share-holders' equity £m	Interest in shares of Reuters Holdings PLC £m	Loans to Employee Share Ownership Trust £m	Total £m
....										
31 December 1992	44	–	36	914	(154)	111	951	(82)	(3)	866
Shares issued during the year	–	–	12	–	–	–	12	–	–	12
Shares repurchased during the year	(2)	2	–	(266)	–	(85)	(351)	–	–	(351)
Loan to Employee Share Ownership Trust	–	–	–	–	–	–	–	–	(5)	(5)
Purchased goodwill written off	–	–	–	–	(67)	–	(67)	–	–	(67)
Retained earnings for the year	–	–	–	220	–	(26)	194	–	–	194
31 December 1993	42	2	48	868	(221)	–	739	(82)	(8)	649

Having demerged from **Imperial Chemical Industries** with a substantial goodwill reserve balance, **Example 14.17 Zeneca** obtains shareholder approval and court confirmation to transfer the balance of share premium account to cancel the goodwill reserve balance.

Example 14.17
Zeneca Group plc *31 December 1993*
Extract from notes to the accounts:

23 RESERVES

	Share premium account	Merger reserve	Goodwill and other reserves	Profit and loss account	Associated under- takings	1993 Total	1992 Total
GROUP	£m	£m	£m	£m	£m	£m	£m
Reserves attributable to parent company							
At beginning of year	–	128	(1,101)	827	21	(125)	81
Profit retained for year				122	(12)	110	(299)
Amounts taken direct to reserves							
Share premiums	1,256					1,256	–
Goodwill (net)			11		–	11	–
Exchange adjustments			(4)	(31)	–	(35)	93
Capitalization of pre-demerger debt		157				157	–
Other movements				(8)	–	(8)	–
	1,256	157	7	(39)	–	1,381	93
Share premium transfer	(1,255)		1,255				
At end of year	1	285	161	910	9	1,366	(125)

....

The cumulative amount of goodwill resulting from acquisitions prior to 31 December 1993, net of goodwill attributable to subsidiary undertakings or businesses disposed of prior to 31 December 1993, amounted to £1,094m (1992 £1,101m) derived by calculating the amount of historic goodwill in the currency of acquisition, at year end rates of exchange.

....

In accordance with the special resolution passed by the Company on 20 April 1993, subsequently confirmed by court order, the share premium generated by the June rights issue of £1,255m was cancelled and transferred to a special reserve included below as "other" reserves in the Company's balance sheet. The special reserve is available for writing off goodwill arising on consolidation and, subject to guarantees given to preserve the rights of creditors as at date of the court order, is available for distribution. In the Group balance sheet goodwill generated from the acquisition of various businesses which at 1 January 1993 amounted to £1,101m, at 1992 year end rates of exchange, has been offset against this reserve.

Example 14.18 Tesco changed its policy with regard to depreciation and reflected the impact on prior year accounts as an adjustment in reserves.

Example 14.18
Tesco plc   *26 February 1994*
Extracts from notes to the accounts:

Note	**Prior Period**	The prior period adjustment arises from the change in
5	**Adjustment**	accounting policy to amortise the premiums paid to acquire food superstore sites over the estimated trading life of the superstore.

Under the new policy the premiums paid for land in excess of the alternative use values on acquisition, which reflect the additional return that may be earned from operating food superstores on such sites, are being amortised in equal annual instalments over a period of 25 years from the date of store opening. This results in a charge to operating profit in the year of £32.1m (1993 – £22.9m, 1992 and prior – £36.5m).

Note 24 **Reserves**

....

	Group		**Company**	
	1994	1993	**1994**	1993
	£m	£m	**£m**	£m
c) Profit and loss account				
At 27 February 1993 as previously stated	**1,691.2**	1,412.1	**513.0**	502.9
Prior period adjustment (note 4)	**(59.4)**	(36.5)	**–**	–
At 27 February 1993 restated	**1,631.8**	1,375.6	**513.0**	502.9
Goodwill arising on acquisition of subsidiary undertakings	**(108.3)**	–	**–**	–
Gain on foreign currency translation	**1.5**	0.2	**–**	–
Retained profit for the financial year	**146.1**	256.0	**44.1**	10.1
At 26 February 1994	**1,671.1**	1,631.8	**557.1**	513.0

By contrast, the prior year adjustment to the reserves of **Example 14.19 Charter** results, not from a change of policy, but from the correction of prior year errors.

Example 14.19
Charter plc   *31 March 1994*
Extract from notes to the accounts:

14 Prior year adjustment – proforma
The comparative balance sheet has been adjusted following the discovery of misstatements by the group's subsidiary undertaking Cape PLC in the reporting of the financial performance of its French insulation business over a number of years. This prior year adjustment has reduced the capital and reserves by £3.9 million, being reductions in stocks £3.3 million, debtors £2.2 million and minority interests £2.0 million and increases in creditors £0.4 million.

....

25 Reserves

Group Proforma reconciliation	Share premium account £m	Revaluation reserve £m	Merger reserve £m	Other reserves £m	Profit and loss account £m	Total £m
At 31 March 1993						
As previously reported	14.4	15.9	–	76.3	481.2	587.8
Prior year adjustment (note 14)	–	–	–	–	(3.9)	(3.9)
As restated	14.4	15.9	–	76.3	477.3	583.9
Retained profit for the period	–	–	–	–	21.3	21.3
Premium on shares issued	0.2	–	–	–	–	0.2
Net effect of translation of currencies	–	–	–	–	(0.4)	(0.4)
Other movements	–	(0.5)	–	0.3	(0.6)	(0.8)
At 22 August 1993	14.6	15.4	–	76.6	497.6	604.2
Effect of Scheme of Arrangement	(2.6)	(15.4)	355.1	(76.6)	(497.6)	(237.1)
At 23 August 1993	12.0	–	355.1	–	–	367.1
Retained loss for the period	–	–	–	–	(0.7)	(0.7)
Goodwill on acquisition of subsidiary under-takings	–	–	–	–	(1.2)	(1.2)
Premium on shares issued	0.8	–	–	–	–	0.8
Net effect of translation of currencies	–	–	–	–	0.5	0.5
Other movements	–	–	–	–	1.2	1.2
At 31 March 1994	12.8	–	355.1	–	(0.2)	367.7

Example 14.20 Highland Distilleries provides examples of reserve movements which we have not specifically classified, together with reserve movements which the company has not classified.

Example 14.20
The Highland Distilleries Company plc *31 August 1993*
Extract from notes to the accounts:

19. RESERVES

	Share premium £'000	Revaluation reserve £'000	Currency reserve £'000	Associates reserve £'000	Profit & loss account £'000	Total £'000
GROUP						
At 31 August 1992	2,102	25,860	1,514	–	86,176	115,652
On issue of shares	883	–	–	–	–	883
Equity accounting uplift	–	–	–	41,320	–	41,320
Profit retained for year	–	–	–	4,209	12,706	16,915
Other movements	–	719	(1,514)	1,394	(432)	167
At 31 August 1993	2,985	26,579	–	46,923	98,450	174,937

....

The Company changed its accounting treatment of Robertson & Baxter Limited with effect from the start of the financial year. The equity accounting uplift represents the Company's share of net assets of Robertson & Baxter Limited at that time, see Note 12.

APPENDIX

INTRODUCTION

This appendix describes the technical characteristics of the selection of the sample of companies on which the survey in Part II is based, and documents the ways in which the analyses are presented. There is also a schedule of the most recent selected topics covered by the survey.

PART II TABLES AND EXAMPLES

CLASSIFICATION OF PRACTICES

In some of the tables, the classification scheme is mutually exclusive and exhaustive; that is, each company can have one and only one practice, and the percentage occurrences add up to 100%. These tables are identifiable by the explicit use of a total line of 100%. The table of practice regarding disclosure of R&D expenditure is an example; in brief, a company either discloses R&D spend or it doesn't.

For the remainder of the tables, the classification scheme is mutually exclusive and exhaustive with respect to the practices; but only exhaustive with respect to companies. That is, each company must have at least one and possibly more than one practice, and the percentage occurrences can add up to more than 100%. These tables are identifiable by the absence of a total line of 100%. The tables of practice regarding complex financial instruments are examples; in brief, a company may have more than one such instrument and each such occurrence is counted.

COMPARATIVE FIGURES

Each table presents comparative figures, where available from the previous year's publication, in parentheses.

ROUNDING DIFFERENCES

The tables are subject to rounding differences. Any apparent errors of addition are attributable only to these rounding differences.

SAMPLE SELECTION CRITERIA

This series of surveys is intended to reflect the financial reporting practices of the largest UK companies. The companies are chosen for analysis on the basis of the following general criteria:

1　they have published their annual report and accounts during the year ended 30 June 1994; and
2　they are not subsidiaries of other companies in the survey.

The companies are divided into three categories, each of which is chosen on the basis of the following additional criteria:

APPENDIX

FT-SE 100 companies
 3 they have an equity listing on the London Stock Exchange; and
 4 they are members of the *FT-SE 100 Index*. This criterion was introduced in the 1992–93 edition and comparison with earlier years should be interpreted carefully. In those previous years, the criterion for the *"Large listed companies"* category was that companies were ranked in the top 250 of *The Times 1000* of that year.

Listed companies
 3 they have an equity listing on the London Stock Exchange; and
 4 they are ranked in the current *The Times 1000;* and
 5 they are not members of the *FT-SE 100 Index*. Following the abovementioned change in criterion, the criterion for the *"Medium listed companies"* category was, in those previous years, that companies were not ranked in the top 250 of *The Times 1000* of that year.

Unlisted companies
 3 they do not have a listing of any securities (equity or debt) on the London Stock Exchange; and
 4 they are ranked in the current *The Times 1000*.

CUMULATIVE LIST OF MOST RECENT SELECTED TOPICS

SECTION	AUTHOR	EDITION
Accounting policies and forecasts	R Montgomerie and D Walker	1991–92
Associated undertakings and joint ventures	D M Whitehead	1992–93
Auditor's report	J J R Mason	1984–85
Auditors' review of Cadbury compliance statements	A Piper and R Jones	1994–95
Brands and other intangibles	D J Tonkin and W R Robertson	1990–91
Cash flow statements	S Hastie	1992–93
Charity accounts	J K Ashford	1989–90
Complex capital issues	B L Worth	1988–89
Consolidated accounts	B Johnson	1991–92
Contingencies	K Wild	1988–89
Co-operative societies	P A Collier and D S Hutton	1988–89
Corporate governance	D A Pimm	1992–93
Current cost accounting	A Steele	1984–85
Deferred tax	R J Munson	1985–86
Disclosure of exceptional and extraordinary items under FRS 3	C Goodhead	1994–95
Environmental reporting	D Butler, C Frost and R Macve	1991–92
European financial reporting	S Archer and S McLeay	1991–92
Exchange rate and interest rate risk	P F Pope and A P Marshall	1990–91
Extraordinary items and prior year adjustments	E Hodgson	1990–91
FRS 3 "Reporting Financial Performance"	D Chopping	1993–94
Fair value accounting	R M Paterson	1987–88
Financial reporting to employees	R Hussey	1990–91
Fixed assets	E Hodgson	1992–93
Foreign currency translation	R M Paterson	1985–86
Foreign currency disclosures	C Roberts	1988–89
Half-yearly reports	R Hussey and S Woolfe	1993–94
Historical summaries	R M Wilkins and A C Lennard	1987–88
Impact of the ASB	W R Robertson and D J Tonkin	1992–93
Investment trusts	S MacDonald	1989–90
Leasing	G F Loveday	1994–95

Leasing and hire purchase	P J Rutteman and F M C Daley	1984–85
Life profit reporting	J W Dean	1994–95
Merger accounting and goodwill	K Wild	1986–87
Off-balance sheet financing	D A Pimm	1990–91
Oil and gas	N H Letchet and J C Norton	1986–87
Operating and financial review	R A Chandler	1993–94
Pension costs	R A Derwent	1993–94
Pension surpluses	R M Wilkins	1986–87
Political and charitable contributions	C J Cowton	1983–84
Privatisation effects on accounting policies	S V Masters and F Faiz	1988–89
Pro-forma accounts	R S Bint	1992–93
Property companies	J S Mellows and K B Hudson	1987–88
Related parties	P R Hinton	1987–88
Research and development	D W Budworth	1987–88
Reserve accounting	R M Paterson	1988–89
Revenue and profit recognition	M Lennon	1991–92
Review of the new financial reporting structures	A Jack	1993–94
SAS 600 auditors and directors responsibility statements	P Chidgey	1994–95
Segmental reporting	R A Padgett	1987–88
Shareholdings	R T Waring	1984–85
Stocks and work in progress	D L Haynes	1985–86
Takeovers	R M Wilkins	1985–86
Value added	P D Bougen	1983–84